Praise for *Selling Through Tough Times*

Successful salespeople know how to make it happen in good times, and in tough times, they also succeed. This book is the playbook they've been using to win, and it's now your playbook. Read it, apply it, and make it happen; your customers will not wait any longer.

—**MARK HUNTER**, "The Sales Hunter," author of
A Mind for Sales and *High-Profit Prospecting*

Each associate in our global sales team found inspiration and practical coaching in Paul Reilly's *Selling Through Tough Times*. Paul's message provided immediate and impactful actions—we pivoted from surviving to thriving using the tough-timer mentality. His lessons easily cross borders and experience levels, making the selling model required reading for all of our sales teams.

—**CHUCK REED**, Vice President and General Manager,
Crane Payment Innovations, Convenience Services

In this rapidly changing world, salespeople constantly face new situations and challenges. In an extremely relatable style, this book brings us real insight and useful instruction on how to provide value to our customers, even when times are tough. I'm looking forward to sharing the book with my sales team and continue using it as a reference in our training.

—**GEORGE H. WINTER**, Commercial Development
Program Director, Ravago Americas

Every company, every seller, every industry faces tough times. This book perfectly captures how to manage the customer experience through a downturn. A must-read for any leader, seller, or service professional!

—**SHEP HYKEN**, customer service/experience expert
and *New York Times* bestselling author

I've made a 30-year journey through engineering to sales. Along the way, I learned the techniques of selling value. I have the good fortune of selling a quality product and learning from great role models. What I did not have was this book. I surely could have avoided many pitfalls, been a better employee, and served my customers better had this been placed in my hands. It's now in yours. Give it a read . . . or two.

—TIM THIESSEN, Vice President, Sales & Marketing, Okuma Americas

Through tough times, you must find a way to differentiate yourself and your solution from the competition. This book goes beyond simply giving you answers, it forces you to think differently and ask better questions. Reilly has created a must-read for sales professionals and sales leaders.

—DAVID STEINER, Stanley Black & Decker,
Vice President, US Commercial Sales

In an age where many are obsessed with ease and comfort and live perpetually searching for hacks or shortcuts to avoid doing real work, Paul Reilly has written a timeless classic for sales professionals and business leaders packed with wisdom and life-truths to help you achieve transformative success.

—MIKE WEINBERG, author of *New Sales. Simplified*
and *Sales Management. Simplified*

Paul Reilly explains how buyers define value differently in a downturn. His book addresses in detail how buyers think and how they act. With a deeper understanding of the buyer, you create a more compelling message. A timely and powerful book.

—DEBBIE BLACK, Siemens Digital Industries Software,
Director, Inside Sales

Your career in sales is going to be marked by incredible tailwinds that make selling easy and devastating tailwinds that will challenge you to keep moving forward. *Selling Through Tough Times* will provide you the mindset and the blueprint to live, survive, and even thrive in tough times.

—ANTHONY IANNARINO, author of *Eat Their Lunch:*
Winning Customers Away from Your Competition

Pre-call planning is a vital part of Honda Power Equipment's field sales process. This book gave opportunities to our team to refine their sales process. Paul mentions that a sales call with no objective is defective; this point ties directly to our core values at Honda. Our sales team benefited from the motivational nature of this book, and it created more focus around refining our sales processes.

—**GARY CHILDRESS**, American Honda Motor Co. Inc.,
Senior Manager, Power Equipment

SELLING
THROUGH
TOUGH TIMES

SELLING
THROUGH
TOUGH TIMES

GROW YOUR PROFITS AND
MENTAL RESILIENCE
THROUGH ANY DOWNTURN

PAUL REILLY, CSP

NEW YORK   CHICAGO   SAN FRANCISCO   ATHENS   LONDON
MADRID   MEXICO CITY   MILAN   NEW DELHI
SINGAPORE   SYDNEY   TORONTO

1 2 3 4 5 6 7 8 9   LCR   26 25 24 23 22 21

ISBN   978-1-264-26656-2
MHID   1-264-26656-1

e-ISBN   978-1-264-26657-9
e-MHID   1-264-26657-X

This publication is designed to provide accurate and authoritative information in regard to the subject matter covered. It is sold with the understanding that neither the author nor the publisher is engaged in rendering legal, accounting, securities trading, or other professional services. If legal advice or other expert assistance is required, the services of a competent professional person should be sought.

> —*From a Declaration of Principles Jointly Adopted by a Committee of the American Bar Association and a Committee of Publishers and Associations*

Individuals' opinions are their own and do not represent the opinions of their employers. Company name is referenced for affiliation purposes only.

Library of Congress Cataloging-in-Publication Data
Names: Reilly, Paul (Sales training consultant), author.
Title: Selling through tough times : grow your profits and mental resilience through any downturn / Paul Reilly, CSP.
Description: [New York] : [McGraw Hill], 2021. | Includes bibliographical references and index.
Identifiers: LCCN 2021025462 (print) | LCCN 2021025463 (ebook) | ISBN 9781264266562 (hardcover) | ISBN 9781264266579 (ebook)
Subjects: LCSH: Selling—Psychological aspects. | Resilience (Personality trait)
Classification: LCC HF5438.8.P75 R45 2021 (print) | LCC HF5438.8.P75 (ebook) | DDC 658.8501/9—dc23
LC record available at https://lccn.loc.gov/2021025462
LC ebook record available at https://lccn.loc.gov/2021025463

McGraw Hill books are available at special quantity discounts to use as premiums and sales promotions or for use in corporate training programs. To contact a representative, please visit the Contact Us pages at www.mhprofessional.com.

He had a troubled adolescence.

He lost his dad as a teenager.

He fought in a war at age 19.

He lost his mom too soon.

He lost his voice to cancer at age 30

(and then became a professional speaker).

Had to rebuild his business after a devastating flood.

And he beat cancer a couple more times.

He is proof that life is what you make of it.

He is a true tough timer.

For you, Dad.

Contents

PART I
TOUGH TIMES

PART II
CRITICAL SELLING ACTIVITIES

PART III

SELLING AND LEADERSHIP TACTICS

Foreword

I know Paul Reilly, and even before reading the manuscript for *Selling Through Tough Times*, I knew two things for certain. First, that I would love and benefit from this book, and second, that it would have tremendous impact on those who read it.

In an age where many people are obsessed with ease and comfort and live perpetually searching for hacks or shortcuts to avoid doing *real work*, Paul has written a timeless classic for sales professionals and business leaders that is packed with wisdom and life truths to help you achieve transformative success. From the very first sentence of the Introduction, readers are put on notice that *Selling Through Tough Times* is a book for adults who are serious about winning at sales and winning in life. I wholeheartedly agree with Paul: "Tough times are good!" I've seen it in my own career and in countless others I've observed. The biggest wins and greatest successes emerged following very challenging times.

Tough times are universal. We all experience them. Whether it's someone new in sales who is stumbling to learn the ropes on the way to becoming effective and confident or a grizzled veteran who's changed industries and is struggling to get a footing in a new environment. Or maybe just someone in a prolonged slump. Or someone whose family life has been turned upside down by cancer or chronic illness. Or maybe it's a tough time created by something unimaginable like trying to sell or lead a sales team through a once-in-a-century pandemic that disrupts marketplaces and forces salespeople to work from home, fill their pipelines, and close deals all while selling virtually and homeschooling their kids!

As with most things in life, it's not our circumstances that determine outcomes; it's how we respond to those circumstances, and this is exactly why Reilly wrote this powerful, practical, hope-filled book—to help you grow both your mental and sales resilience. Looking back with the benefit of hindsight, I can see clearly how the lessons learned and the character built while navigating really hard situations were pivotal for my own personal growth.

Yes, the right attitude is certainly key for surviving and thriving during (and coming out of) tough times, but Reilly does not leave us to rely simply on naive positivity. Rather, he offers hard-hitting, proven sales best practices and provides plenty of helpful tips and tools to attack tough times with a sense of practical optimism.

Reilly's six critical selling activities (select, pursue, discover, persuade, partner, and leverage) should be required reading for all sellers—in good times and bad. Sales pros will appreciate and benefit from his thorough approach to owning and upgrading our sales process.

And while the writer of the Foreword isn't supposed to pick favorites, I cannot stop myself from enthusiastically pointing you to Chapter 14. Sharpening your "sales story" and drafting compelling customer issue- and outcome-focused messaging are the fastest ways to increase sales effectiveness, particularly when your customers are in a world of hurt. Everything in sales becomes easier when your messaging is great, and Reilly's formula provides exactly what you need to sharpen your story, articulate the true value your solution delivers, and differentiate yourself from the competition.

Sales is a tough profession, and it is even more grueling when you are facing strong headwinds, whatever their cause. This book beautifully addresses the required mental rigors for selling during tough times while also providing the necessary fundamental tools to succeed. Reilly delivers big on both the mindset and skill set sellers need not only to survive but also to thrive.

My promise is that *Selling Through Tough Times* will accomplish exactly what tough times do: it will make you better. Implement Reilly's timeless principles. Reap the rewards. And you'll never view tough times the same way again!

Mike Weinberg
St. Louis, Missouri
Author of *New Sales. Simplified* and
Sales Management. Simplified

Acknowledgments

Only having the author's name on a book cover is a bit misleading. So many individuals contributed to this project. To my wife, Lauren, thank you for your unwavering support and commitment throughout this project. To Linda Huizenga, thank you for your dedication and expertise—always willing to go above and beyond. To Amy Li, thank you for championing this project from the beginning. As always, thank you to McGraw Hill for its faith in this message (and the messenger).

Introduction

Tough times are good! Without tough times, the world as you know it today would not exist. Without tough times, the success you enjoy today would not exist. Without tough times, the deep relationships you have built would not exist. Although tough times don't feel good, tough times lead to good in the end. The tough times you experience today lead to tomorrow's success.

At an early age, we are taught that tough times are bad. This continues throughout adulthood. Whether it's from the mainstream media, a boss, colleagues, family, or friends, we are all programmed to believe tough times are bad. So we fear tough times. Tough times are painful, so naturally we try to avoid the pain. Paradoxically, what we are trying to avoid is what we need— pain catalyzes change. By avoiding the pain of tough times, we avoid the benefits of tough times. Instead, when we embrace tough times, impossible success becomes probable. Like manure in a field, the crap you experience helps you grow.

Tough times force you to get better. They expose weaknesses and spark creativity; they refocus your energy and clarify your purpose. Tough times are like physical therapy for the soul. At times, it's uncomfortable and painful, but that pain leads to something far greater. Tough times are good!

Tough times humble you. Good times bring success. That success generates an inflated sense of self. The wave of success only pushes us so far. Momentum is generated by the wave, not the individual. This is why you catch a wave, not create one. When the wave reaches the shore, you exhaustedly paddle back out. Paddling out strengthens us to catch an even bigger wave on our next ride. Tough times humble you and at the same time help you. Tough times are good!

Tough times create unique and unexpected opportunities. In tough times, you create more opportunities than you find. This book is filled with examples of tough times creating opportunities. Good times feel great, but good times obscure our view toward even greater opportunities. When things are good, sellers lack the desire to find something greater. The sting of tough times creates the courage and desire to pursue such opportunities. Tough times are good!

Tough times thin the herd. Tough times are destructive and democratic. Some competitors will not survive tough times. A thinning herd means an abundance of opportunities for you. Tough times are challenging, and some customers and colleagues will not survive. Those are the toughest lessons. The toughest lessons lead to the greatest triumphs. That extreme pain catalyzes the individual to grow and eventually flourish. Tough times are good though not pain free.

Selling through tough times requires the right attitude and the right skills—this book provides the tools to find both. You'll learn the right mental framework and the skills to thrive through tough times. Selling through tough times requires a different mindset and sales approach. Throughout this book, you will gain a deeper understanding of how selling through tough times is different. There are six *critical selling activities* (CSAs) to guide your effort through tough times. The basic principles of selling are constant, but tough times add a new dynamic that forces you to adapt. These CSAs guide you through the tough times and help you prevail once they subside. Success through tough times is about daily progress—moving forward when times are the toughest. This book is filled with exercises that will help you to transfer ideas into daily activities.

Tough times are relative to the industry and the individual. Neither has a monopoly on tough times. Everyone experiences tough times to varying degrees. Some go through them; others *grow* through them. Regardless of how tough your time is, someone always has it tougher than you, and someone always has it easier than you. Don't waste your energy comparing your tough times to anyone else's.

In this book, you'll learn what it takes to be a tough timer. Tough timers thrive mentally and financially during tough times and fly even higher once tough times pass. You'll learn to think and sell like a tough timer. There is a tough timer within all of us, but this inner strength is revealed only through tough times. Don't get frustrated if you don't feel like a tough timer; maybe you haven't experienced enough tough times to reveal your true strength. In this book, you'll learn how to challenge yourself every day and thrive like a tough timer.

Part III of this book provides additional selling and leadership tips. Selling through tough times is an opportunity to get back to the basics of selling and leadership. Included are segments on pipeline management, customer messaging, and leadership. Chapter 16 includes basic principles for leading and coaching your team through tough times.

Tough times are good! I hope that you don't merely go through tough times; I hope that you *grow* through tough times. Take full advantage of the tough time you are currently experiencing. Your progress will be painful and not always visible, but it will be meaningful. Happy selling!

PART I

TOUGH TIMES

W hat are tough times? How do tough times affect our thoughts and actions? How does my customer define value in tough times? These are just a few questions answered in this first section.

Tough times are challenging to define and even harder to predict. In this opening section, you'll learn how to define tough times and understand the relative nature of tough times. You'll appreciate that each individual defines tough times in different ways. Your past experiences, not the experiences of others, determine your threshold of toughness.

Once tough times are defined, you'll discover how they affect your thoughts and your customers' thoughts. You will gain a deeper understanding of how tough times influence your customers' thoughts, which clues you in to their definition of value.

Although tough times are painful, you'll appreciate the positive aspects of tough times. Tough times spark creativity and drive innovation. By embracing tough times, you open your mind to all the possibilities they create.

How do I mentally prepare to sell through tough times? How do I handle the constant rejection? These are the other questions answered in Part 1.

Tough times are mentally fatiguing; they exhaust you. True mental strength is revealed only when it's tested. In this section, you'll gain a deeper understanding of the mental mistakes sellers make in tough times. Identifying these mistakes will help you avoid them.

You'll learn about the Daily Mental Flex® and how to build a foundation of mental resilience. You'll read about tough timers and their characteristics.

Tough timers are individuals who thrive through challenging times. You'll learn how to approach adversity like a tough timer.

You will learn how to muster the mental strength you need to face tough situations. Mental strength is one of the most overlooked and underestimated aspects of selling. In Chapters 4 to 6, you will discover practical ways to build the right mindset. Selling is already tough, and you will learn how to push through the pain and progress forward.

CHAPTER 1

What Are Tough Times?

Today, a salesperson blew a huge presentation, lost the opportunity, and embarrassed himself in front of his peers. His company was depending on this deal to stay afloat. To make matters worse, he had to explain to his boss why he blew the sale. It was the worst day of his professional career.

Later that day, another salesperson from the same company lost her largest customer. She couldn't believe the customer went to a competitor for cheaper pricing. Now she must tell her boss that she lost the company's biggest customer. This will be the toughest conversation of her career.

The CEO of this company is agonizing over whether to initiate layoffs. Profits are suffering, and the company is losing money. Now that the company's biggest customer has left, layoffs are imminent. It's the toughest decision he will ever make.

Last year, another salesperson was diagnosed with cancer. Today she is heading to the hospital for another round of chemotherapy. She is fighting for her life—experiencing pain she has never felt before. This is the toughest battle of her life. What do all these people have in common? They are experiencing tough times. No one person has a monopoly on tough times. Whether personally or professionally, everyone experiences tough times.

Tough times are relative to your experiences, not to the experiences of others. Someone always has it better, and worse, than you. Comparing cancer to a sales slump seems outrageous, and it is. Battling cancer is on a different pain level than losing a sale, but both still cause pain. Viktor Frankl, the famous Austrian psychiatrist, author, and Holocaust survivor, had this to say about suffering:

To draw an analogy: a man's suffering is similar to the behavior of a gas. If a certain quantity of gas is pumped into an empty chamber, it will fill the chamber completely and evenly, no matter how big the chamber. Thus suffering completely fills the human soul and conscious mind, no matter whether the suffering is great or little. Therefore the size of human suffering is absolutely relative.

As a Holocaust survivor, Frankl experienced unimaginable pain and suffering, yet he acknowledges the relativity of tough times. Tough times are as diverse as the people experiencing them. It's useless comparing your tough times with those of other people.

In business, tough times are a steady or sharp decline in economic performance. Tough times are most common during economic recessions or depressions. Economic downturns also impact specific sectors of the economy. These downturns are rolling recessions. An industry facing disruption or stiff competition is facing tough times.

Tough times extend beyond financial hardship to mental hardships. Mental downturns manifest in feelings of helplessness, hopelessness, and general unhappiness for an extended period. Mental downturns and economic downturns often appear together. Sellers feeling hopeless struggle to perform, leading to steeper financial hardships, which lead to stronger feelings of hopelessness, creating a vicious cycle.

Tough times are unrelenting. They stack up on you. When times are tough, they can always get worse. Tough times are indiscriminate and democratic. They happen to anyone at any time. Some people experience more, others experience less. By engaging in life, you experience tough times (and the good times that follow).

Tough times form a foundation of resilience. This foundation enables you to carry heavier burdens with greater ease. Without tough times, your foundation remains unfortified. Novice tough timers face unprecedented challenges that force them to dig deep. First-timers emerge stronger—usually surprised at their newly uncovered strength.

Think of the four people in the opening example. Imagine a cancer survivor experiencing a sales slump. Would a cancer survivor even register a sales slump as a tough time? Probably not. Today's tough times are filtered through your previous experiences. Your previous pain tightens your tough-time spectrum. The more difficult the past, the easier the future.

Tough times are relative to your previous experiences. If you sold through the 2008 Great Recession, a mild downturn wouldn't faze you. Selling through your first recession is more challenging than selling through your third. Previous tough times temper your frustration and strengthen your resolve. Your foundation prepares you to navigate uncertainty. It's challenging to develop toughness when times are mostly good. Powerlifters lift massive amounts of weight because they build a foundation of strength. You wouldn't expect a rookie to shoulder the same load as an experienced bodybuilder. The same is true for someone experiencing hardship for the first time.

Regarding tough times, there are two irrefutable truths: tough times happen, and tough times are temporary. No matter how tough the time, it will pass—as will the good times. Tough times are always on the horizon, but so are the good times that follow. Tough times and good times are fleeting. The average expansion lasts three times longer than the average downturn.[1] So tough times are just a little more fleeting than the good times that follow.

TOUGH TIMES THROUGHOUT HISTORY

A thought for my fellow CEOs: Of course, the immediate future is uncertain; America has faced the unknown since 1776. It's just that sometimes people focus on the myriad of uncertainties that always exist while at other times they ignore them (usually because the recent past has been uneventful).
—WARREN BUFFETT, 2013 Open Letter to CEOs[2]

In 2013, Warren Buffett wrote an open letter to CEOs. Buffett's remarks aptly explain uncertainty and tough times throughout history. Uncertainty is part of sales. Nothing is guaranteed. In this same letter, Buffett mentions, "[W]e are playing a game highly stacked in our favor." In a downturn, it's natural to focus more on uncertainty than on opportunity. In the long term, though, there is always more opportunity than uncertainty.

Downturns and setbacks are part of our history, but our history is also overflowing with expansion and growth. The United States has experienced more than 40 recessions or depressions and several global recessions. Recessions are inevitable, but each downturn is followed by further economic expansion. Balance your uncertainty with hope; the lowest point begins the turnaround. Don't let the current doom and gloom obscure your vision for a brighter future.

Tough times are unique, and so are the opportunities they reveal. Each tough time builds your resilience and bolsters your playbook to manage future tough times. For example, the housing crisis during the Great Recession forced banks to reform lending practices, stabilizing the housing market and mortgage industry. The Federal Deposit Insurance Corporation (FDIC) was created due to thousands of failing banks during the Great Depression. Although tough times are painful, we learn from them.

Tough times are relative throughout history. Imagine living through the Great Depression, constantly reciting the motto, "Use it up, wear it out, make do or do without." This mindset lasted almost four years. Relatively speaking, the Great Recession of 2008 does not seem that bad.

Previous failures are great teachers; we continue learning from them. Previous tough times teach us to manage the next tough time more effectively. In the 13 recessions and depressions prior to the Great Depression, the downturn lasted 16.2 months, and the average expansion was 22.4 months. Since the Great Depression, there have been 13 recessions. The average length of those recessions was 10.4 months, and the average expansion was 59.4 months. Expansions have nearly tripled, while downturns have almost been cut in half[3]—meaning, we are learning to manage downturns more effectively.

Many industries face tough times. Think of small mom-and-pop shops struggling to compete in the wake of Walmart. Think of the oil and gas industry facing regulatory hurdles. In the spring of 2020, the price of crude oil dipped below $0 per barrel. Dairy farmers struggle to stay afloat and compete with large megadairies. No industry is immune to tough times. The only way to inoculate yourself from tough times is to learn, adapt, and grow.

Companies grow through the tough times they experience. Many darlings of Wall Street faced early struggles and emerged stronger. The Walt Disney Company thrives today, but consider the early failures of Walt Disney's career. One of his most notable failures was Laugh-O-Gram Studios in Kansas City, Missouri. Walt Disney was on the verge of a breakthrough, but it did not happen in time. He had to close up shop. He went out to California to build his empire. Shortly after the move, Disney experienced another devastating blow. A distributor stole one of his cartoons and several of his artists. Once again, Disney was on the brink of failure. Only this time he channeled his frustration to create an icon of American optimism. That icon was, of course, Mickey Mouse.[4] There is no doubt that Disney's early failures shaped his success in building one of the most admired companies and beloved characters.

Apple's success today is a far cry from its early days. Apple's current market valuation is more than $3 trillion. Apple is one of the most successful organizations to ever exist, yet the company nearly faced bankruptcy in the late 1990s. Apple was struggling and desperate. At that moment of hopelessness, an unlikely hero saved the company with a $150 million investment. Steve Jobs undoubtedly learned from the experience. In later interviews, he said, "Apple had to remember who Apple was because they'd forgotten who Apple was."[5] Once Apple remembered who it was, the company experienced unparalleled success. If it weren't for that tough time, perhaps Apple wouldn't be in the position it is in today.

Would you start a company during a recession? If given a choice, most people would say no. Why make it any harder on yourself? But those tough times also build a resilient foundation. Wouldn't it be better to have that foundation from the very beginning? History is filled with great companies born through tough times, for example, General Motors, Burger King, Hewlett-Packard, Trader Joe's, Mailchimp, Uber, and of course, Microsoft—the unlikely hero that bailed out Apple with the $150 million investment.

Tough times happen throughout history. Tough times can be unique to an era, industry, or a particular company. Those who adapt and evolve during tough times not only survive but also thrive. We will face more tough times. But we'll also face greater economic expansion as we learn from tough times. George Santayana, the Spanish philosopher, is credited with saying, "Those who don't learn from the past are doomed to repeat it." Conversely, those who learn from their past tough times are destined to expand from them. Tough times are good!

RECOGNIZING TOUGH-TIME SIGNALS

> The stock market had correctly predicted
> nine of the last five recessions.
> —PAUL SAMUELSON[6]

Samuelson's witty comment adequately explains our ability to predict the economic future. We know for certain that tough times happen—determining when is where we struggle. Tough times can appear gradually and predictably or suddenly, without warning. Even when there are signals, those indicators are not completely accurate. There is no crystal ball telling you exactly when the next downturn is coming. Industries are caught off guard by tough times but quickly rebound. It's not uncommon to be out of a recession before recognizing that you were in one.

Tough times are elusive and unpredictable. They are elusive because of our cognitive biases. When things go well, we believe they will continue going well. During good economic times, sellers succumb to the hot-hand fallacy in psychology. The *hot hand* is a basketball reference to a player "on a roll" or "in the zone." As spectators, we believe that the player is more likely to make his next shot because he made his previous shots.

The hot-hand fallacy explains the surprising nature of tough times. If we're hitting our targets and continue putting in the work, we expect performance to follow. Just as the basketball player believes he'll make the next shot, we believe that we'll keep performing well. If we're expecting to perform well, we're likely to miss tough-time signals—until we start missing shots.

No one can predict tough times with 100 percent accuracy. However, there are indicators that signal that tough times are on the horizon. Some signals are tangible, others not. Some factors are leading indicators, others are lagging indicators. Some indicators are company and industry specific, whereas others are broad. Company- or industry-specific indicators could be intracompany challenges, a tough competitor, or industry disruption. Broad economic indicators focus on the overall health of the economy. Recessions are defined as a period of temporary economic decline during which trade and industrial activity are reduced, generally identified by a fall in gross domestic product in two successive quarters. Here is a list of economic indicators to monitor when you sense tough times:

- **Unemployment rate.** A rising unemployment rate indicates that tough times are on the horizon. The inverse is true for good times. Ironically, extremely low unemployment rates also create challenges.
- **Consumer Confidence Index (CCI).** This index provides a window into consumers' attitudes and purchasing intentions. A falling CCI indicates tough times.
- **Purchasing Managers' Index (PMI).** This index measures supply-chain activity in the manufacturing and services sector of the economy. A number below 50 indicates economic decline.

- **Federal Reserve interest rate (FED rate).** Lowering the FED rate generally means that the Federal Reserve is trying to stimulate the economy, indicating tough times.
- **Housing starts.** This is the number of new residential construction projects starting in a period of time. Fewer starts indicate less confident consumers in the economy.

There are other common signals within your company or industry that indicate that tough times are coming. There could be a decline in sales, customer attrition, layoffs, or shrinking profits. For individual sellers facing tough times, indicators include missing sales targets, losing customers, and a decrease in selling activity.

There are less tangible signals of tough times. These signals are less concrete but still provide a window into the future: customers claiming business is slow, repairing versus replacing equipment, and cost-cutting campaigns. You might experience more price objections from your customers. Discretionary spending decreases, and people may start saving more money. Ask your UPS or FedEx driver if he or she is staying busy. You might notice a general decline in business activity: fewer meetings, less interest in products, lower conference attendance.

A general sense of unease can be a leading indicator of tough times. Have you ever had the feeling that things are going too well? Everything seems to be going your way. You're on a roll. As things continue going well, you wonder if the universe is going to knock you back down to reality. This is sometimes called the *law of averages* or *regression to the mean*. We think, "Things are going great. Is something bad going to happen to balance out all this good stuff I'm experiencing?"

In the beginning of *Meet the Fockers* (Universal Pictures, 2004), Greg (Ben Stiller) and his wife Pam (Teri Polo) are headed to the airport. A stranger gives up his cab so that Greg and Pam can get to the airport quicker. They magically hit all green lights on the way to the airport. Coach seating is overbooked, so they receive complimentary upgrades to first class. While they are waiting in a long security line, a TSA agent opens another line for them. Everything is going great. In fact, Greg feels so confident about his trip that he doesn't buy rental car insurance. Shortly after the opening credits, the universe knocks Greg down a few notches. As you're watching the opening scene, you know something bad is *going* to happen.

A "feeling" that a slowdown is coming is not a certainty, but it is concerning. This happens after an elongated period of expansion. A feeling something bad will happen sounds like an overly pessimistic mindset. Although this indicator is not scientific, it is real. Be aware of this signal, but don't let it influence your attitude.

Tough times are hard to predict; there is no start or end date. Tough times arrive and go like a mild headache. With a mild headache, the onset of pain is gradual, and then it becomes noticeable. You're not sure exactly when the headache started, but you're experiencing it now. You take some medicine for the pain, and the headache goes away. Do you remember the exact moment it subsided? Probably not. After a while, you simply notice the pain is gone. Tough times subside like a headache; they gradually enter and leave. When you're going through tough times, you eventually notice that the pain is gone, and then, suddenly, you're back in good times.

Tough times are always on the horizon, and so is greater economic expansion. Even experts cannot accurately predict the next downturn. Be aware of the signals, but don't get too frustrated by them. Instead, use these signals as a trigger to prepare. You may not be able to predict tough times, but you can prepare for them.

THE ONSET OF TOUGH TIMES

Tough times appear in different forms and on different timelines. Businesses are built on a continuum of growth and decline. This continuum is shaped in the four phases of the business cycle: expansion, peak, contraction, and trough. Viewing tough times as a business cycle normalizes and stabilizes the uncertainty we face in tough times. There is also a mental cycle we experience during tough times. As we experience peaks and valleys, there are waves of uncertainty challenging the mentally toughest sellers.

Some tough times appear slowly and steadily. For example, your industry faces mounting competitive pressure as it matures or continuous pressure from regulations. This pressure causes a slow, steady, and sometimes unnoticeable decline. The gradual onset deteriorates at a slow, digestible rate. Slow and steady declines invoke the *boiling frog effect*. If you put a frog directly in boiling water, it leaps out of the pot. If you put the frog in a pot with cool water and then bring it to a boil, the frog complacently sits in the water waiting to be boiled alive. You're more likely to accept a slowly deteriorating environment than change it. The pain involved in change exceeds the pain of the deteriorating environment. Pain extended over a longer time frame is less intense. Like the frog in the pot, we're not likely to change. Tough times that appear gradually do the most damage.

Other tough times shock our system, for example, losing your largest customer, tectonic industry shifts, natural disasters, and a global pandemic. You face a tsunami of change (and pain) in a matter of days, weeks, and months rather than years. Like a slow and steady tough time, you experience pain, but the pain window is smaller—meaning, the day-to-day pain is more intense. This acute pain acts as a stronger catalyst for change. This is one of the few benefits of sudden and unexpected tough times.

THE MENTAL PHASES OF TOUGH TIMES

In 1907, Bill Klann worked for a Detroit ice company. It was hard work with low pay, but Bill was happy to have a job. Unfortunately, Bill was laid off later that year. Out of work and out of patience, Bill contacted his previous employer—an automobile manufacturer. It was harder work for less money, but again, Bill was happy to have a job. For several years, Bill worked hard and was a model employee. Bill's boss assigned him a special project to speed up production.

In 1913, Bill visited a slaughterhouse in Chicago. He watched the workers systematically dismember hogs and cattle as they went down the line. This might have been an unpleasant experience for some people, but Bill found it inspiring. He thought to himself, "If you can take something apart this way, you can put something together this way." Bill quickly rushed back to his boss to present his idea. His employer eventually bought into Bill's idea. Both Bill and his employer experienced greater success.[7]

Tough times are as unique as the people experiencing them, but Bill's story provides a template for managing tough times. There are three mental stages every person experiences during tough times: *acknowledge, act,* and *adapt*. Bill had to acknowledge his tough time—getting fired. Bill took action—found a new job. He then adapted and improved.

Acknowledge

Acknowledgment is a far cry from acceptance. Acknowledge tough times without accepting tough times. Denial is not a strategy; there is no benefit to ignoring tough times. You can't realize the hidden benefits of tough times unless you admit that you are experiencing them. The key is to acknowledge without accepting. Acceptance is too permanent.

Acknowledgment is the bare minimum of recognition. When you fall on tough times, don't dwell on them. Recognize reality, but choose not to accept it. As one business owner said at a company meeting, "Apparently, there is a recession, but we've decided not to participate in it." The crowd erupted. That's acknowledgment, not acceptance. Tough times are temporary, and so is the associated pain, but the benefits can last forever. Acknowledge tough times with the expectation of taking action.

Act

In tough times, people are tempted to pause. When people feel stuck, some wait for help or for the situation to improve. This doesn't work. Sales is an action-oriented profession. You can't wait your way out of a rut. Bill could have sulked and waited for things to improve, but he didn't. He took action and found another job. When you're in a rut, you need to gain traction. If you want to gain traction, take action.

Newton's first law: An object at rest stays at rest, and an object in motion stays in motion unless it's acted on by an outside force.[8] In good times, you're in motion, and you'll stay in motion. You are taking action, and it's paying off. Then you experience tough times—the outside force. Some people let this outside force slow them down, whereas others judo-flip that outside force in their favor. Once tough times slow you down, take more action to stay on your intended course.

Increasing activity is challenging in tough times. You may feel like you're working twice as hard to produce half the results, which is frustrating. Focus more on progress in tough times, not just performance. Multiple setbacks will tempt you to wait it out, but you cannot wait your way to success. To stay motivated in tough times, change your focus. It's less about performance and more about progression. Take action to achieve progress. Progress is a leading indicator of future success.

Tough times are positioning opportunities. Your goal is to attain mind share and market share by taking massive action. Position yourself to emerge faster and stronger from tough times. Within each of us there is a deep desire to grow, evolve, and move forward. Progress is the same as achievement, no matter how minimal it may be. Achievement breeds confidence, encouraging us to do a little more. When you're stuck in a rut, any progress pushes you closer to your goal.

Adapt

Failure is a great teacher. Failure forces us to adapt. Consider your career progression from your first sales call to your last. You adapted only because you failed. Failure not only motivates you to improve, but it also provides the feedback to improve.

Painful failures motivate us to tweak our approach and try new things. As you fail through tough times, don't shy away from the pain; embrace it. Harness that pain and let it stimulate change. We eventually become numb to the ill-effects of pain. The sting of pain is temporary, but the positive change it creates is permanent.

Think of Bill Klann's experience, and apply the acknowledge-act-adapt approach. Bill acknowledged his tough time of getting fired; then he took action to find a new job. He continued to act and adapt and was eventually given a special project. He continued acting and adapting, developing an idea for systematically putting things together. Bill's employer, Henry Ford, eventually bought into the assembly-line idea. The assembly line significantly lowered the Model T's price, doubling Ford's market share.

Bill persevered. As with any success, we often marvel at the achievement but forget other factors leading to the success. There were two significant events that set the stage for Bill's and Ford's success. And those two events have one thing in common—tough times.

Let's analyze the timing of the two main events in this story: Bill's firing and Bill's discovery of the assembly line. In 1907, there was a run on one of the nation's largest banks that led to a recession. Bill was fired from that ice company because of the economic fallout from that recession. If there had been no recession, would Bill have been fired?

In 1913, Ford assigned Bill to improve productivity. This initiative was during the recession of 1913–1914. Ford was facing tough times and looking for ways to reduce costs. If there had been no recession, would Bill have been tasked with this cost-cutting project? Not likely. Ford's assembly line revolutionized the manufacturing process. Tough times ushered in new ideas and concepts leading to Ford's success. Tough times are good!

Tough times are filled with uncertainty but also opportunity. Uncertainty either clouds your vision or acts as the lens to explore the depths of what is possible. Some people use uncertainty as an excuse to wait it out, whereas others use it as motivation to press on. Have you ever met a successful person who waited his or her way to success? No. When you fall on tough times, you either wait it out or you gut it out. The choice is yours.

There is no denying that tough times are frustrating and painful. In life, we are taught to avoid pain. To avoid the pain of tough times, people give up. This is a mistake. Pain acts as a catalyst for positive change. When tough times knock you down, you either give up or you stand up. Again, the choice is yours.

Tough times are inevitable in business and life. How you manage the valley of tough times determines your peak in the good times. Through tough times, don't pause; press on instead. Your action might not deliver the desired result, but take action anyway. Your progress is proof of achievement. Your tough-times prescription is simple: acknowledge the tough time, take massive action, and adapt as necessary. Whether you see it or not, you're moving in the right direction. Your progress is not always visible and pain free, but it is always meaningful. Tough times are good!

SUMMARY

Tough times come in many shapes and forms. Tough times could be a broad economic downturn, a tough competitor, or anything in between. Tough times are not limited to a financial downturn but also include a mental downturn. Tough times are part of life. By actively engaging in life, you experience them. No matter how painful they are, tough times are temporary. However, the positive change they create can be permanent.

Our previous tough times are great teachers. Previous downturns provide new tools to better manage recessions. Despite our advancement, we still can't predict tough times with absolute certainty. However, there are metrics that signal that tough times are on the horizon. Look for those signals. Like the business cycle, there is also a mental cycle. This mental cycle begins with acknowledging the tough time, taking action, and adapting as necessary.

Tough times are as unique as the individuals who experience them. Your previous tough times build a foundation of resilience. Tough times are relative to your previous experiences, not the experiences of others.

CHAPTER 2

How Tough Times Impact
Our Thoughts and Actions

Thoughts and actions run on a continuous loop. Tough times influence our thoughts, which, in turn, influence our behavior. Buyers think differently and buy differently in tough times. They have different priorities, needs, and concerns. This new mindset leads to new buying behavior. Sellers also think differently and sell differently in tough times. Sellers have different priorities and concerns. This leads to new selling behavior. This chapter focuses on how tough times affect our thoughts and actions.

In some cases, buyers and sellers have similar mindsets. This synchronous mindset creates an opportunity for sellers to deeply understand their buyers. The underlying motivation behind their thoughts and actions is the same. Although mindsets are similar, these thoughts manifest differently in their behavior and, in certain cases, contrary to one another.

Newton's third law: For every action, there is an equal and opposite reaction.[1] Newton's law has implications for selling through tough times. Selling through tough times is a constant push and pull. As sellers push to sell more, buyers pull back resources to spend less. Buyers and sellers are concerned about economic uncertainty. In response, a buyer might cut spending to conserve resources, whereas sellers may sell aggressively to create more resources. Tough times force sellers to be more aggressive and buyers to be more conservative. The action is different, but the behavior stems from the same scarcity mindset. The same fundamental mindset is driving both behaviors. Therein lies the opportunity for sellers to think like their buyers on a deeper level.

Buyers use different criteria and motives in a downturn. These new motives and criteria influence how they define value. Sellers are challenged with understanding buyers' new thought processes and then redefining value in more relevant ways. After reading this chapter, you'll understand *how* buyers act and *why* they act.

Sellers think and sell differently through tough times. The seller's new mindset influences behavior both positively and negatively. In this chapter, you'll discover the common mistakes sellers make through tough times. These mistakes are easy to recognize but challenging to overcome. Prevailing in tough times requires greater control of your thoughts leading to positive behavior. Control your thoughts, control your actions.

HOW BUYERS THINK IN TOUGH TIMES

Your success in a downturn rests on your ability to understand how buyers think. Are you confident that you fully understand how your buyers think? Research at Tom Reilly Training revealed that 80 percent of salespeople implied they clearly understand their buyers' needs. However, a follow-up study shows that three out of four buyers believe that salespeople *don't* fully understand their needs or buying process.[2] There is a disconnect between how sellers think and how buyers feel. Most sellers believe that they do a good job; most buyers believe that they do not.

We do not completely understand our buyers' needs, but there is a fundamental truth to guide us: buyers want value. Value is a constant. How it's defined is not. Value is relatively defined by individual buyers. Understanding your buyers' mindset provides a deeper understanding of how they define value. Customers define value, and their definition is the only one that matters. In tough times, customers think differently and define value differently. Your success depends on your ability to understand these differences.

Uncovering the inner thoughts and desires of a buyer can be challenging. What buyers do and say can differ from how they feel. Feelings are not as transparent as words and actions—especially in tough times. Buyers conceal their thoughts and feelings for several reasons. They don't want to appear vulnerable in a negotiation. They are fearful of misusing their company resources. They are uncertain about their future or their company's future. Savvy buyers conceal information that hurts their negotiating leverage. These concealed insights are attainable through a deep understanding of how buyers think.

Buyers need sellers who create value. Whether buyers show it or not, they need you through tough times. Buyers rely on you to craft solutions that address their hidden concerns and desires. This depth of understanding requires a full immersion into the customer's world. You can only focus at this level by taking the focus off yourself.

Empathy is taking the buyers' perspective—imagining what it's like to be them. Empathy is necessary for any sales success, but especially during tough times. Struggling buyers need you to see their perspective, not merely sell your product. Empathy is a dynamic selling trait. Empathy is a skill that needs constant development. Empathy is ever evolving, like your buyer's definition of value. Customers define value relatively based on their unique situation. Sellers constantly face new situations requiring new perspective. Developing this skill in tough times helps you succeed long after the tough times pass.

You'll notice a common motivator as you immerse yourself in the buyers' minds: fear. In tough times, buyers are filled with fear. Buyers are unsure when tough times will pass and what the world will look like after. This stems from fear. In tough times, buyers are concerned about wasting money or time and missing opportunities. Fear of missed opportunity (FOMO) stems from fear.

Fear is a powerful motivator in good times and more potent in tough times. Fear drives our thoughts, which drive our actions. As you read, ask yourself, "How are my buyers demonstrating uncertainty, scarcity, and FOMO?" Compile a list, and use it to explore the depths of your buyers' minds. Volumes have been written on how we think. This chapter provides a basic understanding of the buyer's mind in tough times.

Uncertainty

Imagine that you are the driver on a road trip. You're cruising along, and the GPS stops working. You reach a fork in the road. You can turn right or left. All the passengers are glaring at you wondering which way you'll turn. The suspense and anxiousness are taking over. Inside your head, you're screaming, "Which way should I go?" If you turn the wrong way, you will veer off course. With no GPS, you could be lost for hours. Everyone is depending on you, but you don't know what to do. So do you turn left or right?

Tough times are like a road trip. Decision makers are driving the organization—under a constant cloud of uncertainty. The car is full of team members expecting the decision makers to make the right decision. In these decisions, there is more at stake than simply turning around.

Buyers, like most humans, want things moving on a steady and predictable path. However, "Challenge the status quo" is a common mantra among business leaders and corporations. As we are encouraged to challenge the status quo, we also take comfort within it. This new level of uncertainty impacts buyers' decisions—clinging to anything familiar and stable. With the weight of *their* world on their shoulders, buyers ask, "Should I turn left or right?"

The future is always uncertain. It seems more uncertain in tough times because we lack the information we need to navigate the uncertainty. Buyers don't have answers to the questions swarming in their minds. Therefore, buyers pause and delay their decisions. Tough times highlight the buyers' information gap, creating an opportunity for sellers. As buyers look for stability, sellers can provide stable footing and close the information gap.

Dig for the root cause of a buyer's uncertainty. Understanding the root cause helps you to understand the buyer's uncertain world. When assessing your buyer's world, ask yourself the following questions:

- Why is their world so uncertain?
- What's leading to their uncertainty?
- How can I demonstrate stability and certainty in my messaging?
- What tectonic shifts are going on in their world?

Scarcity

In business, resources are scarce. Through tough times, those resources seem a little scarcer. It's natural to protect and hoard what is scarce. Companies reduce spending, cut costs, and decrease budgets. When buyers' resources are scarce, they take a myopic view. They focus on satisfying their basic and immediate needs rather than maximizing their value in the long run.

People are fearful of misusing scarce resources like money. As resources become scarcer, buying decisions are scrutinized. Nobody likes making decisions under a microscope. Because of this heavy scrutiny, buyers question and challenge different aspects of the solution, including price. Buyers operating from an abundance mindset take greater risks. Buyers adopt the mindset of a gambler playing with house money: *it's okay if it doesn't work out; there are other ways to make it up.*

Scarcity-minded buyers are fearful of spending too much or overpaying. They're not cheap, just concerned about protecting their scarce resources.

Money provides stability. Ample resources stabilize uncertainty. When a company loses that stability, everyone is on edge. Through tough times, buyers view saving dollars as job security for themselves and for fellow employees. More dollars saved equals more jobs saved. To alleviate your buyers' concerns, demonstrate how your solution gives them more of the resource they're afraid of losing. That resource could be more money, cash flow, or time.

Opportunity FOMO—Fear of Missing Opportunities

A crisis is a terrible thing to waste.

—PAUL ROMER, Stanford economist, referring to
the unexpected opportunities of tough times[3]

Tough times are filled with fear, uncertainty, and scarcity. Paradoxically, tough times are also filled with opportunity. Buyers are equally concerned about missing opportunities as they are about misusing their resources. The fear of wasting a resource compels buyers to conserve and hoard. Because opportunities are resources, the fear of missing an opportunity just as easily compels a buyer to act. The same way a dip in the stock market represents an investment opportunity, an economic downturn represents a growth opportunity. To paraphrase Romer's point, a tough time is a terrible thing to waste.

Buyers focus on what is visible to them, that's why uncertainty and scarcity run amok in tough times. Where some buyers see uncertainty and scarcity, others see opportunity. These buyers view tough times as opportunities to gain traction and invest in their business. These buyers are more confident in their future and willing to take chances. These abundance-minded buyers represent growth opportunities in tough times.

How often do buyers use time as an excuse? They tell you, "We like your idea, we just don't have time to make it happen. Someday we'll revisit this opportunity." Someday is today. Tough times create unique opportunities. The scarcest resource, time, is now available. Buyers might have long-term initiatives they were planning to roll out or new projects to implement. This available time is an opportunity to act.

Tough times create investment opportunities. Baron Rothschild, British nobleman and member of the renowned Rothschild banking family, said, "The time to buy is when there's blood in the streets."[4] Any savvy investor looks for buying opportunities, not selling opportunities. Buy low and sell high. This sounds great, but the best time to buy is often the time filled with the most uncertainty and pain.

There are decision makers patiently and prudently looking for these opportunities. Forward-thinking buyers view tough times as purchasing opportunities. They view tough times as opportunities to gain a competitive edge. They invest in new equipment, new buildings, their people, and so on. They opportunistically invest through tough times; that's one of the reasons for their success.

Your goal is to understand the fear buyers experience. Live in it, breath it, and see it through their eyes. You can only understand your buyer by fully immersing yourself in their world. Buyers face uncertainty, scarcity, and opportunity with every decision they make. Fear is the root cause of these emotions: the fear of what *could* happen; the fear of wasting a resource; and the greatest fear, missing an opportunity. Tough times will pass, the fear you and the buyer feel will subside. Until it does, remember that the most repeated phrase in the bestselling book of all time is "Don't be afraid."[5]

WHAT BUYERS DO IN TOUGH TIMES

Fear is the motivator that drives our thoughts. Our thoughts drive our actions. How buyers think determines how they act. Action is a manifestation of thought. Fear is why they think how they think, and how they think determines what the buyer will do. Fully immersing yourself in the buyer's mind gives you an understanding of the *why* behind what they do. The previous section focused on the *why*; this section focuses on the *what*.

Pause

"When you don't know what to do, do nothing."[6] Although Mark Cuban was referring to his number-one rule of investing, he could be describing buyer decision-making. When buyers are unsure about the future, they hit the pause button. This is a natural response to fear and uncertainty. Buyers tell themselves, "When you don't know what to do, do nothing. Hold your ground and hunker down."

It's common for buyers to delay projects and purchasing decisions through tough times. This pause is due to the uncertainty of the current situation. When buyers feel less certain about the future, they take fewer risks.

Why would a buyer make a long-term investment if they have trouble seeing the future? It's hard buying into a better future if the buyer can't visualize that better future. Once the future stabilizes, the comfort of reality sets in. With this newly found certainty, buyers become more open to your ideas. In Chapters 9 and 10, you'll discover new ways to influence the buyer and open their mind to your ideas.

Cost Cutting

Cutting cost is a prudent strategy in tough times. When tough times hit, companies conserve cash. Businesses analyze spending habits to identify cost-cutting opportunities. Buyers review vendor relationships, look for cheaper alternatives, adjust purchasing timelines, and request discounts. Some companies freeze their spending. The degree of the freeze is determined by the necessity of your product. If the buyer must have it, they'll keep buying. But, if they can live without your product, then you'll notice a drop-off. In tough times, buyers clarify purchasing priorities, focusing on what they must have versus what is nice to have.

Cost-cutting is really an opportunity masquerading as a challenge. Buyers (and sellers) often misread cost-cutting campaigns as price-cutting campaigns. Buyers focus on reducing overall cost by requesting discounts. Over 70 percent of the time, sellers are going to cave in, destroying profits and setting expectations for future discounts. Price is tangible but it's only one aspect of cost. Cutting cost opens the conversation to all the ways you reduce cost. What if you viewed cost-cutting as an opportunity to create value rather than cut price?

Cost-cutting campaigns start new conversations with buyers leading to additional opportunity. Think of the ways your solution reduces the buyer's costs: labor costs, logistical costs, engineering costs, reducing downtime, energy costs, maintenance costs, and so on. Cost is bigger than price. Cost includes everything the buyer sacrifices in addition to price. These campaigns are opportunities to explore new ways to create value for your buyer. Tough times are good!

In cost-cutting campaigns, buyers falsely believe every dollar saved is pure profit. However, a dollar saved doesn't account for the value forfeited to save that dollar. In tough times, buyers look for low-hanging fruit to cut. Buyers analyze what they save compared to the value they receive. It's easier to cut a solution that creates less value. Cost without value diminishes you in good times and destroys you in tough times. If your solution is in danger, demonstrate how cutting your solution would lead to a greater cut in profitability. Remind the buyer they cannot cut their way to success.

Self-Preservation (Survival)

When tough times appear, buyers shift to survival gear. People are fearful of losing what they have: money, resources, their job. It's natural to focus on your own survival through tough times. The severity of your previous tough times determines the intensity of these survival instincts. The tougher the times, the stronger buyers focus on self-preservation.

Buyers hit hard during previous tough times scrutinize their decisions through the prism of self-preservation. These buyers ask, "Is this decision more likely or less likely to get me fired?" Buyers asking these questions stay below the radar and out of the spotlight. These decision makers distance themselves from any failure while clinging to any success. Be wary of such buyers because they won't hesitate to throw you under the bus. These risk-averse decision makers are careful when making highly visible decisions.

Other buyers view challenging times as an opportunity to stand out. These decision makers take chances and make bold decisions. These bold decisions enhance their career trajectory or propel their company forward. These decision makers are eager to prove their value. They're not looking to survive; they want to thrive. They are more motivated to prevail than they are afraid to fail.

Too many buyers worry about survival—theirs or their colleagues—in tough times. Remind buyers that survival is simple: find ways to create more value. Self-preservation is a function of creating value. Companies keep employees who create value, and buyers partner with sellers who create value.

Remind buyers (and yourself) of their role in creating value. In a training seminar, one seller expressed her frustration trying to persuade a buyer to change. The buyer acknowledged that the solution was better and saves the company money, but she was hesitant to change because of the tough times the company was experiencing. I encouraged the seller to evoke the buyer's self-preservation motivation. After more discussion, we crafted a strategy.

The seller went back to the buyer with this message: "I understand, during these uncertain times, that decisions are heavily scrutinized. Your industry is accustomed to tough times, and every employee is tasked with creating value for their organization. This is an opportunity to further demonstrate your value. Right now, your company is looking for cost-saving ideas. You have a unique opportunity to make that happen."

When buyers face tough times, they are concerned about themselves. This is a natural response to tough times. Buyers are concerned about how they are impacted. How could they not be? This survival instinct affects their decision-making. Buyers aren't selfish or greedy; they're just concerned about their future. Help your buyers preserve their positions and create value for their companies.

Herding

Many animals, like goats and sheep, travel in herds. There is strength in numbers. If they are attacked by a wolf, herding offers a greater chance of survival. The same is true for buyers. *Herding* is a tactic where buyers surround themselves with additional decision makers. Just as with sheep and goats, herding is a survival technique. This is most apparent in decision-making. It's common for buyers to incorporate more decision makers in tough times. It's easier to spread the risk over the group. Research also shows that the group is smarter than the individual. In a famous experiment, Sir Francis Galton demonstrated that a group more accurately guesses the weight of a cow than an individual.[7] On the show *Who Wants to Be a Millionaire?*, contestants have the option to ask the audience or phone a friend. Asking the audience yielded the correct answer 91 percent of the time. Phoning a friend (an individual) yielded the correct response 65 percent of the time.[8] Group decision-making is not a bad thing, but it does add a new dynamic. Key decision makers can spend as they see fit, but don't be surprised if they add other decision makers.

Companies also herd around other companies. Organizations look to market leaders for guidance in tough times. For example, if a market leader in the oil and gas industry decides to lay off employees, don't be shocked if other companies take the same approach. Market leadership doesn't happen by accident, and many buyers look to those leaders, assuming that their decisions are the right ones. Market leaders set the tone in good times and provide guidance in tough times.

WHAT SELLERS THINK ABOUT IN TOUGH TIMES

In an old Native American proverb, an elder tells a young boy, "There are two wolves fighting inside of us. One wolf is evil, filled with anger and despair; this wolf wants you to do bad things. The other wolf is good, filled with hope and kindness; this wolf wants you to do good things. These two wolves constantly fight each other." The boy then asks the elder, "Which wolf wins?" The elder responds, "Whichever wolf you decide to feed."[9]

This proverb aptly explains the importance of our thoughts. We move in the direction of our thoughts. Two wolves already exist inside of us. It's naive to think that you can avoid doubt and negative thoughts in tough times. Whichever wolf you feed determines which will prevail. Thoughts matter.

In tough times, sellers and buyers have similar thoughts. Sellers experience uncertainty and scarcity. Sellers also fear missing out on unique opportunities. Just as with buyers, this mindset is driven by fear. Buyers and sellers experience similar feelings during tough times, and this section focuses on how sellers think during tough times.

Uncertainty

During tough times, you face uncertainty that wasn't there before. This uncertainty causes sellers to lose confidence and competence. You're uncertain about future opportunities, future projects, and future performance. Does this sound familiar? Our fear exacerbates the uncertainty we face. There is a better way to approach the uncertainty of tough times.

If you're feeling uncertain in your profession, consider this: When has sales ever been a stable and certain profession? Never. There is no other profession better equipped to face uncertainty than the sales profession. Uncertainty is what makes sales the best profession in the world. Uncertainty is why it feels so good to close that big deal. The uncertainty of success compels you to work harder. Uncertainty strengthens your resolve. If success were certain, it wouldn't taste as sweet. Don't fear uncertainty—embrace it!

When you chose sales, you traded comfort and stability for a chance at greater success. Take pride in knowing that most people can't handle the uncertainty of sales. This is the only profession where you face more rejection than acceptance. Uncertainty doesn't drain you; it motivates you. Be the positive beacon of light for your customers, your prospects, and your team during uncertain times. Use these uncertain times to become the best version of yourself.

Scarcity

In tough times, there is a general decline in business activity. As resources become scarce, so do sellers' opportunities to sell. In tough times, sellers are more likely to miss their targets. This creates an obvious problem because sellers are expected to produce. As sellers miss their targets, they obsess over those targets. This creates a vicious cycle where sellers focus more on themselves and less on their customers. Through tough times, sellers become target obsessed rather than customer obsessed.

Sellers face a scarcity of resources within their organization. Sellers have to support their customers with fewer resources. This leads to obvious support issues and customer attrition. Customers are forgiving to a certain point, but eventually they'll look for support somewhere else. Imagine the frustration of their sellers. They're fighting to keep customers, but circumstances that are out of their control are forcing their buyers to leave. Think of the mental toll this takes on sellers.

Not all sellers struggle during tough times. Scarcity in one area leads to opportunity in other areas. Some sellers thrive in this challenging environment. These sellers focus on the unexpected opportunities that surface during tough times. Tough times create a new challenge that sparks creativity. The pain of tough times forces you to pursue new opportunities. Sellers tweak their solutions, find new opportunities in nontraditional markets, prospect more, and build stronger relationships. These tough timers rise to the challenge and thrive.

WHAT SELLERS DO IN TOUGH TIMES

Thoughts drive actions. How sellers think influences their behavior. Selling is an action-oriented profession. It's not enough to do things the right way; you must think the right way. This section highlights the common mistakes sellers make in tough times. As you read this section, be aware of your own behavior. If you are guilty of these common mistakes, don't just change your behavior, change your attitude.

Reduce Activity

Salespeople seem to reduce their activity at the same rate buyers reduce their costs. With less buying activity, sellers reduce selling activity. Salespeople reduce their activity for several bogus reasons. In tough times, sellers say, "Nobody is buying right now, so why should I try to sell?" Just because fewer people buy doesn't mean you stop selling. A higher activity level positions you for the turnaround that follows tough times.

Some sellers reduce activity because they don't want to appear opportunistic when buyers are struggling. It's understandable wanting to avoid this label. But salespeople are there to create value, and dollars follow value. Whether good times or tough times, buyers need sellers to support them and create value. By reducing your activity, you're doing more harm than good. If you appear too opportunistic, refocus your motivation on serving and helping customers, not selling to them.

Other sellers don't want to bother buyers during tough times. If you think you're a bother, rethink your entire approach to selling. Sellers create value, not interruptions. Salespeople solve problems. They do not create problems. Sellers make their customers' lives easier. If you don't, then rethink your approach.

Other sellers complain that buyers are less open to meeting in tough times. This is a legitimate concern. In tough times, buyers are shuffled around, asked to work from home, furloughed, or laid off. Selling is more than just face-to-face meetings. It includes all the ways you interact with buyers. Creatively surround your customers with your message of value. Every interaction, whether they respond or not, is an opportunity to create value for your customers.

There is a common theme with all these explanations—a negative view of your role. Sellers exist to create value for their customers, prospects, and their companies. If you can help your buyers or prospects, then be persistent and diligent in your approach. Don't let the deafening silence of no response frustrate you. Dig deep and innovatively think of ways to create more value for your buyers.

In tough times, you experience more setbacks. When you feel down, don't slow down. Instead, look for ways to do more. Take a page from J. J. Watt's playbook and do more. J. J. Watt is one of the most dominant defensive ends to play in the National Football League. He has experienced his fair share of tough times. He's experienced several injuries and surgeries. Watt developed an interesting habit when he was coming back from an injury. When his team was scrimmaging, he would increase his activity instead of taking it easy. After each play, he would sprint an additional 20 yards and then run back to his defensive huddle. After an injury, his fitness level declined, so he worked harder to get back to where he was. What if you gave a little more effort to bounce back stronger? In an article, Watt explained that when you look back on your struggle, there is beauty in it. You see how far you've come.[10] Tough times are good!

Seller-Focused Behavior

When tough times appear, sellers shift to survival gear. In tough times, sellers feel a stronger sense to sell than serve. They're more focused on solving their own problems rather than their customers' problems. As salespeople feel pressured to sell, they focus on themselves rather than their buyers. Successful sellers view the world through the eye of their buyers—understanding how they define value. This customer-focused approach guides their sales process. Customers respond favorably to such an approach.

When you operate from a scarcity mindset, you wonder, "Where is my next deal coming from?" You desperately look for any opportunity with a pulse. Once you find the opportunity, you pursue it with a seller's mindset, wondering, "How can I close this deal?" This seller-focused behavior appears desperate to buyers. Buyers don't partner with desperate sellers.

Customer-focused sellers look for opportunities to make a difference, not just a deal. In tough times, prospects remember your approach. Would you rather be known as the deal maker or the difference maker?

Buyers need you the most when times are the toughest. They need your support. They need your expertise. Now is the time to double down on your customer-focused approach. Customers don't remember everything you do for them during tough times, but they remember how you made them feel. If you made your customers feel like a priority, they will reward you with their loyalty—both now and in the future.

Cut Price versus Sell Value

For some sellers, tough times create a vicious cycle of poor performance and deep discounts. Sellers struggle to hit their numbers, so they entice buyers with deep discounts. These sellers experience some success, so they discount more to entice more buyers. Compound this with the added price resistance from buyers, and profits quickly evaporate. This discounting happens during a time when your company can least afford to give up profit. There is a better way to respond.

Price is only an issue in the absence of value. Instead of looking for ways to decrease your price, look for ways to increase your value. Use tough times as a trigger to create value in new and unique ways for your customers.

One of my clients used tough economic times to introduce several new value-added services for its customers. The company's sales team held a brainstorming session to discuss new ways to create value. The group discussed questions such as, "What's missing from our current offering?"; "What do customers hate doing that we can do for them?"; and "What feedback are you hearing from our best customers?" These questions generated new and innovative ways to serve those customers. Tough times were the trigger for this brainstorming session. While implementing these services, pricing wasn't an issue. Customers didn't complain about price; they were thrilled with these value-added services. In fact, this company attracted new prospects it never had a chance with before. Tough times are good!

Demanding discounts is a common tactic of opportunistic buyers. Beware when buyers insist that your pricing is too high. Buyers often use tough times as an opportunity to gain negotiating leverage. A savvy negotiator notices when you experience the added pressure of tough times. The more pressure you face, the more concessions you are likely to make. Balance the pressure you feel by uncovering the pressure your buyers are feeling.

The number-one reason sellers discount is because they can. The best way to eliminate discounts is to remove the seller's ability to discount. Stop the bleeding and apply a tourniquet to keep your team from hemorrhaging profit.

SUMMARY

Tough times impact us on multiple levels. This chapter focused on how tough times impact our thoughts and actions. Buyers and sellers have similar mindsets through tough times—full of fear. Fear creates uncertainty and a scarcity mindset. This mindset forces buyers to hoard their resources. Viewing the world through the eyes of buyers helps you to understand the motivation behind their actions. A better understanding makes clear why there is a strong focus on cost cutting, self-preservation, and hoarding of resources.

Understand your mindset before attempting to understand that of your customers. How can you influence another person's thoughts if you don't control your own thoughts? Tough times are uncertain, but there is no other profession better equipped to handle uncertainty than sales. Nothing is ever given in sales. Success has always been optional. Use the uncertainty to motivate you to increase your activity level. Let your competitors sit at home and wait it out.

The underlying motivation through tough times is fear—fear of misusing a resource or missing an opportunity. Sellers succumb to the pressure of fear. Sellers fear being too opportunistic, so they reduce their activity. Sellers fear losing an opportunity, so they push harder to close a sale—switching to a seller-focused approach. Sellers fear losing a deal and offer discounted prices out of desperation.

Fear causes inaction. Acknowledge your fear but embrace courage. Courage is not the absence of fear; it's the management of fear. Fear tempts you to pause versus press on. Too many people let fear run their lives. Fear only overwhelms you if you let it. Control your fear; don't let your fear control you. Consider Eleanor Roosevelt's take on fear and belief:

> Believe in yourself. You gain strength, courage, and confidence by every experience in which you stop to look fear in the face. . . . You must do that which you think you cannot do.[11]

CHAPTER 3

Redefining Value
in Tough Times

Your customers define value, and their definition is the only one that matters. Although customers define value, the prevailing times define your customers. A buyer's experiences greatly influence his or her definition of value. This chapter focuses on how and why buyers redefine value through tough times.

Value is an outcome. Buyers compare what they sacrifice with what they gain. If the gain is greater than the sacrifice, that's value. The bigger the gain, the greater the value. The degree of value is determined by the gap between sacrifices and outcomes. The wider you extend that gap, the greater the value.

Value is also personal. It's not always rational because we're not purely rational, we're emotional. Tough times are chock full of emotions, exaggerating the irrational tendencies of buyers. Emotions greatly influence a buyer's definition of value in tough times. Emotions play a stronger role in tough times but a central role in all decision-making—especially buying decisions.

Consider the irrational behavior that you witness regularly. People jump from airplanes without parachutes, climb mountains without safety gear, and walk across hot coals with no shoes. Value is rational, emotional, logical, and irrational all at once. You may never fully understand the irrational side of buying, but you will understand the emotions triggering it.

Whether rational or irrational, customers define value. And their definition is the only one that matters. To understand your buyers' definition of value, ask yourself, "What are they trying to accomplish and why?" To further clarify, ask yourself, "What are buyers willing to sacrifice to achieve what they want to accomplish?" To be successful in tough times, redefine value in your customers' terms.

Value is bigger than basic needs. Any seller recognizes what a buyer is trying to accomplish. For example, a buyer has a need to increase productivity. *What* that buyer is trying to accomplish is the logical side of purchasing. Most salespeople adequately understand buyers' logical needs. Logical needs are straightforward and obvious. Few sellers question why a buyer wants to increase productivity. *Why* that buyer wants to increase productivity is the driving factor. Understand your buyers' *why*, and they're more likely to buy.

Value is bigger than price. Price is what you pay; value is the outcome you receive. Price is a short-term sacrifice. It's tangible, logical, concrete, and straightforward. Price is easy to understand. Value is long term, less tangible, and harder to comprehend. Because price is short term and tangible, it's more focal than long-term value. It's more challenging for buyers to accept a potential outcome when the future seems uncertain. Accepting long-term value means seeing past the uncertainty. Remind your buyers that although the future seems uncertain, it is more promising than the prevailing tough time.

Value is bigger than what buyers sacrifice to attain it. The more someone is willing to sacrifice, the more value he or she places on something. Help your buyers see past what they sacrifice and focus on what they gain. It's natural to focus more on what you give up versus what you gain. Losses loom larger than gains. This is called *loss aversion*, and it's a powerful motivator. It's more painful to give up something than it is satisfying to gain something. Couple your buyers' loss aversion with the uncertainty of tough times, and their threshold of sacrifice becomes smaller.

Just as value is bigger than price, total cost is also bigger than price. Total cost encompasses everything buyers sacrifice. Total cost includes labor costs, energy costs, logistics costs, maintenance costs, training costs, and time, frustration, and service costs, just to name a few. These costs are less tangible than price and are difficult to quantify, but they are real. To enhance value, look for ways to reduce the cost associated with your solution. By reducing the sacrifice of your buyers, you widen the gap between what they sacrifice and what they gain—creating greater value.

Your value is greater than your buyers' sacrifice, but is that value worth it? Is the juice worth the squeeze? The sweeter the juice, the harder you'll squeeze. Total cost is everything buyers sacrifice, including the cost of switching to your solution. These costs could include more paperwork, additional training, potential risk, fear of the unknown, and processing costs to name a few. Is the long-term value of your solution greater than the switch-out costs to attain it?

Is your buyers' gain worth what they must sacrifice? This depends on what they gain. Gains include the utility and impact of the solution. *Utility* is what your product or service does, but *impact* is how it really affects buyers. Impact includes the emotional effects and economic impact of your solution. The buyer's impact must vastly exceed the buyer's sacrifices. If what your buyers receive is equal to what they sacrifice, would they buy? This is the equivalent of trading a dollar for 10 dimes. Is such a trade worth it? Maybe, if you needed exact change—value is personal. For most of us, though, the answer is no.

Price is to *cost* as *utility* is to *impact*. The utility of your solution is simple, straightforward, and tangible, just like price. Impact is like cost: less tangible, complex, harder to calculate. But as cost is to price, impact is greater than utility, only less tangible (harder to prove). Too many salespeople focus on utility; it's easier for buyers to comprehend utility. Utility is easier to explain and understand, but it is the more commoditized part of the solution. Focusing on utility inadvertently leads to a price discussion. Connect the utility of your solution to meaningful impact to your customer. This is aligning the outcome of your solution to the customer's definition of value.

Value is constant, but the variables defining value are not constant. The following value equation was originally published in the ground-breaking book, *Value-Added Selling*. This equation provides a more formalistic view of how buyers define value:

$$\text{Price} + \text{Cost} + \text{Utility} + \text{Impact} = \text{Value}^{[1]}$$

Price and cost are the input variables—what buyers sacrifice. Utility and impact are the outcome variables—what buyers gain. These variables change with the times. Use this equation to redefine and calculate value in customer terms.

HOW BUYERS DEFINE VALUE IN TOUGH TIMES

Charles Darwin famously said, "It is not the strongest of the species that survives, nor the most intelligent that survives. It is the one that is the most adaptable to change." Although Darwin is describing how species survive, he could be describing how businesses survive and thrive through tough times. Sellers and buyers must adapt based on the prevailing circumstances. As buyers adapt, their needs change, and so does their definition of value. As sellers adapt, so will their sales approach.

Buyers define value differently in tough times. Their priorities shift. Buying priorities offer a glimpse into how customers define value, outcomes they expect, and what they will sacrifice to achieve those outcomes. As a customer-focused seller, adapt with your buyer to understand why and how he or she defines value.

Whether buyers reveal it or not, they need your help to adapt in tough times. Buyers don't know what they don't know. Buyers rely on you to educate and deliver insight and sometimes help them get out of their own way. In certain cases, the buyer may not fully understand how to define value. Buyers clue you in to their definition of value, but they expect you to connect the dots. As you connect the dots, you might receive pushback from your buyers. Buyers push back for several reasons: they fear change, uncertainty, lack of information. Just because a buyer pushes back does not mean that you fall back. Dig your heels in deeper to better understand your buyer's motives and definition of value.

In tough times, organizations shift direction. This new direction is driven down from the top. The buyer's needs shift to be consistent with the new direction. These shifting needs force sellers to be nimble. Shifting needs create new opportunities. If your customers pivot to a new industry, their needs completely change, creating new opportunities. As customers adapt, so will their definition of value.

Customers define value in unique ways. Value includes a buyer's needs, wants, fears, and desires. In tough times, people default to survival mode. Buyers focus on what they *need* to have versus *want* to have. Buyers streamline purchasing to reflect necessity. Buyers simplify their needs and opt for solutions that are merely good enough. They substitute the niceties of your solution for its basic utility. They even minimize the impact of your solution to further justify their decision. They'll tell themselves, "Given the tough economic climate, we don't need these extras." This simplistic approach provides short-term relief but does more damage in the long run. As buyers simplify their needs, provide them with a holistic view emphasizing the long-term impact of their decisions.

As buyers question the necessity of your solution, they strip away the value added. As your solution is stripped to its basic utility, price becomes more focal. As buyers strip the value-added extras, they expect a proportional discount. This frustrates sellers who understand how their buyers previously defined value. Tough times shift buying priorities. Value-focused buyers are seemingly more price sensitive. Although this tendency is temporary, you're forced to ardently defend your value and justify your price.

Groups of buyers define value differently than individual buyers. Buyers recruit other decision makers in tough times. This herding tendency adds a layer of complexity to their definition of value. Each different decision maker redefines value in his or her own unique way. One buyer's definition of value might conflict with the previous decision maker's definition of value. As a seller, you must be flexible. Collaborate with new decision makers as they get involved. Help new buyers conform to the previous definition of value. Groups naturally want to generate consensus.

Understanding your customers' definition of value is a dynamic, ever-changing process. As buyers redefine value, stay light on your feet and explore new ways to create value. A challenging customer forces you to adjust and adapt to meet his or her growing expectations. Your most challenging customers serve you well in tough times. Your capacity to create value expands to the expectation customers place on you. You elevate to your customers' rising expectations, making you better in the long run. Tough times are good! This section provides some direction as you promote and communicate value in tough times.

Certainty and Stability

Remember the Chevy "Like a Rock" campaign? I'm sure you're reciting those Bob Seeger lyrics right now. What an exciting campaign. It highlighted the certainty and stability of the Chevy brand. You could depend on your Chevy truck. It was strong, solid, and certain, just like a rock. The content was spot on given the timing of the campaign—during the recession of the early 1990s.[2]

Tough times are filled with uncertainty. Buyers look for steady footing as they navigate uncertain terrain. What is reliable in good times can be shaky in tough times: supply chains are disrupted, people are shuffled around, and resources are scarce. Amid the uncertainty, buyers crave stability. "Like a rock," your value added should highlight the stability of your solution. Stability creates peace of mind. Translate your stable message into meaningful impact for your buyers.

Other companies demonstrate their stability by investing in a downturn—like Procter & Gamble. P&G has endured several tough times. P&G has emerged stronger through each downturn, giving you confidence in the brand. It should be noted that during tough times, P&G has a history of taking action. While other companies were cutting their advertising spend during the Great Depression, P&G actually increased it. Although the company's message focused on the brand, the act of investing during tough times sent a strong message of stability.[3]

Support

Customers want to know that you have their backs. They need support when times are tough. Support is critical in tough times because buyers face more challenges. During these tough times, your buyers expect your support.

Herding is a common response to tough times. People find strength in numbers but support through individuals. During any tough time, buyers want to know that you have their backs. Customers need support before, during, and after the sale. It is critical that buyers know that you're there in lockstep with them. Nothing irritates a buyer more than a seller who over-promises on the front end but fails to support on the back end. Detail your support strategy with your customers. Share examples of how you help other companies during tough times. Demonstrate support during tough times, and customers will reward you with their loyalty.

Flexibility

"Have it your way." Burger King launched this campaign to highlight its flexibility. It also highlighted the rigidity of its rival, McDonald's. Burger King realized that customers wanted a Whopper their way. This campaign was launched in 1974, in the middle of a recession.[4] Customers want flexibility in tough times.

Buyers adapt during tough times and expect you to adapt with them. Being a flexible partner shows buyers that you're willing to work with them. Too many organizations adopt rigid policies and procedures designed to serve their company, not their customers. In tough times, buyers have zero patience for rigid policies and procedures. These policies are frustrating in good times and outright wrong or insensitive in tough times.

New York Times bestselling author Shep Hyken highlights the importance of flexibility and convenience in his book, *The Convenience Revolution*. "Friction kills the customer experience—and those who do the best job of reducing or removing it are most likely to win in the marketplace,"[5] he writes. Reducing friction and increasing flexibility go hand in hand.

Anything that dissuades the customer from buying creates friction. Customers want to work with companies that make it easy. Every touch-point within your customer experience either eases the transaction or creates friction. Increase your flexibility to accommodate the changing needs of your buyers. Review your terms, policies, and procedures through the eyes of your customers. Experience your solution as your buyers experience your solution. Change or challenge the rigid or unnecessary policies hindering the customer experience. After reviewing your process through the eyes of your customers, ask yourself, "Would I buy from my company?" If you're not convinced, your buyers aren't either.

Longevity

"Do customers really care about our 90-year history?" A salesperson asked me this in a training seminar. This was not a pessimistic question; it was a customer-focused question. We were analyzing the salesperson's company, trying to identify the unique aspects of its solution. The company's longevity was unique compared with its competition. Your past creates a timeline into the future. If your company has been around for 90 years, it'll likely be around tomorrow. Longevity is important through tough times—you can share your security with your customers.

In tough times, companies fail. Your customers have likely experienced this failure with past providers. Instill confidence in the minds of your buyers. Let them know that you can weather the storm of tough times. Buyers partner with companies that are going to be around. Demonstrate your long-term sustainability to give your buyers peace of mind. Consider this example from Northwestern Mutual, a financial services company. "There never was a time in all these trying months that Northwestern Mutual could not have met every demand that was made upon it with business promptness, in full, and without the sacrifice of a dollar of its securities."[6] Michael Cleary, past president of Northwestern Mutual, was commenting on the Great Depression. Northwestern Mutual was a financial safe haven for many policy owners during this period. Since 1872, Northwestern Mutual has paid a dividend every year to its whole-life policy owners.[7] What a powerful example of longevity and stability into the future this is.

Find subtle ways to remind your customers of your company's longevity. Selectively share your company's plans. Imagine the impact this information has on buyers. Give the buyers peace of mind today and instill greater confidence in where you're headed in the future.

By discussing your plans, you can draw a parallel to your customers' plans. For example, "Mr. Customer, after discussing your company's future,

I can't help but think of our company. They're so similar. Two companies this similar should be working together. We're already traveling the same path."

Buyers need security in tough times. They need to know that your company will prevail through tough times. Management and leadership play a significant role in instilling this confidence. Bring your manager or leader on joint calls. This show of support provides buyers with greater security. Highlight the longevity of your company to show more stability. If you have been around, you're going to stay around.

Reduce Risk

"Nobody ever got fired for buying IBM."[8] This common phrase emerged in the early days of the IBM computer. IBM set the benchmark for personal computing. Buying an IBM computer was a safe decision. How safe is your solution?

Given the uncertainty of the economy or certain industry segments, buyers look to reduce risk however they can. Position your solution as the low-risk alternative. Highlight the safety of your solution. Explain features and benefits so that every member of the organization benefits. Emphasize the widespread benefits of partnering with your organization.

Decisions are made under a microscope. Even routine decisions are heavily scrutinized in tough times. Position your solution as a safe, reliable, and sensible choice. Yours is the solution that anyone in the buyer's organization would choose. Buyers want to keep their powder dry in tough times. Reduce the risk of selecting your solution.

Cash Flow

Cash flow is the lifeblood of any organization. In tough times, credit tightens, sales drop, and cash becomes king. Help your buyers gain more of what they are afraid of losing—cash. Many buyers focus on discounts to solve a cash-flow problem. You create value by addressing the root cause. Identify ways you can solve this problem.

Look for ways to positively impact your customers' cash flow in tough times. Can you offer favorable payment terms in tough times? Can you offer special financing options or extended terms? Customers remember these small acts of consideration. If you help cash flow to them, they are going to continue flowing more cash to you (instead of your competitors).

HOW SALESPEOPLE CREATE VALUE IN TOUGH TIMES

What value do you *personally* bring? This is a gut-check question. It forces you to think of all the ways you add value to the buyers' businesses. Some sellers can easily answer this question, whereas other sellers struggle. For top-achieving salespeople, this question is easily answered. Top achievers demonstrate their value and remind buyers of the positive impact they have on their customers' businesses. Sellers struggle to sell their personal value because they create none, or they're unsure how to articulate it.

If the extent of your value is a weekly drop-in asking buyers, "You don't need anything today, do you?"—you are creating zero value. You're actually creating negative value because you have wasted your buyers' time. These sellers typically mask their ineptitude under the blanket of service and support. Every interaction is an opportunity to create personal value for your buyers. Some sellers seize the opportunity, whereas others do not.

Salespeople create personal value out of necessity. If you're selling in a commoditized industry, you become the unique aspect of the solution. Sellers must find a way to stand out. In contrast, other sellers don't create enough personal value because they don't have to. They let other aspects of their solutions create value. This happens when you are selling a high-demand, unique product—hence the expression, "a product that sells itself." The product might sell itself, but you still need to create personal value. Selling a unique and innovative product is a bonus, but don't use it as a crutch. When it's easy to sell a product, it's just as easy to forget about the personal value you bring. In tough times, sellers need more than just the value of a product.

Other sellers create immense value, yet very few get the credit they deserve. Top sellers are hungry and aggressive but also humble. To them, promoting their personal value might sound like braggadocio and arrogance. This is understandable. However, customers forget about your personal value unless they are reminded of it. Your personal value is a significant part of the overall solution. Demonstrate your personal value. If you don't, you're missing a significant opportunity to sell a bigger solution. In tough times, customers want more. Your personal value enlarges the total package.

Our research shows that a salesperson can represent a significant amount of value. Buyers were asked how much of their buying decision is weighted on the product, the company, and the salesperson. Buyers indicated that the company represents 18 percent, the product represents 57 percent, and the seller represents 25 percent.[9] If you're not selling your personal value, you're missing out on 25 percent of the reason why customers buy. What if your competitors are doing better at demonstrating their personal value?

Have you noticed that when top sellers leave an organization, their customers often follow them? It's because they create value. The salesperson is essential to the total solution. You become essential by creating value. The only limit to the value you create is the edge of your imagination. There are as many ways to add value as there are sellers to create it. Here are some ideas to create more personal value.

Knowledgeable Expertise

Theodore Roosevelt said, "People don't care how much you know until they know how much you care."[10] This platitude may be true, but not if you're in sales. In our research on top achievers, customers selected knowledgeable expertise as *the* most important attribute of a salesperson. Knowledge even ranked higher than trustworthiness.[11]

So what is knowledge? Is it knowing your product? Your customer? Your industry? Yes, yes, and yes. It's not enough to just know your product or service. Immerse yourself in the customer's business, your business, and the industry. Get to know every facet of the industry. Get to know the nuances of your company and the customer's business. Your currency to the customer is your knowledge. In tough times, the value of this currency increases. Buyers partner with knowledgeable sellers to navigate this uncertain world.

Sellers who understand their customer's business have a unique advantage. Big companies have complicated purchasing processes. If buyers continuously need to educate you on their processes, they'll look for more knowledgeable sellers. One seller we trained consistently won business because he understood how to navigate the customer's purchasing department. That seller transferred his expertise into meaningful impact for his customer.

How well do you know your top competitors? Competitive knowledge is critical. What you don't know holds great power over you, including what you don't know about your competition. Research your competition—both the company and the salespeople. Gather intelligence on your competition from your customers and colleagues.

Knowledge is critical even if you are new to your industry or the sales profession. This frustrates new sellers as they struggle to build their expertise. Do not let the knowledge gap frustrate you—let it spark your curiosity. Commit to growing your knowledge, and you can quickly close the gap. Embrace what you don't know and begin the process of building your knowledge.

Are you a student of your profession? Do you dedicate enough time to research your company, products, and industry? Top achievers build an inventory of insights. You gain an encyclopedic knowledge through your career that creates value for your customers. What you learn is like inventory on the shelf. That inventory of knowledge continues growing throughout your tenure. With knowledge, you never run out of room, and it never expires. At the right time, you simply pull that inventory. Fill those shelves!

Priorities change in tough times. You have more choices on how you spend time. For sellers, this is a time to study, research, and fully immerse yourself in your profession. Dedicate time every day to developing your most important attribute. It's amazing what 15 minutes can do every day. All this knowledge only creates value when you transfer it into meaningful insights that positively impact your customers. Customers care how much you know, but they care more about how your knowledge impacts them.

Problem Solving

Within every problem is an opportunity to create value. The more pain the problem causes, the greater is the opportunity. Customers like doing business with people they like and trust. This platitude is the mantra of many sellers. Although trust is key in good times and bad, likeability takes a backseat to sellers who create real value. One of the most impactful ways to create value is to solve a customer's major problem. Good sellers solve problems when their customers ask for their help. However, customers are often unaware of a problem. Great sellers partner with customers and uncover problems they didn't know existed. The hidden problems often have the greatest impact on the buyer's business.

Problems don't magically appear for sellers to solve. For this reason, many sellers struggle to identify problems. A more passive approach is seen in a seller who claims, "Buyers never call me when they have a problem." Passive problem solving is simply an inclination to help customers. Proactive problem solving requires a relentless desire to help customers succeed.

Solving problems is more than providing customers with proposals. Don't look for products to quote; look for problems to solve. Explore problems like an investigative journalist. Ask questions, do research, talk to new contacts, and expose problems. In tough times, buyers face more problems and challenges than they do in good economic times. Problems are prioritized, meaning that some are overlooked. The best sellers identify and solve those ignored problems.

In our training seminars, salespeople often say, "It's hard to find problems to solve." Be thankful that it is difficult. If it were simple, your competitors could just as easily find problems to solve. If problem solving were easy, it wouldn't be as impactful. Problems are difficult to find and challenging to solve. This is why most salespeople give up. The key is to open your eyes. Problems hide in plain sight. Salespeople can be blinded by their own ambition. Ambitious sellers focus more on making a deal than on making a difference. Identifying and solving problems is more about attitude than any sales tactic. What if you approached an opportunity with the mindset of solving problems versus selling product? Rather than leading with the right product, lead with the right mindset.

Yogi Berra said, "You can observe a lot by just watching."[12] Open your eyes and ears. One tried-and-true method to identity problem-solving opportunities is a walk-through on a project, process, or current methodology. This is a physical or virtual walk-through. Spatial awareness allows you to uncover new ideas and insights in your and the customer's mind. The best sellers illuminate a problem their buyers didn't know existed.

Yogi would agree, you can also hear a lot just by listening. Deeply listen to your customers for additional problem-solving opportunities. Deep listening is seeking to understand your buyers, not just waiting for your turn to speak. Deep listening requires suspending your assumptions and opening your mind. Approach every customer interaction as if it were your first. It's amazing what a fresh set of eyes can see and a fresh set of ears can hear.

Reliability

How dependable are you? In tough times, buyers need a sure thing. When tough times push on customers, they need somebody to lean on. During tough times, customers are facing a world of uncertainty. Their concerns mount higher every day. Reliable sellers give their customers one less thing to worry about and eliminate a few other worries.

Reliable salespeople go the extra mile to conscientiously serve their customers. Reliability is tricky. An unreliable person is more noticeable than a reliable one. When sellers reliably deliver on their buyers' expectations, the buyers don't think much about it. They move on to their next task. They take it for granted. Reliable salespeople demonstrate their value by processing requests urgently and correctly. Reliable sellers follow up impeccably with buyers. They conscientiously perform their work in a timely manner. Reliable sellers are the benchmark on which other sellers are graded. They generate a stable and predictable experience in front of the backdrop of an uncertain world.

Get Things Done

In tough times, companies are strained for resources—forced to do more with less. This leads to hiccups in the customer experience. Sellers have to make the same promises to customers but with fewer resources, creating a bottleneck in the customer experience. Salespeople must step up and expand their capabilities to meet their customers' expectations. Sellers need to get things done.

This requires a deeper understanding of how your organization operates. Getting things done for your customers requires working with your internal customers. Internal customers are team members that support the customer—directly or indirectly. Internal customers include inside sales, customer service, engineers, tech support, operations, and the credit department, to name a few. Learn the nuances of your internal processes. Identify ways to make your internal customers' lives easier. Work with your team, not against it, to get things done.

During tough times, customers expect sellers to make things happen. If there are supply shortages, you need to deliver. If you need managerial approval, get the approval. If your team needs a kick in the tail to deliver, then start kicking. Customers want to work with sellers who get things done.

Professionalism

Julius Erving once said, "Being a professional is doing the things you love to do on the days you don't feel like doing them."[13] Dr. J is one of the best to ever play in the National Basketball Association. Selling in tough times requires a higher degree of professionalism. Make it a habit to do what your competitors aren't willing to do. True professionals care about their work and how it impacts their customers.

Professionalism means putting your best work on display for the world to see. It means carrying yourself with integrity and going the extra mile for your customers. Professionals are the total package for their customers.

Professionals operate at a higher standard and hold themselves accountable to deliver results. When their plan doesn't work out, professionals look in the mirror first rather than out the window. Professionals seek feedback from their customers, colleagues, and managers so as to improve. They're looking to complement their strengths and improve where they're weak.

Buyers aren't aware of all the little things you do to improve, but they recognize the end result. Professionalism is demonstrated in the way you manage your business and yourself. Professionals build a reputation and become the benchmark by which other sellers are graded. Just imagine if you were the benchmark seller in your industry.

SUMMARY

In good times or tough times, buyers want value. Value is constant, but the prevailing times help define it. Value is determined by the needs, wants, and fears of buyers within the backdrop of current times. These factors are dynamic and ever changing. As a customer-focused seller, you are also ever changing. Your customers define value, and their definition is the only one that matters.

Adaptable sellers look for ways to improve. Tough times create new demands, constraints, customer expectations, and opportunities. Buyers raise their expectations in tough times. Tough times force you to expand your capabilities to meet the ever-growing demands of your buyers.

Ralph Waldo Emerson wrote, "The mind, once stretched by a new idea, never returns to its original dimensions."[14] In a similar way, your capacity to create value is stretched through tough times. But when tough times subside, your new capacity to create value remains. Tough times broaden and elevate your capabilities. Tough times are good!

CHAPTER 4

Mental Mistakes
in Tough Times

The biggest mistake in tough times is not losing a sale—it's losing hope. Hope is the fuel that propels you through tough times. The moments our hope is challenged are defining moments in our life and career. Tough times force you to question your hope. If you haven't experienced hopeless moments, then you haven't experienced tough times. Almost everyone experiences hopeless moments in tough times—it's how you manage them that matters. Your response at these moments determines the depth and degree of hopelessness. A strong foundation of hope keeps sellers on the right path as they navigate tough times. Protect your hope at all costs.

In tough times, sellers experience a cycle of failure and frustration. To find success, they'll assess their performance, try new skills, and review their techniques. Success through tough times is more than changing your technique; it's shifting your mindset. A skills-focused approach only addresses 50 percent of the problem. No professional can peak by improving only half of what matters.

Mental preparation is as important as preparing your technique. Sellers focus on methods rather than mindset. Methods are tangible and tactile, whereas the mental aspects are more abstract. Most sellers agree that attitude drives behavior and impacts performance, but few can explain how to develop the right attitude.

Sellers use a process to guide their sales efforts. We like process because it produces a predictable outcome. Sales processes address the tactical side of selling but fail to address the mental rigor placed on the seller. In tough times, your mental process is more important than your sales process. What process do you use to guide your thoughts and beliefs? Your mental preparation empowers you to transition from hopeless moments to a hopeful mindset.

This chapter prepares you to manage hopeless moments by recognizing and managing common mental mistakes. The first step is recognizing your mental mistakes and then preventing their damaging effects. Use this chapter to guide your mental preparedness. Although these times are trying, these tough moments are defining moments in your career and life.

Chapter 3 highlighted the common mistakes sellers make in tough times. Some sellers reduce their activity, and others offer deep discounts. It's easier to prevent mistakes if you are aware of them. This chapter focuses on identifying the mental missteps sellers experience through tough times. Assess your thoughts as you read this chapter. Be aware of the mental challenges you face. Tough times reveal inner strengths—and weaknesses—we didn't know existed. Our strengths will carry us through; our internal weaknesses create opportunities to improve.

LEARNED HELPLESSNESS

Have you ever felt helpless? You believe your actions don't matter. It's not worth trying because it's never going to happen. You're stuck, and that's just the way it is. Your window of opportunity has shut. This is a tough spot to be in. It's like being stuck in a nightmare. Have you ever had a dream where you try to wake up but can't? Someone's chasing you, and you cannot escape them? You try screaming, but you don't make a sound? This is what hopelessness feels like. You eventually wake up from the dream, but at the time it feels like you never will.

At some point, almost everyone enters this place of despair. Our mental dexterity and the relative toughness of the situation determine how long we stay there. Many people can bounce back from these hopeless moments, mustering the strength to press on. For some, though, they get stuck there, unable to press on.

When we're stuck in this place, we ask ourselves, "How did I get here?" Or we tell ourselves, "This is just the way it is. . . . I guess I'd better get used to it." Although no one would choose to be stuck in this hopeless place, why do people stay there? Do they have a choice?

Before answering this question, consider Martin Seligman's groundbreaking experiment with dogs.[1] Seligman and his colleagues were experimenting with two sets of dogs. Prior to the experiment one set of dogs received random electrical shocks; the other set did not.

For the next part of the experiment, the two sets of dogs were placed in a large box separated by a low barrier. The experimenters charged the floor on one side of the barrier and noticed something interesting. Some dogs jumped over the barrier to avoid the shock, and other dogs did not. The dogs that stood there accepting the shock were the same dogs that received random electrical shocks before.

These dogs developed an expectation that electrical shocks were normal. The dogs didn't jump over the barrier because they didn't know that they could escape what they believed to be normal. These dogs accepted their reality rather than looking for ways to escape. Seligman calls this tendency *learned helplessness*.

Seligman found similar results in other experiments and later concluded that humans also experience learned helplessness. When people believe that they are helpless, they stop trying. The opportunity to escape their environment could be right in front of them, but they believe nothing will change, so they take no action.

Salespeople experience failure and success. Sellers expect this. But during tough times, failures keep mounting, and successes dwindle. Traditional selling activities are not producing the expected results. In certain cases, added activity produces no results. Nothing seems to work. This depth of failure deflates even the strongest-willed sellers. These sellers begin to feel helpless. If this helplessness is not addressed, it blinds the sellers to future opportunities. Although tough times are temporary, learned helplessness can create permanent damage or lengthen the tough time.

Learned helplessness doesn't appear as you think, with complaining and griping. At least complainers are passionate enough to vent their frustration. They still care. Learned helplessness manifests as apathy. Helpless sellers have given up. They have mentally checked out and don't care. Be aware of the seller who doesn't care enough to complain.

Tough times are temporary and short-lived. Helplessness extends the length of tough times because you are blind to the opportunities in front of you. Helpless sellers choose to do nothing, missing their opportunity. Let your competitors sit and wait it out. They are the ones who will miss the train as it leaves the station.

Because helplessness is a learned behavior, you can also unlearn it. Replace learned helplessness with *learned hopefulness*. Learned hopefulness is maintaining an unwavering belief that things will get better. No matter the depth of your despair, you must believe that things will get better, and eventually they will. Believing in something opens your eyes to greater possibilities.

At these tough moments, it's tempting to look forward past the pain of the present. Instead, look to the past. Look for a previous tough time in your life. It could be the loss of a job, a terrible failure, or a monumental tragedy. Ask yourself, "How did I hold on to hope?" or "How did I make it through?" Don't rush the response. Patiently observe that previous tough time. As you reflect on that tough time, you'll realize that it was only temporary. It may have been painful, but it was not permanent. Your previous tough time puts your current tough time into perspective—realizing that today isn't all that bad. Progressing from that tough time is proof that your current tough time will also pass.

Internalizing Failure

Who do you blame when you fail? You might expect this question to segue into a discussion on accountability, but it's not. Think of this question as you analyze previous failures. Who do you blame, or how do you blame? If you solely direct blame on yourself, you could be doing more harm than good.

Too many sellers internalize failure, believing that they are solely to blame. Failure is rarely permanent. But internalizing a temporary failure can lead to long-term effects. Internalizing failure is believing that you are the failure rather than a person who happened to fail.

Failure is a necessary part of success. Failure, just like success, is due to internal and external factors. During tough times, you experience a supply and demand issue. You have more to supply, but there is less demand. During tough times, buyers buy less. If you internalize this setback as a personal failure, you start believing that you are a failure. You start looking for additional evidence supporting your belief, which you are sure to find. Confirmation bias proves that you're more likely to find evidence to reinforce your initial impression or belief.

If you can internalize failure, you can internalize success. Internalizing success invokes the same confirmation bias, only confirming success, not failure. Seek information to reinforce the belief in your success, not your failure. With the right mindset, you begin viewing failure as feedback.

Internalizing failure leads to a defeatist attitude. You own the effort and the inputs; you cannot control the results. Accountable sellers focus on what they can control. You control your effort, not the outcome. Don't go easy on yourself; challenge yourself to get better. Focus on what you can control. In tough times, your energy and effort define you, not your results.

SELF-PITY

"I never saw a wild thing / sorry for itself. / A small bird will fall frozen dead from a bough / without ever having felt sorry for itself."[2] This is one of D. H. Lawrence's shortest and yet most powerful poems. One of the most memorable renditions of this poem is from *GI Jane* (Caravan Pictures, 1997). The master chief (Viggo Mortensen) reads this poem for a select group of Navy Seals during their Basic Underwater Demolition/SEAL (BUD/S) training.

Have you ever felt better after feeling sorry for yourself? Probably not. Wallowing in self-pity and adopting the woe-is-me mindset does no good. Self-pity is useless. It distracts. It robs your productivity and drains your energy. Self-pity victimizes you, leading to further helplessness.

Self-pity takes many forms, but it's most recognizable with the question, "Why me?" If you've been in sales, you've asked this question in various forms: "Why did this happen to me?"; "Why did the customer not buy from me?"; "Why can't they meet with me?" Rather than asking, "Why me?" ask, "Why not me?" Is there a reason you should be spared the pain of tough times? Remember, tough times are democratic and unbiased.

Self-pity leads to incessant complaining among sellers. There is always one seller who would rather complain than make positive change. Such a seller would rather have an excuse than an opportunity. He or she verbalizes the woe-is-me mentality in a way that attracts other complainers. Misery loves company, and complainers want a crowd.

Self-pity is a habit. You get to choose how you respond. Feeling sorry for yourself serves no purpose and hampers your ability to sell more effectively. Self-pity is a thief robbing you of the positive actions you could take to improve your situation.

If someone approached you and said, "I feel sorry for you," how would you respond? You might get defensive or angry. You might confront that person and express your frustration. In your response, you would let the person know that he or she cannot talk to you that way. You would not accept expressions of pity from anyone, so why accept them from yourself?

SCARCITY MINDSET

Have you ever been working an opportunity and thought, "I'm screwed if I don't get this deal"? Like most sellers, you've been in this position. Your pipeline is drying up, and there's not much on the horizon. You desperately need to close this deal. The buyer senses your desperation. There is just too much riding on this one opportunity. This is an unsettling feeling.

You attract what you think about. Why think about the scarcity of your situation when you could just as easily focus on the abundance? With a scarcity mindset, you look for information to reinforce your belief. You're more likely to focus on what's missing rather than on what's in front of you. This creates a vicious cycle where you see fewer and fewer opportunities. What you view as scarce, your competition may view as abundance.

Tough times create several long-term positioning opportunities. When opportunities are scarce, sellers focus on short-term concerns. It's hard for sellers to see long-term opportunities if they're fighting for short-term scraps. Sellers act in a manner best serving them now, even at the expense of better long-range opportunities, for example, salespeople pushing a less optimal solution but one that is easier for the buyer to accept. Selling with a scarcity mindset leads to desperation. Desperation leads to deeper discounts. Sellers think, "I am better off discounting today than getting nothing tomorrow."

A scarcity mindset hinders an honest pipeline review. When sellers have fewer deals in their pipelines, they desperately keep deals alive. This bloated view creates a false sense of security. These sellers are more fearful of admitting that a deal is dead than they are motivated to find another deal.

A scarcity mindset is a perception sellers create to justify poor performance. For every salesperson short on opportunities in tough times, there are sellers with an abundance of opportunity. Scarcity exacerbates a problem existing long before tough times. Tough times make us realize that we should've been prospecting more all along.

In good times, you're closing deals, the phone is ringing, and the pipeline is full. Everything is great, and there is an abundance of opportunity. Because of your belief in abundance, you find more opportunities—your perception fosters reality. Then tough times hit, and things change. Opportunity doesn't come knocking like it once did. This frustrates sellers and creates a scarcity mindset. When scarcity sets in, get creative and make things happen. If opportunity doesn't knock, build a door, not a limiting mindset.

OVERCOMING MENTAL MISTAKES

Have you ever been in a bad mood and someone tells you, "Just cheer up!" Although those words are well intentioned, you find them annoying. You would like to cheer up, but it's not that simple.

To cheer up, you need to embrace a new attitude or emotion, but right now, you're at capacity with negativity—and it's one in, one out. You cannot let positivity in until negativity gets out. You cannot be happy until you stop feeling frustrated and peeved.

Overcoming mental mistakes is about stopping the negativity. Chapter 5 focuses on building mental strength and positivity, but you cannot build positivity until you stop breaking down. There is no scarcity of emotions in tough times. Through tough times, you experience the full range, but not all at once. We can only experience so many emotions at once. Our attitude reflects whatever emotion we currently experience.

In tough times, you feel overwhelmed with emotions. This pressure is constantly weighing down on you. As this weight mounts, it wears you down. Combating this negativity requires more effort, fatiguing you even further. Eventually, you are completely exhausted.

You need a release, an outlet to channel these thoughts and actions from your mind. The longer you wait, the more pressure builds. What fills your mind consumes you. If you're filling your mind with the wrong stuff, then it's time to get rid of it. You get rid of mental waste the same way a garbage truck gets rid of trash. A garbage truck can only compress so much trash. When the truck is full, it visits the dump. Dump all those negative emotions. Don't compress those negative feelings anymore. There is a better way to avoid these missteps.

The first step in overcoming mental mistakes is admitting that there *are* mental mistakes. Use these questions to identify your current mental state:

1. Do you ever feel hopeless?
2. Do you give up easily?
3. Are you too reliant on your top opportunities?

4. Are you too hard on yourself?
5. Do you feel sorry for yourself?
6. Do you talk negatively to yourself?
7. Do you ever agonize over previous failures?
8. Is it easier for you to notice negative events than positive events?

If you answered yes to several of these questions, it's time to visit the mental trash dump.

The following exercises prevent further mental fatigue. These measures are applicable whether you are facing tough times or simply a tough moment in time. Use these countermeasures at the first sign of mental fatigue and frustration. You can't get on the right path until you stop going down the wrong path. Chapter 5 focuses on building mental strength once you're on the right path. Here are seven tips to overcome the common mental mistakes made during tough times.

Acknowledge (Not Accept) Your Current Reality

Would you stand soaking wet in a storm and deny that it's raining? No. Similarly, as you experience the mental storms of tough times, you cannot deny the mental rigor you experience.

You can only solve a problem that you believe exists. The first step in overcoming a mental mistake is to realize that there is one. The key is to acknowledge without accepting. Acceptance leads to helplessness. Acceptance is too permanent. It's harder to move something that is permanent. The tough time you experience is temporary, not permanent.

Sellers don't admit when they struggle because it seems weak. They don't want to be vulnerable. Vulnerability is necessary because it exposes what you need to fix. You can't make it right unless you acknowledge that it's wrong.

Admit when you face tough times. It takes the pressure off. Acknowledging tough times keeps you hopeful. Acknowledge the external factors impacting your success. Be aware of your words as you acknowledge tough times. Consider the following examples of acknowledgment statements:

"Things are tough right now. Some customers have halted their projects. This could create some temporary pain."

"This customer currently doesn't have the budget to move forward. This is not reflective of my effort or ability. Things will improve. In the meantime, I will look for ways to adapt."

"We are currently in a recession. In the short term, this will impact my performance."

Here are the same statements, only with a tone of acceptance versus acknowledgment:

"Things are tough. This project is *never* going to happen. What can I do? Will this ever change?"

"This customer has no budget. There is no point in trying to sell my solution."

"We're in a recession. I'll wait until things get better to start selling."

Acceptance statements are too definitive. Accepting temporary setbacks as permanent reality leads to helplessness. Accepting tough times is the equivalent of giving up. You can acknowledge external factors without blaming the external factors. Focus on what you can control.

Look at the Facts

When you are filled with negativity and self-doubt, focus on the facts, not the emotion. I was working with a sales team experiencing tough times. One seller was hit especially hard and seemed hopeless. This seller had a track record of success but was in a slump. She was selling in a new territory to an unfamiliar group of customers while their industry experienced tough times. Customers weren't buying; projects were halted. The seller was obviously frustrated and defeated. She was internalizing the failure and felt hopeless.

The only way I could convince this seller that she was wrong was to look at the facts. I asked the seller to walk me through her performance over the past several years. I said, "Imagine that you are in court defending the claim that you are a good salesperson. What evidence do you have to support this claim?"

She responded by saying:

"I have hit my sales target for the past three years."

"I receive glowing performance reviews from my sales managers."

"Salespeople reach out to me when they need help."

"I have received awards at our sales meetings based on my performance."

This seller not only is a good salesperson, but she is also an award-winning salesperson. The facts disproved the notion that she is a bad salesperson. The facts proved that she is a good seller facing bad times. Your past performance is proof positive of your success. But your past is also not your potential. You can still become more successful.

After this fact-finding session, the salesperson felt better. Her mind clearly reoriented to a more positive place. Start with the assumption that you are successful, and look for evidence to support that premise, but don't dwell on that previous success. Last year's sales don't count for this year's targets.

Step Outside Yourself

What if you viewed your tough time as a story? Everyone loves a good story. Stories are filled with heroes, villains, and challenges to overcome. Naturally, we like to be the hero of our own story—especially when times are good. However, it's more important to be the hero through the tough times. To gain perspective, step outside of your story and the struggle. Create distance between you and the tough times you are experiencing. What if you were the narrator in your story instead of the main character?

Have you wondered what your struggle looks like from the outside? During tough moments, it's not only okay, but it's necessary to step outside yourself. This new vantage point provides perspective in tough times. You depersonalize the story and view the circumstances more objectively. As you narrate the story, you are likely to portray yourself in a more positive light. You influence your attitude from the outside working in. You are letting negativity flow out while positivity flows in.

In a dramatization, an actor plays the main role instead of the actual person. What if someone else played your role through this tough time? What if the mentally toughest person you know played you? It could be a colleague, teacher, coach, family member, or friend. How would that person respond to your challenges? If you want to be mentally strong, do what mentally strong people do. Use the mentally toughest people you know as role models through these tough times.

In his book, *Rejection*, James Sherman offers sound advice on handling tough times. He writes, "You can't go back and make a new start, but you can start right now and make a brand new ending."[3] Through tough times you cannot change the beginning of your story; it's already played out—but your actions today determine how you write the ending.

Hard Resets

Have you ever had issues with your cable box or receiver? When you call your service provider for support, what is the representative's first suggestion? The rep recommends a hard reset. A hard reset means cutting the power, waiting for an extended period, and then reconnecting the power. With power restored, the box is updated and starts working more optimally.

Like your cable box, you occasionally need a hard reset. You need to disconnect from the negative energy you experience. Think of the negativity you experience daily: lost orders, customer issues, financial concerns, pressure from your boss, competitive pressure, internal strife—the list goes on and on. Even the mentally toughest sellers need to unplug and remove this negative energy.

When you are overwhelmed with negativity, simply unplug for an extended period. Take a break from the negativity. It will recenter your state back to normal. Once you plug back in, you have a new baseline of energy and a renewed sense of optimism. Don't feel guilty taking a break. Sellers struggle with taking breaks because they feel that their performance doesn't merit a break. These are the sellers who need to unplug the most.

Use all means necessary to remove negativity. For some sellers, it's hitting the gym. Others meditate and focus their energy in a more positive way. Others will journal. The act of putting pen to paper creates an outlet for your thoughts. Writing down your problems and negative emotions is a physical outlet for your negativity. You cannot fill a full mind until you make some space available. Whatever your method, unplug, rest, and find a more positive outlet to plug into.

Minimize Your Problems, Don't Magnify Them

Are your problems really that bad? How would someone else manage the tough times you are experiencing? Tough times are relative in their severity and their importance. Taking an outside perspective can right-size the challenge you face. Some of our challenges are small when placed in the broader context of our lives and our world. It's okay to compare your tough times with those of other people if you're trying to gain perspective.

Tough times are relative. Somebody always has it better and always has it a lot worse. Several years (and pounds) ago, I ran marathons. I trained for months for one marathon. I followed a strict training regimen getting ready for the big day. My training peaked with an 18-mile run four weeks before the marathon. At about the thirteenth mile, my knee started hurting. The pain intensified with each mile. Eventually, I had to walk the rest of the way home. I took a few days off and tried running a few miles, but the pain returned. I was mad and thought, "All this work, and I won't be able to run the marathon." I took a few weeks off in the hopes I could participate.

On the day of the race, I was filled with anticipation and a lot of pasta from the night before. I wasn't sure how I would do. I thought, "Will I finish? Will the injury force me to walk? Did I overdo it on the fettuccine Alfredo?"

I started the race and felt okay for the first few miles. At mile five I felt great. At mile seven I was humming along. But at mile 10, the familiar pain returned. A few more miles and I was done, forced to walk the remaining miles. I was furious. I was the victim, screaming inside my head, "Why me?!" I put so much work in for nothing. In hindsight, my frustration got the best of me, and I was pouting like a cry baby.

At my lowest point, though, I gained some perspective. A wheelchair marathoner passed me, and with a smile on his face, he yelled, "Keep going, man!"

What was I really complaining about? What that individual would give to experience my pain! Although I couldn't run out the race, I finished, the whole time realizing it could be worse. Perspective helps you right-size the emotion associated with the tough time. Somebody always has it better and someone else always has it worse. When you're experiencing tough times, gain some perspective. View your pain through someone else's prism.

Fuhgeddaboudit

"Fuhgeddaboudit" is a common expression of New Yorkers and New Jerseyans. There is some debate on the true meaning of the phrase because it is used in several different ways. The most literal translation and most common meaning is simple. It means "forget about it." Whatever you are worried about or concerned about, it's not worth the worry. So leave it alone.

Have you ever replayed a failure or rejection over and over in your mind? You meticulously review every step, highlighting what you did wrong. It consumes you, and you can't move forward. In these instances, develop a positive amnesia. It's okay to forget the failure once you have extracted all the value from it.

During tough times, salespeople experience multiple setbacks. That's part of sales. Some sellers easily brush off failure; others take it to heart. For those taking it to heart, realize that every rejection means that you're that much closer to success. This refers to the *law of averages* or *regression to the mean*. The world naturally balances itself back to the middle. Even if you are in a slump, you're eventually going to close another sale. Imagine that there is a predetermined number of noes you must hear before hearing yes. The sooner you plow through the noes, the sooner you'll hear yes. You're going to make another sale. Just remember, every no gets you that much closer to a yes.

Once you experience the positive benefits of failure, move on. The pain of rejection motivates us to change. Failure provides feedback to grow and develop. That pain forces us to adapt and evolve. A failure doesn't mean that you lose, unless you fail to learn something along the way. Our minds have a limited capacity. The more you ruminate over previous failures, the less capacity you have for future success. Once you learn all you can from that failure, fuhgeddaboudit!

Operate with a Mindset of Abundance

Operating with an abundance mindset opens your eyes to the opportunities others cannot see. You view the world through a lens of opportunism. You find what you are looking for. This mental hack invokes a self-fulfilling prophecy. Those who see the abundance in the world find more opportunities. It's a biblical mandate:

For to everyone who has, more will be given and he will grow rich;
but from the one who has not, even what he has will be taken away.
(Matthew 25:29 [New American Bible Revised Edition])

Operating with an abundance mindset trains your brain to view the opportunity in every struggle as opposed to seeing the struggle in every opportunity. Like a microscope, an abundance mindset creates the focus you need to see the next opportunity. Train your brain to view things abundantly, and that is what you will perceive—abundance.

An abundance mindset means pursuing opportunities with the knowledge that your effort is worthwhile. You operate with complete confidence, knowing that opportunities exist and that your effort leads to those opportunities. In your mind, it's clear that the opportunities exist—it's simply a matter of finding them. Opportunity is found at the intersection of preparedness and timing. Opportunity shows up when the timing is right. Be prepared to recognize it. An abundance mindset motivates you to press on instead of pausing.

Abundance-minded sellers make more calls knowing that opportunity is there. They willingly make one more call because it could be their next big opportunity. Abundance-minded sellers have an extra bounce in their step and passion in their heart. They attract more opportunities because they put their effort, eagerness, and excitement on display for the world to see. They are a magnet for prospects believing in the same abundance. Imagine waking every morning knowing that there are endless possibilities to achieve your desired success. That is operating with an abundance mindset. The universe gives you what you give it. If you don't like what you're getting, look at what you're giving.

SUMMARY

Selling in tough times is half mental and half skill. You need both to prevail in tough times. Tough times reveal the mental strength that has atrophied during good times. When tough times hit us, we never seem completely prepared. Tough times can rock our world. We experience this initial shock, and it serves as a trigger to monitor our mindset and correct our course.

Use countermeasures to overcome the common mental mistakes. Feeling helpless is a learned behavior, and so is feeling hopeful. The disproportionate amount of failure in tough times challenges the mental prowess of the strongest sellers. Acknowledge that times are tough, but do not accept it. Acknowledge the external factors without using them as an excuse. The failure you experience is not completely on your shoulders (and neither is your success). Be aware of this fact, but don't let external factors be a crutch. Focus on what you can control, which is your inputs, your energy, and your effort.

CHAPTER 5

Building Mental Strength

“I'm at the edge of a 2,000-foot cliff. If I keep drifting over, I'm dead.” That's what I was thinking as my dad and I navigated the winding roads of Custer State Park in South Dakota.

Every year, nearly half a million bikers congregate in Sturgis, South Dakota, for a motorcycle rally. This rally attracts bikers from around the world. This eclectic group includes notable motorcycle gangs like the Hell's Angels, various Christian motorcycle gangs, doctors, lawyers, and other weekend warriors.

Several years ago, my dad and I embarked on a father-son trip. It was great. We experienced most (but not all) of what Sturgis had to offer. We explored the Badlands, Black Hills, Deadwood, Mt. Rushmore, Crazy Horse, and, of course, the legendary burnout pits at Full Throttle Saloon. The most galvanizing experience was navigating the sharp turns of Custer State Park.

While riding through the sharp turns, I struggled to keep up with my dad. At each sharp turn, I slowed down, and my dad zipped right through. I was starting to lose ground, so I throttled up on a straightaway. I quickly made up some ground. There was a sign indicating a sharp turn ahead. I was going way too fast.

I tried slowing down, but I kept drifting out to the edge of the turn. I drifted toward the edge of the cliff and panicked. I thought, “I'm at the edge of a 2,000-foot cliff. If I keep drifting over, I'm dead.”

I hit the brakes harder and leaned toward the road. Finally, I moved back toward the middle of my lane, away from the cliff. I was safe, but now I couldn't see my dad. I thought, “Not a big deal. I'm safe. I'll catch up with him.” (It wasn't a near-death experience, but it was too close for my comfort.)

After a few turns, I noticed that my dad had pulled over to wait for me. Over the bellowing engines of the bike, he yelled, “You have to speed up!”

How's that for fatherly advice to a son: go faster on your motorcycle. His advice was for good reason. There was a line of angry bikers riding my tail and losing their patience.

I'm yelling over the roar of the engines, "I'm trying to catch up, but you're going too fast through the turns. My bike keeps drifting to the outside, and then I have to slow down."

My dad shut down his engine signaling me to kill mine. As the engines muffled out, he asked me, "Where are you looking when you go through the turns?"

I responded, "I'm looking at the 2,000-foot cliff telling myself, 'Don't go there!'"

He responded, "Don't you get it? Your bike naturally moves in the direction you are looking. If you look at what you're trying to avoid, your bike drifts in that direction. You move in the direction of your thoughts. Let's go through the turns again. Only this time, don't look at what you're trying to avoid—look at where you want to end up."

We rode through the same turns, and sure enough, the old man was right. I looked through the turns, and that is where I ended up.

> **Thought:** Look through the turn.
> **Behavior:** Bike turned in the direction of my thought.
> **Result:** Easily navigated the turn.

We move in the direction of our thoughts. We behave as we believe. You might learn this on a motorcycle or playing a sport like golf.

I remember like it was yesterday. There he was, Tiger Woods. I could not believe I was standing next to Tiger.

Over the past decade, no other PGA golfer has experienced the mental and physical challenges Tiger Woods has endured. Yet he has persevered. Growing up watching Tiger play was incredible. He seemed superhuman, unflappable. All the other players were fighting for second. Witnessing Tiger's greatness made it harder to watch his physical and mental decline. Woods went from barely touching his toes and five back surgeries to reminding the golf world just how great he is.

So back to the story . . .

It was me, Tiger Woods, and well over 100,000 people at the 2018 PGA Tour Championship at Bellerive Country Club in St. Louis, Missouri. I attended the final round to watch Tiger nearly beat Brooks Koepka for the title. My friend and I tracked Tiger all day. On the fifth hole we watched Tiger from the fairway gallery, an ideal spot to watch his approach to the green.

Unfortunately, Tiger hit his drive into the trees. Fortunately for me, though, the ball landed right next to me. The crowd swarmed around the ball, knowing that it was Tiger's shot. A few minutes later, Tiger walked up. He was five feet away. Everyone silently watched, full of awe and anticipation. I thought, "How is he going to hit the ball around these trees?"

Tiger had a difficult shot. He had several trees in his path, but if he launched a high iron, it might go over the trees. Tiger was focused. For 10 seconds he just stared at his target. Another 10 seconds went by, and he is still staring. Tiger just stared at his target for 20 to 30 seconds, thinking about his shot. It was a vivid image, the sun shining on the silhouette of Tiger as he stared at his target the way an actual tiger stares at its prey. It was the most inspiring moment of the entire tournament.

Once Tiger finished visualizing his shot, he approached the ball and took several practice swings, committing his thoughts to action. He swung from his mind and muscle, forcefully launching the ball over the trees. Tiger saw the shot before he took it. The roar of Tiger's clan echoed throughout the entire course.

> **Thought:** Visualize the ball flying over the trees.
> **Behavior:** Swing consistently with the vision of the shot.
> **Result:** Ball lands pin high.

Whether navigating the sharp turns of Custer State Park or launching a golf ball over some trees, thoughts drive behavior, and the behavior drives the result. You undoubtedly have similar metaphors in your life. Have you ever focused on what you want to avoid versus what you want to achieve? How often have your thoughts manifested into action? The most important conversation you have is the conversation with yourself. To predict your future, listen to your thoughts.

You move in the direction of your thoughts. You become what you think about. You behave as you believe. Building mental strength requires belief. Have you ever met a successful person with a lousy attitude that didn't believe?

A positive attitude is easy in good times. Think about it. In good times, you face less struggle. Your behavior is easily linked to the success you experience. Your success reinforces your behavior. Although attitude is important in good times, your attitude remains unchallenged. It's easy to stay positive when you hit every metric of success. Maintaining the right attitude is more challenging in tough times. There are certain challenges that you only face in tough times. This is why tough times are more difficult. The sheer magnitude of setbacks overwhelms the mentally toughest sellers.

Salespeople are often considered to be the elite athletes of the business world. They're the rainmakers, the movers and shakers that make things happen. Elite athletes put an enormous amount of pressure on themselves, just like elite sellers. But unlike professional athletes, salespeople don't have an off-season. The relentless pressure mounts during tough times, and our season has no end date. You can see how this could wear you down.

The unrelenting pressure is exhausting. Those moments of exhaustion are the moments that matter. Although it's more challenging to thwart negativity when you feel exhausted, it's more meaningful when you do. This is the true test of mental strength.

Why do we let negativity prevail, knowing that it impacts our behavior? Often we are programmed to view things a certain way. You're conditioned to view things either negatively or positively. How you're conditioned influences your thoughts and actions.

Environment influences attitude. Family and friends influence attitude. Upbringing influences attitude. Everything influences our thoughts, but you must be the filter. You get to choose what you let in and let out. No person has more control over your thoughts than you. You get to choose.

For some people, that choice is more challenging. Some people are conditioned to view events more negatively. Imagine growing up in a house where your parents constantly complained. You witness the incessant complaining about their bosses, their jobs, paying taxes, extra work, not enough work, spending too much money, or not having enough money. How could this not impact your mindset?

Now imagine growing up in a house where your parents inspired you to think and act positively. Imagine parents celebrating their mortgage payment, thankful for their home; parents who are genuinely thankful for their jobs and the lifestyle they afford their family; and parents who are thankful for what they have instead of focusing on what they do not have.

Do your best to control what you can control. You can't always choose your circumstance, but you can choose your responses. For some people, this choice is more challenging than others, but it's still a choice. Consider the following quotation from Viktor Frankl: "Everything can be taken from a man but one thing: the last of the human freedoms—to choose one's attitude in any given set of circumstances, to choose one's own way."[1]

This statement comes from a man who was tortured and survived three different concentration camps. He witnessed and experienced unimaginable hardship. If Frankl can choose his attitude in Auschwitz, you should have no problem choosing yours. The choice is yours regardless of the pain and suffering you experience.

POSITIVE MENTAL PROGRAMMING

Our brains are like computers. We process information to deliver an outcome, the key words being *process information*. The way you process information is determined by how you are programmed. If you don't like how you process information, reprogram your mind.

If a software designer gets the wrong outcome, he or she rewrites the code. Most of the time it's human error; someone missed a parenthesis or an apostrophe. One issue causes an error. A computer cannot perform at full capacity with an error, and neither can we. A computer does what it's programmed to do, and so will you.

Mental programming explains how we process information and events—either positively or negatively. You program your mind to respond in a certain way. Mental programming works both ways, just like computer programming. Garbage in yields garbage out. Just like computer coding, you can rewrite the code and change the outcome. Condition yourself to think more positively. If you're struggling to see past the negative, it's time to rewrite the code.

Positive mental programming (PMP) is steadily conditioning our mindset to move in a more favorable direction leading to better outcomes. PMP leads to greater opportunity. Programmers restructure code for better performance from a computer. PMP is about restructuring our code to reach our potential. Recoding enables you to view the once impossible as possible, and eventually the possible becomes probable. Program your mind to see past the struggle and focus on the opportunity.

Here are five ways you can more positively mentally program yourself.

Develop a Positive First Response

Think of a recent setback. What was your immediate response? How did you react? What emotions did you experience? You gain mental strength through an immediate positive response to adversity.

Your initial response to adversity is a window into your mental programming. Some people face adversity and immediately feel defeated. These individuals quickly give up and move on to something easier. Others respond negatively and slowly recover from their initial reaction. They pause, refocus, and eventually get back on track. Still others experience a negative event and instantaneously push through adversity.

How do you respond to adversity? Assess your current programmed state by tracking your immediate response to adversity. For a few days, carry a pen and paper around with you. Track your immediate response to adversity. For this exercise, adversity can be anything from losing your job, losing a small order, breaking a shoelace, or simply completing a bothersome task. Recognize the adverse moment, and track your response. For example, you procrastinate on a task that you don't want to complete or you ignore a problem that you need to address. Responding positively to adversity builds mental strength.

Tracking negative responses to adversity generates self-correction. You're more likely to respond positively if you notice your negative tendencies. Program yourself to respond positively and immediately to adversity. The goal is to train yourself to view adverse events more positively.

Jocko Willink, Navy SEAL, author, and podcaster, exemplifies the positive immediate response on the Jocko Podcast. In one episode, Jocko shares his thoughts on overcoming adversity, struggle, and previous failure. His advice is simple: when you face a setback, respond by saying, "Good." Jocko explains, "When things are going bad, there's gonna be some good that's gonna come from it."[2] When your competitor beats you, say, "Good." You'll be able to learn from the experience. The "good" is not getting beat—it's learning from that experience.

For example, if your customer buys from the competition, say, "Good." Now you can analyze which failure led to the switch and fix the problem. If you fail to hit your quota, say, "Good." Now you can work on your skills to become a better seller.

Tough times lead to greater outcomes. To attain those greater outcomes, embrace the right immediate attitude. Immediately view each setback or failure as an opportunity to improve. Tough times are good!

Monitor Your Self-Talk

Self-talk matters. Self-talk is the ongoing conversation you have with yourself. In good times or tough times, we constantly talk to ourselves. Have you listened to yourself lately? It's amazing what we tolerate from ourselves that we wouldn't tolerate from other people. We would not allow others to say, "You're terrible at this" or "You'll never achieve this." If you wouldn't allow another person to talk to you like that, why tolerate it from yourself? You control what you accept from others; control what you accept from yourself.

Negative self-talk leads to self-sabotaging words and behaviors. Imagine that you were preparing a friend for a tough time in his or her life. Your friend is facing a personal struggle. Would you break your friend down or build him or her up? You would build your friend up. Build yourself up!

Review your self-talk and identify what triggers negativity, for example, words or phrases like, "It can't be done" or "They'll never go for that" or "It's impossible." Everything is impossible until it's not. Decisively negative statements blind you to opportunities and trigger you to give up or quit.

Have you ever talked trash to yourself? It's easy to pump yourself up when things are great. Trash talking shows up when times get tough. The most important conversations are the ones with yourself. How's that conversation going? Do any of the following phrases sound familiar?

"There are no opportunities in my territory. This sucks."

"No prospects are willing to schedule an appointment. This sucks."

"It's impossible to get anything done. This sucks."

"I can't sell that solution right now. This sucks."

If this is how you talk to yourself, congratulations! You are appointed the captain of the "Suck Brigade." In your mind, everything sucks, and it always will. From this day forth, you have final ruling over all things that suck. Feel free to elaborate on all the little things that suck. Feel free to drag people down to your level. You now have the ability to find what sucks in the most positive circumstances.

It's doubtful that you fall into this category. You wouldn't still be reading this book (unless you're trying to find what sucks about it). When the captain of the Suck Brigade starts recruiting, don't participate. The captain will complain and nag until you join. Such people show up at your weakest mental moment. Don't get sucked in.

It's not a question of whether we talk negatively to ourselves or not. We all experience negative self-talk. The key is to reframe the conversation positively. Positively shifting our internal dialogue requires more mental strength than simply maintaining a positive conversation. Positive self-talk is not all sunshine and unicorns—it's positively reframing the trigger phrase and then driving accountability with a personal statement.

There is a better way to talk to yourself. Notice the content and structure of these statements:

"There is opportunity out there; I just need to find it."

"The prospect will meet; I just need to craft a compelling message."

"This tough time will pass. I can positively control my attitude in the meantime."

"It can be done; I just need to find another way to make it happen."

In each example, you reframe the negative statements more positively and add an accountability statement. If your mind is filled with negative self-talk, follow this three-step process to refocus positively:

- **Step 1.** Recognize and acknowledge the negative self-talk.
- **Step 2.** Positively reframe the negative self-talk.
- **Step 3.** Connect the positive self-talk to an accountability statement.

Be aware of your self-talk, and use this three-step process to reframe the conversation. Use the accountability statement to focus on what you can control. My company teaches sellers to take positive control of the sales conversation and guide it down a path of value. How can you control that conversation if you cannot control the conversations with yourself?

Success has no constraints, so don't add one with negativity. Negative statements could just as easily be positive—just change a few key words. Stop focusing on failure when there is nothing absolute about the future. Your future has yet to be written, so the possibilities are endless. In good times and tough times, the future is never certain. This should provide you with more hope than despair. You rarely get exactly what you expect. Sometimes you get more.

Selectively Focus Your Attention

Selective attention involves focusing on certain information or stimuli in the presence of other stimuli and information. If you're eating dinner with friends and everyone at the table is talking, it's conversational crossfire. There are several distractions, but you focus on the conversation with your neighbor. You selectively focus on that one individual. You're able to filter out the background noise and focus on one thing.

You can also selectively focus on what is positive and good and ignore what is negative and destructive. How many articles have a negative title? How many news broadcasts have a shocking, negative lead? Hence the old news expression, "If it bleeds, it leads." You are not doomed to focus on the negative. Set your filters to let the positive flow in and the negative flow somewhere else.

It's hard to focus on the positive in tough times because of the sheer amount of negativity. In those instances, consider the famous quote from Mr. Rogers: "When I was a boy and I would see scary things in the news, my mother would say to me, 'Look for the helpers. You will always find people who are helping.'"[3] Take a page out of Mr. Rogers' playbook and look for the positive.

Through tough times, you're surrounded with negativity. Selectively focus on the positive instead. You control your focus. In any negative event or setback, there is an opportunity for growth. Positively focus your attention on the myriad opportunities, not the magnitude of your struggle.

Challenge Yourself

When elephants are born in captivity, it's common to restrain the animal using a rope attached to a small stake driven into the ground. The newly born calf does not have the strength to break free. As the elephant calf grows, the same rope and stake are used to restrain the mighty elephant. Although the elephant could easily break free, it does not. The elephant is conditioned to believe that it can never break free. Elephants are one of the largest and strongest land mammals, yet they can be restrained by a rope and stake driven only a few inches into the ground.

Do you feel like your current tough time is your stake and rope? How often do we allow a rope and stake to hold us back? How often do we condition ourselves to accept the limitations placed on us?

Remember the elephant when you set your goals during tough times. It's common for salespeople and sales managers to lower their expectations in tough times. Instead of driving that stake into the ground, look for opportunities to break free. To do this, challenge yourself and your assumptions. Become aware of your inner dialogue, and challenge yourself to think differently. Challenge yourself to cross boundaries and take chances.

Challenge the things deemed to be unchangeable or impossible. Impossibility is relative; something is always impossible until someone else does it. How often do rookie sellers land a prospect no one else could? That rookie seller is often told, "Don't bother going after that opportunity. Those people will never buy from us." This is another stake being driven into the ground.

Tough times are the times to challenge yourself and your assertions. What do you have to lose? The only thing you risk losing is future regret, which is worth avoiding. When the stake is driven and the rope is tight, keep going.

Develop an Attitude of Gratitude

If there was one simple thing you could do to feel healthier, happier, and reduce stress, would you do it? The answer is obvious. Yes!

All of this is achieved through gratitude. Numerous studies highlight the benefits of gratitude. Robert A. Emmons, professor of psychology at the University of California, Davis, found that gratitude is linked to 23 percent lower levels of the stress hormone cortisol.[4] Tough times are filled with stress. Imagine lowering your stress by focusing on what you're grateful for. In a separate study, Emmons and Michael McCullough noticed that participants focusing on gratitude showed signs of enhanced well-being and positivity and felt healthier.[5] Attitude drives behavior. Gratitude-focused people behave as they believe. If you believe that you're healthy, you make healthier decisions. If you believe that you're positive, you will be more positive.

Sales leaders, expressing gratitude to your team leads to more activity and enhanced performance. Consider this fund-raising study by Adam Grant and Francesca Gianino.[6] Fund-raisers were separated into two groups. One group received thanks and praise from the director of fund-raising. The second group did not receive thanks and praise from the director. The weekly call volume of the thanked group increased by 50 percent.

An attitude of gratitude serves you well in tough times. In tough times, you experience an overwhelming amount of negativity, setbacks, and adversity. Adverse events are more salient, whereas positive events are more subtle. If you can't change the adverse events, change what you see through those negative events.

It's hard to be grateful when you're jealous of other people. Comparisons invoke jealously and envy; neither is helpful in tough times. Comparing yourself with others spotlights what is missing instead of what you have. Salespeople compare their territories and opportunities with those of other sellers. Focus and be thankful for what you have, not what you don't.

Negativity is a by-product of comparison. Envy and frustration appear as we compare our success to that of others. Success, like tough times, is relative. Success is more than your achievements; it includes the struggle you overcame to garner those achievements. Success easily earned is not as sweet as success hard fought. Stop comparing your success to the success of others. If you find yourself saying, "They have it all!" or "How did they get there? Why am I not there?" take a step back to realize where you are compared with where you were. The greater the distance traveled means the greater the success. Success is relative.

Develop an attitude of gratitude. The moment you start comparing, shift the focus to what you have. When you experience negative events, find the blessing in the burden. Look for the positive outcome generated from the negative event. Reprogram your brain to find the positive in everything. It takes the same amount of energy to focus on the positive outcome as the negative event that caused it.

Put gratitude into action. Consider starting a gratitude journal. Every day, fill a page with what you are thankful for. Imagine having a tough day but then writing a page of reflections leading to gratitude. This would be enough to lift anyone. And if the day was especially challenging, simply read your journal for an extra dose of gratitude.

POSITIVE ENVIRONMENTAL PROGRAMMING

The timeless classic *Mary Poppins* (Walt Disney Productions, 1964) is filled with powerful self-help nuggets. Consider Mary Poppins' famous quote, "Well begun is half done," which means a task or activity started the right way is easier to complete. A more contemporary translation is, "Half the work is beginning the task the right way." To be successful, set yourself up for success.

Success is not as hard as we make it seem. You can proactively eliminate barriers. People unknowingly place obstacles on their paths to success. They're not trying to sabotage themselves; they're just making it harder than it has to be. This often manifests as poorly managed time or priorities—electing to do what is easy or urgent versus what is challenging and fruitful.

Positive environmental programming (PEP) is setting yourself up for success. PEP is about controlling and influencing your surroundings to more easily attain success. There are internal aspects of our environment that we control and external factors that we cannot control. PEP is focusing on what you can control and not wasting energy on what you cannot control. There is no benefit to hyperfocusing on what you cannot control. *Positive mental programming* (PMP) is controlling the content of your mind. PEP is controlling the *context* of your mind. You shape your mind just as much as your surroundings. Think of this section as your personal PEP talk to help you positively shape your environment.

Conduct a Barrier Analysis

What gets in the way of your success? This is not a leading question to invoke a clever response of "nothing" or "myself." Really think. Is it your activity level, lack of prospects, fewer opportunities, your technology? Asking and answering the opening question is a basic barrier analysis. A *barrier analysis* identifies what gets in the way of your success. You can't remove a barrier you don't know exists. Once the barriers are identified, the next step is to remove them. People are more motivated if they face fewer—not zero—obstacles along the path to success.

Sellers facing obstacles need the right skills to confidently overcome those challenges. If sellers lack confidence in their ability, they are likely to stall out and call it quits. Sellers need the right level of skill to match their will so that when they do face a barrier, they break through not break down.

Barriers are easier to find than you think. For example, a seller is missing his or her sales targets because he or she lacks qualified leads or opportunities. This barrier gets in the way of the seller's success, so the salesperson must decide how to remove it. He or she could request more leads from the sales managers, more effectively qualify leads as they enter the pipeline, or pick up the phone to find more leads. The focus is on removing the barrier. Barrier removal is not achieving the goal; it's just one small win on the path to goal achievement.

Tough times reveal the root cause of the barrier. For example, salespeople highlight the difficulties of meeting with customers in tough times. Some salespeople tell me, "Nobody is meeting with sellers right now" or "My customer is furloughed and can't respond to me." This barrier seems out of your control, but it reveals another barrier within your control. The perceived barrier is the furloughed employee, but the real barrier is having too few relationships within this opportunity.

Tough times clarify the real barriers. Some barriers are misperceived as purely external when the root cause is internal. In those instances, tough times reveal barriers we didn't know existed. Remember, a good economy masks bad sales behavior. Anyone can be successful in good times—it's the tough times that reveal our strengths and weaknesses. This is one of the benefits of tough times. Tough times reveal new barriers to break down. This better positions you for the good times that follow. Tough times are good!

Reduce Friction

Have you ever told yourself, "Tomorrow morning I'm taking a run"? Then, the next morning, your alarm rings and you hit the snooze button instead. The bed is just too comfortable, and the blankets feel so warm. It's just too tempting to stay in bed. What if there were a better way to prepare? What if you could proactively set yourself up for success?

If you were planning to run tomorrow morning, what proactive measures would ensure that you complete the workout? You could set the alarm on your phone and place the phone out of arm's reach so that you must get up to turn it off. Once you're out of bed, it's harder to get back in. You could lay out your clothes and running shoes the night before. That's one less thing you have to do in the morning. You could plan your route. You could even place your headphones next to your workout clothes. When you wake up, you're ready to run. You reduced the friction between you and your goal.

Success is not as hard as we make it. Reducing friction is setting yourself up for success. When challenged at a moment of weakness, how do you respond? Some people face these moments and press on; others give up. By reducing friction, you move forward with greater ease and less frustration. Reducing friction is different from removing barriers. A barrier, by definition, stops progress. Friction just slows you down. The more friction there is, the closer you get to stopping. By removing friction, you travel faster and generate more momentum to break through any barriers along your path.

Reducing friction positively programs your environment. Many salespeople view prospecting as a hassle, so it takes a backseat to other activities, like taking care of existing customers. What if you could reduce the friction? Let's say that the afternoon before your prospecting campaign, you develop a preestablished list of prospects and contact information. You preplan these calls with objectives, a list of probing questions, and call-to-action items. You block off your calendar for these times. Reducing friction reduces the hassle associated with bothersome activities.

Reducing friction reshapes your attitude. Although attitude drives behavior, behavior can also reshape a negative attitude. By removing some hassle the day before, the activity doesn't seem so bad. You're removing the difficulty that drives negativity. Now prospecting isn't so bad. Reshape the environment, which, in turn, reshapes the attitude.

Create a Positive Perimeter

Crabs behave differently based on their environment. A single crab placed in a bucket will find a way to escape. If you place several crabs in a bucket, something unusual happens. If one crab tries to escape, the other crabs fight and claw, dragging the crab back into the bucket. If the escaping crab persists, the other crabs snap its claws and eventually kill it.[7] So much for helping your fellow crab. How often do you feel like the crab in a crowded bucket?

PEP is creating a positive perimeter. Set a boundary, and surround yourself with the right people—people who build you up, not pull you back down. Were your parents ever hesitant to let you hang out with certain kids—you know, the troublemakers deemed the "wrong crowd"? Your parents did this for good reason: you become who you surround yourself with. Who are you surrounding yourself with?

One study in New Zealand showed that graduate students' performance was 18 percent higher than average, but only if they were unaware of their rank.[8] Those students only performed above average when they didn't know the average. When made aware of the average, graduate students underperformed, lowering their scores to average. Students did not want to appear too smart. Whether intentionally or not, groups can pull you down. Be wary of who you surround yourself with.

Sellers unknowingly create an environment that pulls them down. We do this by putting more "crabs in the bucket." In every aspect of your life, people build you up or break you down. It's easier to spot those building you up. They're committed to your success. They provide a helping hand and constructive feedback. They challenge you when you need it, even if you don't want it.

Those breaking you down are more subtle. They shower you with undue praise and convince you that you're "just fine." They tell you to stay the same. Other behavioral cues may be more insidious. They encourage you to fail by lulling you into a false sense of security. They claim your failures are out of your control. They are quick to wallow in self-pity with you. These individuals are there at your weakest moments. Success is a continuum, mostly moving forward, but also backward. Cut ties with those who hold you back. Find another group to propel you forward.

Who and what we surround ourselves with create our environment—positively or negatively. I worked with a company that needed positive reprogramming in its entire organization. Every day, the company ran a shipping report to track the number of shipments not leaving the warehouse on time. The report was called the "Shipping Failure Report" (SFR). Imagine beginning your day reviewing a report that highlights your failures. It's not a question of whether you failed, just a question of how much. Whoever designed this report had to be the captain of the Suck Brigade. Every day the captain would ask, "How bad did you suck yesterday?"

One small change could dramatically improve the team's attitude. Call it the SSR for "Shipping Success Rate." Imagine beginning work every day knowing you're already a success; it's just a question of how much.

There are some things that you control and some things that you cannot control. You have more control over your environment than you think. Stage your environment to set a positive tone. Surround yourself with positive affirmation: customer testimonials, gratitude lists, awards. Create an environment with things that motivate you: posters, pictures, quotes. Positive elements create a positive environment.

Surround yourself with people who lift you up, not hold you down. Do you have certain customers who lift you up, customers who demand your absolute best? The same is true for others in your circle. Are there leaders in your organization who build you up and make you want to become better? Surround yourself with these individuals in tough times. Through osmosis, you absorb their characteristics.

In contrast, there are individuals to avoid. Through osmosis, you absorb what flows from them too. These colleagues are hard to be around in good times, let alone bad times. Misery loves company, and they bring you down to their level. Avoid these people altogether.

Jim Rohn, motivational speaker, famously said, "You are the average of the five people you spend the most time with."[9] Who are you spending your time with? You control the environment you create. If you don't like your current environment, create a new one.

SUMMARY

Attitude drives behavior, and your behavior is what drives your success. We move in the direction of our thoughts and behave as we believe. Of all the things out of our control, the one thing that we can control is our attitude. This process begins with positive mental programming. Train your brain to positively process information, which leads to the right attitude, which, in turn, drives the right behavior. Program your mind to drive you forward, not hold you back. Positive environmental programming is setting yourself up for success; it's reshaping your environment to remove barriers and surrounding yourself with the right people.

Sun Tzu said, "Every battle is won before it's ever fought."[10] He could've been referring to the mental battle in our head. The battleground in tough times exists between your two ears. The battle is won first mentally and then fought in the marketplace.

CHAPTER 6

Characteristics
of Tough Timers

I n tough times, why do some salespeople struggle and others thrive? Why do some accept failure and others remain hopeful and resilient? Why do some merely *go* through tough times and others *grow* through tough times? After reading this chapter, you will be able to answer these questions. You will learn to succeed through tough times like a tough timer.

Mentally tough sellers draw from a wellspring of attributes that help them thrive in good times and grow through tough times. Tough timers, with or without titles, are leaders among their colleagues and customers. Their leadership stems from something deeper than titles. Their leadership is deeply rooted in their ability to act and inspire change.

Tough timers are resilient; they stretch and adapt with the prevailing times. They are visionaries who deeply believe in their success. Tough timers do not question if they will succeed—it's only a question of when. Tough timers are pragmatic optimists. They believe in a better future, acknowledging that success does not come without struggle. Tough timers view their world opportunistically. Winston Churchill could have been describing tough timers when he said that "an optimist sees the opportunity in every difficulty."[1]

Tough timers are adventurous in their approach. They take chances. Their success is all but certain. Why wouldn't they find other routes to success? Whatever path tough timers choose, they travel it with a tone of humility. Tough times humble everyone. Tough timers are already traveling a path paved with humility.

Who did you think of when you read the last few paragraphs? Did one individual come to mind? If your colleagues were reading this book, would they think of you? Whoever you pictured is the mentally toughest person you know. If you want to be a tough timer, then do what they do, and think how they think.

Every seller needs a role model, especially in tough times. Sellers who struggle are more open to coaching, advice, and development. More reason to have a mentor or be a mentor in tough times. Some sellers mentor by telling. Tough timers mentor by modeling. Tough timers demonstrate what to do and how to think while carrying themselves with quiet confidence. Look for a tough timer to emulate.

This chapter provides a detailed description of tough timers. These characteristics were collected and observed over more than 40 years, dating back to the founder of Tom Reilly Training. Over this period, we have worked with the best sales organizations and the mentally strongest salespeople.

As you read each characteristic, ask yourself, "How many of these words describe me?" You may have some, but not all, of the tough-timer characteristics. Don't let this gap frustrate you. Let it motivate you. Use the gap as feedback to strengthen the areas where you are weak. Certain strengths only appear once they are tested through tough times.

RESILIENCE

When you fall on tough times, do you bounce back higher? Resilience is the ability to bounce back higher than where you fell from. Resilience means busting through obstacles and setbacks. Tough timers are resilient; they quickly recover from failure and press on. Tough timers bounce back to a higher level of performance. They experience failure, reflect and learn, and then come back stronger. Tough timers arm themselves with new skills and tactics to approach their next challenge. They take all the benefits of failing without dwelling on it.

Success in any field requires resilience, but especially in sales. In sales, you face more failures, more adversity, more competition, more of everything. Each setback is an opportunity to gain resilience. In tough times, you'll face even more opportunities. How do tough timers face setbacks? These sellers don't get emotional or upset—they simply get to work. Giving up doesn't cross their minds. Others waste energy on emotion; they focus their energy on solving the problem. Resilient sellers embrace the new challenge.

When I was a young seller, my dad shared a story with me. As a psychology graduate student, he reached out to one of his professors to discuss a new business. While making small talk, he explained how his selling model was going to help other salespeople succeed. At that point, his professor asked, "I don't know why anyone gets into sales. How can you deal with all that rejection?" My dad responded, "I never really thought of it." That's resilience.

How resilient are you? Do you give up easily? Over the next few weeks, monitor your resilience. How do you respond to the mildest adversity? It could be something as simple as a prospect going silent or losing a large customer. The key is to understand how you respond.

Resilient tough timers are flexible. Any seller can see a problem, but tough timers are flexible and adapt to see the solution. The problem is a necessary pathway to their success. Tough timers abide by the motto "Persistence beats resistance." They stubbornly go after their goals and handle difficulty along the way. When things get difficult, most people give up. Tough timers don't. When tough timers are challenged, they push harder, making them stronger for the next challenge.

VISIONARY

Tough timers push through adversity because their positive vision of the future is more powerful than the pain of the present. Visionary salespeople see no wasted effort today because they firmly believe in a more positive future. Tough timers know that the future is better. The road may be different through tough times, but they know that they are headed in the right direction. Tough timers are visionary because they deeply believe in their success. Because their success is certain, their actions today are consistent with the success they expect in the future. It is easier to take a risk and work hard when you know that your effort leads to your success.

Visualize your success. Imagine that you're pursuing a prospect. From the beginning, you pursue this opportunity with the belief that you will be successful. You've imagined and dreamed about your success to the point where it's real. Accepting this future success encourages you to take the right action today.

While speaking at a kick-off meeting in Texas, one sales leader introduced me to his top performer. The top achiever sold in a market experiencing tough times. His business was off 70 percent from the prior year. During dinner, I asked the seller, "How do you feel about this year?" I wanted to gauge his attitude. He explained, "This type of year is not uncommon in my industry. I know what I need to do. Support my top customers as they struggle. Go after new opportunities as they develop. If there are no opportunities, I'll create some. I have been through this before. I know what to do." There wasn't a hint of doubt in his demeanor. This is what it means to be visionary.

PRAGMATIC OPTIMISTS

> This is a very important lesson. You must never confuse faith
> that you will prevail in the end—which you can never afford
> to lose—with the discipline to confront the most brutal
> facts of your current reality, whatever they might be.
> —ADMIRAL JIM STOCKDALE[2]

This quote became known as the "Stockdale paradox" in Jim Collins' book, *Good to Great*. Admiral Stockdale was captured and tortured during the Vietnam War. Stockdale explained to Collins how he survived this experience. The Stockdale paradox is relevant to any tough time and rings true today, just as it did during the Vietnam War. This powerful paradox addresses the dichotomy of tough times: you must maintain faith that you will prevail, even if—and especially when—your current reality is contradictory to your ability to prevail.

Pragmatic optimism is like the Stockdale paradox: remain optimistic despite the harsh realities you face. Tough timers are positive while acknowledging the realities of their situation. A pure optimist keeps his or her head in the clouds. These clouds obscure that person's view to reality. It's harmful to face tough times with naive optimism. Tough timers positively address their challenges.

Tough timers view the world pragmatically. They approach tough times with tenacity, knowing that it won't be easy. You cannot ignore the realities of tough times; those realities won't ignore you. You cannot overcome a challenge that you don't believe exists. Tough timers don't sell in a bubble. They acknowledge their challenges and adapt accordingly.

Optimistic tough timers embrace the good qualities of a pessimist while ignoring the negative ones. A pessimist spotlights the holes in any plan. A tough timer does the same, but they go a step further and fill in the holes.

Tough timers are genuine. They lift people up with their sincere and pragmatic optimism. They inspire hope with their positive nature yet paradoxically remain grounded enough to address the challenges of tough times.

OPPORTUNISTIC

In 1898, a batch of wheat-based dough was left out overnight, causing it to ferment. The baker decided not to throw it out. Instead, he rolled out the dough, creating large, thin flakes. The baker, Will Kellogg, experimented with these flakes and eventually created Kellogg's Corn Flakes.[3]

In 1918, a California restaurateur accidentally dropped a customer's sandwich roll in a pan of meat drippings. Rather than throwing out the sandwich, the customer still ate it and raved about the "dipped" sandwich. The French dip sandwich was born.[4]

In 1924, a restaurateur was overwhelmed with crowds on a holiday weekend. He was running out of food, but people were still showing up. All he had left was lettuce. Not wanting to turn people away, the owner concocted a dressing using basic ingredients. Caesar Cardini poured the dressing over the lettuce and served the first Caesar salad.[5]

Although these stories are fascinating, what's more fascinating is the timing. In 1898, the United States was on the tail end of the depression of 1893. As World War I was ending, we experienced another recession in 1918 (not to mention the global pandemic of the Spanish flu). Although the 1920s were "roaring," there was still a recession in 1923–1924. The success stories that began this section are proof positive that you can prevail in tough times. Maybe tough times provided the opportunistic lens for these entrepreneurs to visualize their creations. Tough times are good!

A skeptic would claim that dumb luck led to these successes, but that's only half true. Yes, these entrepreneurs experienced good fortune, but they had to act on it. They viewed their accidental innovations through an opportunistic prism. You, too, can prevail if you are opportunistic.

Opportunistic sellers adapt and apply their skills to the prevailing circumstances. It's seizing opportunity from the jaws of defeat, finding gain amid pain. Tough timers view the world through an opportunistic lens—finding an advantage in the struggle. Tough timers are surrounded by opportunity—they simply need to find it.

Hopefulness and optimism are prerequisites for opportunism. Remember, learned helplessness blinds you to the opportunity, whereas learned hopefulness blinds you to the struggle. Tough timers are so convinced of their success that they manufacture opportunities out of their own belief.

Opportunists run from the herd and pursue new ideas, whereas others seek the security of the status quo. Tough timers test the boundaries of their comfort zones. They realize that you cannot stand out if you blend in with the crowd. Tough timers boldly stand out with hope, optimism, and a willingness to do what others consider a hassle or too risky.

ADVENTUROUS

Have you noticed that children are more open to new ideas? They willingly take risks. When you ask children, "Would you like to go on an adventure," they enthusiastically respond, "Yes!" An adventure represents a new set of possibilities (and challenges).

The older we get, the less likely we are to embrace adventures. Whatever happened to our childlike wonderment? When adults are asked if they want to take an adventure, they'll likely say, "Well, that depends. What is it?" A common response with a hint of skepticism. The unknown motivates children but creates fear for adults. The fear of what could happen overwhelms the excitement of what might happen.

Most people are risk averse. Think about what happens during tough times—you "stay under the radar" or "keep your powder dry"—*you play it safe*. This is like staying calm as the ship sinks to save your energy for the swim rather than fixing the hole. If you're saying, "That's not me," ask yourself, "When was the last time I stepped way outside my comfort zone?" If it takes you too long to answer this question, you're playing it too safe. Too many salespeople play it safe in tough times. They take fewer chances, missing opportunities. One thing is sure, playing it safe in tough times doesn't ensure that you'll be playing for long.

Tough timers try new techniques, sell in unchartered waters, and take on new challenges. Tough timers risk failure for a greater chance at success. They go higher and deeper into their opportunities at the risk of offending lower-level contacts. Tough timers are adventurous and willing to take risks—especially when their competitors are playing it safe.

Tough timers love a challenge and thrive in the face of adversity. A tough timer's success is all but certain, so tough timers view their turbulent path to success as an adventure. What if you treated your profession more like an adventure than a job?

STEADFAST

Unwavering, unyielding, and immovable. Steadfast means to be firm and resolute in your pursuit. Tough timers are determined to be successful. They are resolute in their effort because they know that their actions lead to their success. They operate with a quiet confidence and comfort, knowing that today's action creates tomorrow's results.

Tough timers are steady and consistent with their effort and approach. They consistently execute the tried-and-true selling fundamentals. Have you ever noticed the pace of top achievers? They march toward their goals at double-time. There is no variable speed. They are fully in pursuit of their goals. There is no wavering in their belief or their effort.

Tough timers remain steadfast in their focus. During tough times, it's tempting to chase shiny objects. When there's so much doom and gloom, shiny objects are more distracting. Even though such objects shine like gold, this doesn't mean that they are valuable. Tough timers steadfastly approach opportunities that are a good fit. Although tough timers adapt and evolve, they don't waiver from their intended goals.

It's easy to remain steadfast when your activities produce the desired result. True commitment is tested when your effort leads nowhere. Tough timers remain steadfast, even if that effort doesn't produce immediate results. Tough timers work through today's pain for progress tomorrow.

When I think of a steadfast approach, I think of farmers. Farmers are dependable; they do the work. They are unwavering in their process. It's common to characterize salespeople as hunters or farmers. However, the skills required to be great at both are not mutually exclusive. Some of the best hunters I know are literally farmers. Regardless of your role, the key is to remain steadfast in your approach.

Think of a goal to which you are deeply committed. You steadfastly do the work, even when you can't see the results. When you're deeply committed, you know that your action eventually produces the desired result. The way you feel in goal-achieving mode is the way tough timers operate.

It's easy maintaining a steadfast approach during good times. Everything is going your way. The outcomes motivate you to keep going. Tough timers distinguish themselves when those results are not visible. They believe in the goal and remain focused. When others hit the road, they kick into a higher gear.

HUMBLE

The most important characteristic of tough timers is also the least noticeable: humility. Humility is an interesting characteristic because it is hard to recognize. Arrogance and pride are easily recognizable in salespeople. It's not like people can brag about being humble. Humility is more noticeable in its absence than its presence.

Humility is often misunderstood in sales. The word *sales* conjures images of a confident, gregarious, outspoken seller. Therefore, notions of humility run contradictory to our idea of the typical seller. Many people associate humility with weakness. But for every outspoken and arrogant top performer, there is a top performer who is humbly plodding his or her way to success, quietly going about their work.

It is naive to think that there is only one archetype that generates success. Tough timers are diverse, and so are the roads that lead to success—especially in tough times. There are many routes to achieve sales success. Tough timers travel the lowly path of humility to achieve theirs.

Humility means embracing a modest view of oneself. Humility precedes strength. You can't get stronger until you first acknowledge your weakness. Humble sellers recognize that it's not all about them. Value is defined by the customer—independent of the seller. Only a humble salesperson steps outside himself or herself to truly understand the customer's definition of value.

Tough times humble us all. Whether it's a pandemic, a recession, a tough competitor, or industry concerns, they all kick us in the teeth. High-flyers are grounded by an anchor of reality when tough times hit. Even the most prideful and arrogant sellers acknowledge the humbling effects of tough times.

Pride is more apparent in good times. Prideful sellers let their performance go to their heads, thinking they've reached their peak. How can you get better if you're already at the top? When these sellers are humbled by tough times, it's a harder fall. Hence the old adage, "The bigger they are, the harder they fall." Humble tough timers fall a much shorter distance in a downturn. For tough timers, the humbler you are, the softer you land.

Humility begins with admitting that you can improve. Take an honest look at your successes and failures. When they analyze success, too many sellers overemphasize their efforts and ignore the external factors. The opposite is true for failures. Many unsuccessful people overemphasize the outside influences while minimizing their role. Humble salespeople look for ways to improve. They ask their sales managers for help. They own their successes and failures so that they can learn and grow while maintaining their modesty. Tough times humble us all. Like many of these characteristics, humility serves us well in good times and bad.

SUMMARY

Tough times reveal your true character. Look for these characteristics as you experience tough times. Think of individuals who encompass all the qualities of a tough timer. Model your behavior after them. Look to them for advice. Pursue these individuals with the same tenacity you pursue a prospect. You are who you surround yourself with.

Tough times don't last, but tough people do. Tough timers endure when others give up or give in. Tough timers view their struggles as opportunities to improve. Not everyone's path to becoming a tough timer looks the same. There are different paths for different people. It's only during tough times that your character is fully revealed.

Tough timers are resilient and bounce back higher from where they fall. They are pragmatic optimists taking their challenges head-on. They are adventurous and opportunistic, finding new ways to be successful. Tough timers deeply believe in their success; they sense it and see it before it happens. Tough timers are steadfast and humble. They push forward even when they cannot see their progress.

How many of these words describe you? As you read this chapter, you may have seen that some of the characteristics described align with who you are, whereas others do not. Refer to Table 6.1 to help you recognize which characteristics are present and which are not. View this exercise as a mirror. This mirror highlights where you need to improve. Rate yourself in each of the characteristics. Then think of ideas to further align your actions with those of tough timers.

TABLE 6.1 Tough-Timer Self-Assessment

Tough-Timer Attribute	Ranking (1–10)	Improvement ideas
Resilient		
Visionary		
Pragmatic Optimist		
Opportunistic		
Adventurous		
Steadfast		
Humble		

Daily Mental Flex®

P rofessional bodybuilders and power lifters are the embodiment of physical strength. The current world record for the bench press is 770 pounds,[6] and for the squat, it is more than 1,000 pounds.[7] These individuals work out daily to build their strength—spending up to four hours at the gym. What if you could build your mental strength to the same level that power lifters build their physical strength?

Whether it's walking, running, or weight lifting, physical exercise is part of any healthy routine. The CDC recommends 30 to 45 minutes of exercise per day. Committing to this rigorous exercise routine means that you are one of the 23 percent of people who exercise enough on a regular basis.[8] Imagine if you were as committed to your mental strength as you are to your physical health.

Prevailing through tough times requires daily commitment. Condition your mind every day to get stronger mentally. Each day you can handle a little more adversity. You don't start off squatting 1,000 pounds; you work your way up.

This Daily Mental Flex® (DMF) is your daily guide to building mental strength. It's a collection of exercises inspired by positive mental programming, positive environmental programming, and tough-timer characteristics. You'll notice the common themes presented in the six DMF exercises. The DMF requires commitment. Positive change only happens through commitment and dedication to the process. It is foolish to think that one workout leads to your desired physical health. The same is true for this DMF. The right activities executed continuously lead to the desired results.

One workout doesn't lead to your desired health, but skipping a workout detracts from it. The negative impact of skipping a workout is greater than the positive impact of making each workout. Skipping one DMF is not detrimental, but skipping one means that you're more likely to skip the next DMF and the one after that. Eventually, the DMF is something you used to do.

Your mental progress is not always visible, but it is meaningful. Because you don't always see the immediate benefit of completing this flex, it can be challenging. The especially challenging days are the ones that matter the most.

DMF INSTRUCTIONS

Do what is uncomfortable and you become stronger. Each exercise is designed to condition one element of mental strength. There are six exercises focusing on gratitude, continuous improvement, discipline, pruning negativity, positive reframing, and reducing friction.

Begin your DMF in the morning before you start your day. You don't need to complete the DMF in one sitting, but you do need to complete each exercise before the end of the day. This requires focus and commitment. The DMF is available for download at www.ToughTimer.com. Just as you would lay out your shoes, clothes, and earbuds the night before a run, set your DMF where it's easily visible.

The DMF includes a weekly focus. Bodybuilders target certain muscles. The same is true for tough timers. Focus on one area where you need extra conditioning. For your focus area of the week, you'll double up on your exercises. For the sake of clarity, *every day you must complete all six exercises*. Every morning, write down your DMF focus for the week. Each exercise is critical, but it is most critical to focus on the areas where you need the greatest improvement. For example, if your weekly focus is discipline, then you should repeatedly strengthen this area to build on it. It is important to switch your weekly focus. Switching focus creates balance and a strong mental foundation.

Exercise 1: Gratitude

Journal a half page of what you are thankful for. If gratitude is your focal exercise, journal a full page.

Tough timers have an attitude of gratitude. Being grateful reduces stress and enhances health and happiness. Can you think of a better way to begin your day? The key is not just to answer the question, "What are you grateful for today?"—but to think about the answer.

For example, you write down, "I'm thankful for my family." That's great; me too. Don't simply lift the bar; put a little weight on it. Think about specifics. Was there an occurrence that led you to be especially thankful today? Did your child hug you in the morning? Did your spouse do something special for you? Recall the details that led to your feelings of gratitude.

Exercise 2: Continuous Improvement

Spend 15 minutes on a continuous-improvement activity. If continuous improvement is your weekly focus, then spend 30 minutes.

Tough timers look for ways to improve. Develop an attitude of enhancement. Tough times expose your weaknesses so that you can become stronger. Tough times are painful, and that pain acts as a catalyst for positive change. Highlight one area you need to improve. This area of improvement could be personal or business related. For example, spend 15 minutes improving your sales presentation. Spend 15 minutes reading a sales book or role-playing an upcoming call. Tough timers challenge themselves to get better daily. Here are several other continuous-improvement ideas: read, listen to a podcast, role-play a presentation, get organized, improve your writing skills, do some product training, tweak your messaging, or improve selling skills.

Exercise 3: Discipline

Complete a task that you don't feel like completing. If discipline is your weekly focus, then complete two tasks that you don't feel like completing.

Tough timers have the self-discipline to complete tasks that they don't feel like completing. Self-discipline is crucial in tough times. In tough times, you act today for achievement tomorrow. This means doing things today that you don't feel like doing.

What is the one thing you don't feel like doing today? On your to-do list, the bothersome tasks are at the bottom of the list. For some salespeople, it's making a tough call, cold-calling a prospect, completing a call report, or scheduling next week's appointments. Do the things you do not feel like doing. Every time you do, you become mentally stronger. The simple act of completing a task motivates you to complete another.

Exercise 4: Pruning and Planting

List one way you will prune negativity or plant positivity. If this is your focus exercise, then list two ways.

Tough timers prune negativity and plant positivity. Pruning a tree removes the dead branches. Once the dead branches are removed, the tree reaches its full potential. Negativity is like those dying branches—it limits us. Pruning is removing negativity whenever and wherever you can. For example, if a colleague is negative, prune him or her from your day. You cannot expend energy on those who are negative. Monitor your self-talk for negativity. If you notice negative self-talk, replace that negativity with more positive thoughts and feelings.

At the same time, surround yourself with positivity. Plant positivity around your newly pruned tree. This includes positive people and positive messages. Surround yourself with positive people and messages that inspire you. These messages include positive affirmations, quotes, positive videos, posters, and podcasts. Every day, prune negativity or plant positivity.

As you continue this exercise, you'll notice less negativity in your life. Some days it will be hard to find anything negative to prune. This is a positive sign that you are reaching your full potential. On those days when you can't find negativity to prune, be a positive inspiration to someone else.

Exercise 5: Positive Reframing

Think of something negative that happened today, and find a positive outcome resulting from this negative event. If this is your weekly focus, think of two events.

Tough timers achieve positive outcomes through negative events. In tough times, bad things happen. You experience an onslaught of negative events. Most people focus too heavily on the negative and cannot see the positive. Focusing on the negative impedes your ability to push through. There is a better way.

Tough timers train their brains to find opportunities through adversity. For example, you lost a sale, which is obviously negative. Instead of moping over the loss, learn from it. You conduct a review of the loss and realize you weren't prepared. As a result, you take positive action. You practice, role-play, and prepare for your next opportunity. You think, "I lost the sale, but now I'm better prepared for the next one."

Another negative event: The prospect says, "I'm not interested." You persist and follow up, but he still says no. After analyzing the negative situation, you realize that your messaging was flat. You take positive action and work on your messaging. You think, "The rejection stung, but that pain helped me craft a more compelling message."

In both examples, you train your brain to view negative events more positively. Complete this exercise at any point throughout the day. It may be easier in the evening as you reflect on your day. Think of a negative event. How can you positively reframe that event?

Exercise 6: Reducing Friction

Complete one activity today to make tomorrow's goals easier to achieve. If this is your weekly focus, complete two activities today to make tomorrow's goals easier to achieve.

Tough timers reduce friction between themselves and their goals. Success is not as hard as we make it. Tough timers proactively set themselves up for success. Your daily success does not begin that morning—it begins the day before.

Reducing friction is proactively taking control of your environment and making it easier to be successful. Everyone begins the day well intentioned, but soon we are bombarded with distractions that derail our efforts. As Mike Tyson said, "Everyone has a plan 'til they get punched in the mouth."[9] This punch in the mouth takes many shapes: a customer crisis, internal requests, the constant ding of your inbox. Each distraction creates friction between you and your target.

Prepare today for tomorrow's success. For example, your goal is to make 10 prospecting calls before lunch. How would you prepare today to accomplish tomorrow's goals? You could prepare a list of prospects in advance, research those prospects, and preplan each one of those calls.

Another example: You have a critical presentation tomorrow. You may review your notes, practice the presentation a couple of times, and think of potential objections. Or you have an early start the next day. Clean and organize your desk tonight, have your lunch already made, and lay out your clothes so that you are ready to go.

Ask yourself, "What is the most important thing I need to accomplish tomorrow?" Then ask, "How can I reduce friction to accomplish my goal?"

Tough times require your absolute best and reveal your best. This DMF is your daily guide for managing the mental rigors of tough times. The Daily Mental Flex is available for download at www.ToughTimer.com.

PART II

CRITICAL SELLING ACTIVITIES

Marcus Lemonis is the star of the critically acclaimed show, *The Profit*, on CNBC.[1] On this show, Lemonis partners with small-business owners to help them achieve greater profits and improve their business. He saves numerous small businesses in multiple industries. Although each company is unique, there is a common thread—tough times.

Lemonis helps struggling businesses. These businesses are facing financial troubles, tough competition, a recession, industry disruption, and/or other tough times. Lemonis has three principles to guide his turnaround: people, product, and process. He believes that you need great people, a great product, and a systematic process. Lemonis often acknowledges that struggling businesses have a good product and good people, but they lack a systematic process. Process is a sequence of actions to deliver the desired result or outcome. A structured process is critical in every facet of business, especially sales.

Selling is a dynamic and ever-changing process. Most business processes deliver the expected outcome with precision. In manufacturing, if you meticulously follow the right process, you deliver the desired result every time. There is the occasional hiccup, but most of the time, everything is working like a well-oiled machine. Unfortunately, sales is not like this. You can meticulously follow the process but get the desired result only a third of the time (and that would be wildly successful). Multiple external factors influence a sale, mainly the buyer and his or her decision-making environment. Buyers follow their purchasing process, not your sales process.

It's easy to trust a process that works. In tough times, your success rate declines along with your certainty. Your winning techniques are no longer winning at the same rate. In these tough moments, a structured process keeps you focused. A systematic process provides the stable footing needed through uncertainty. Sellers question whether they're doing the right things or embracing the right techniques. Out of frustration, sellers try new techniques or look for the silver bullet and abandon the basics.

In his book, *Call Sign Chaos*,[2] Jim Mattis explains the importance of the fundamentals. He commonly says, "Be brilliant in the basics." This mantra applies to both soldiers on a battlefield and salespeople facing tough times.

There are six critical selling activities (CSAs) that make up the tough-times sales process: select, pursue, discover, persuade, partner, and leverage (see Figure 1). The CSAs focus your effort on selecting the right opportunities, advancing the sale, and partnering with the buyer. Each CSA requires continuous commitment regardless of where you are in the sales process. For example, understanding a buyer's needs is still important even if you're past the discovery phase. Meeting with the right decision makers is still important even when you're past the pursuit phase. As you advance to the next CSA in this process, the previous CSA must remain complete.

FIGURE 1 Critical selling activities

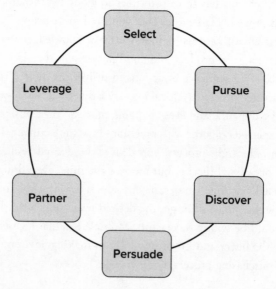

Select. Establishing the right targets and building a target-specific plan. Tough times are full of uncertainty. Planning and selection build a base of certainty and confidence for the seller.

Pursue. Approaching your target opportunities the right way. This includes focusing on the right decision makers and entering the buyer's process early. Pursuing business in tough times creates new challenges and opportunities. Entering the opportunity the right way increases your likelihood of success.

Discover. A continuous process of understanding the buyer's needs. The buyer's needs change in tough times. As you travel the unchartered waters of tough times, you and the buyer will discover something new together.

Persuade. Convincing the buyer that you are the ideal partner with the ideal solution. Buyers decide differently in tough times, forcing you to persuade differently.

Partner. Working with your customers to help them achieve their goal. Tough times are opportunities to build an unshakeable bond with customers. As you and your customer traverse through tough times, you'll develop a deeper connection.

Leverage. Expanding your solution with the customer to protect and grow your business. The goal is to protect your profit, enhance the customer's profit, solve problems, and grow your relationships.

This is your process for selling through tough times. You might be wondering, "How is this different from my normal sales process?" The overall stages of the process are similar, but there are tactical differences within each CSA. The difference is not in the elements of the sales process; it's in the execution. In sales, it's always about execution.

CHAPTER 7

Select

Your list of sales targets is like an investment portfolio: well balanced with investments that align with your overall investment goals. If your goal is to grow, you should invest in stocks with huge upside potential and high risk. If your goal is to protect, you should invest in securities with less upside potential and less risk. Regardless whether your strategy is to grow or protect, you'll need high-quality investments to achieve your goals.

The same is true when you are managing a portfolio of prospects and customers. As a seller, the currency you invest is your time, and you only have so much. The key is to ensure that you are investing that time and energy with the most viable opportunities. Whether your goal is to protect or grow, you should invest your time in quality targets.

Like a downturn in the stock market, tough times create similar investment opportunities. Downturns are opportune times to invest in your target opportunities. Focusing more time on your ideal opportunities positions you to emerge stronger for the good times. However, when target opportunities don't yield the expected result, sellers get frustrated. As sellers get frustrated, they desperately look for any opportunity. Sellers become lax in their definition of good business. Review your pipeline in tough times and ask yourself, "Will these targets lead to my success?" Even when times are tough and opportunities are lean, focus with laser-like intensity on good business.

Sellers, like buyers, are instant gratification–seeking individuals. A seller's short-term desire to produce will trump his or her commitment to more fruitful, long-term opportunities. Those long-term opportunities progress more slowly. Short-term (less ideal) opportunities seem to generate progress more quickly but lack long-term viability.

During tough times, sellers are more susceptible to price shoppers. Some sellers develop a take-what-I-can-get mentality. These sellers are more likely to offer discounts in tough times, attracting price shoppers. Once you fill your pipeline with price shoppers, it's hard to purge them. Price shoppers are quick to quote, which feels like a short-term win, but they unknowingly create long-term issues.

Other salespeople take a shotgun approach, pursuing every opportunity with a pulse. There is no focus. Seneca, the Roman philosopher, said, "To be everywhere is to be nowhere." Going after all opportunities is an attempt to be everywhere. It's a fool's errand and a seller-focused approach—believing that your solution is a good fit for everyone. If your solution is a *good* fit for everyone, then it's a *great* fit for no one.

Even during good economic times, sellers get frustrated when pursuing an ideal opportunity. Converting an attractive prospect can be a long, frustrating, but rewarding process. During tough times, the process is longer and more challenging. Resilient tough timers persist as they pursue their targets, even in a challenging environment.

Time is our most precious resource. Invest your time wisely in the most viable sales opportunities. In this chapter, you'll learn how to select the right opportunities and avoid the wrong ones. Once you select the right targets, you'll learn to build a plan to pursue that opportunity. The first step is knowing which targets to pursue; the second step is knowing which targets to avoid.

DEVELOP THE IDEAL TARGET PROFILE

Only 18 percent of sellers focus on pursuing ideal targets. Only 20 percent of sellers have a well-defined profile. Our research shows that sellers struggle to focus on the right opportunities.[1] How can sellers invest their time in an ideal opportunity if they are unaware of what they are looking for? Zig Ziglar famously said, "If you aim at nothing, you'll hit it every time."[2] Our research shows that nearly 80 percent of sellers are unaware of what they are aiming for. Without a target profile, sellers are easily distracted by the wrong opportunities. They're not sure what to look for, so any opportunity looks good. Sellers with an unclear profile chase what is shiny and new instead of chasing what is viable.

There is a better way to identify target opportunities. The first step is knowing what you are looking for. Talk to your sales manager and ask,

"What is good business for our company?" You're trying to understand the look and feel of good business. Your ideal target opportunity could be a prospect or existing customer. Ideal targets represent strong growth opportunities. Whether an existing customer or new prospect, select an opportunity with significant growth potential.

You can define good business by analyzing your current customer base. Brainstorm with your colleagues, and review your best customers. Identify what these customers have in common. The term *best* can mean several different things: most profitable, largest revenue, and so on. These are the types of customers you want to duplicate.

Orchestrate a small group discussion with your top sales performers and management team. Have each salesperson list his or her three best customers. Keep the list to the top 10 customers. As a group, discuss what these customers have in common. This list of common criteria is your profile. Here is a sample list of criteria for your best customers:

1. Our best customers are financially viable, even in tough times.
2. Our best customers are innovative and forward thinking.
3. We converted our top customers from the same competitor.
4. We have strong, layered relationships with each customer.
5. Our best customers are family-owned businesses.
6. Most of our best customers are in the same industry.
7. Many of our best customers are large-volume opportunities.

When analyzing these criteria, look for qualitative and quantitative criteria. These examples show both. The qualitative criteria are mainly sensory and subjective. For example, our best customers are innovative or relationship oriented. Quantitative criteria are more objective and easier to identify, for example, company size or industry segment.

Notice the third criterion on the preceding list. Salespeople often target certain competitors because it's easier to pick off their customer base. These competitors often neglect their customers or cannot provide a solution that fully satisfies the buyers' needs. Through tough times, target your weaker competitors. These weaker competitors struggle to support their customers. These competitors' customers are more vulnerable in tough times and need support. You can provide that support, or your competition can.

In tough times, your competitors will make desperate moves, especially regarding price. These competitors might not survive the tough times. As one seminar participant explained, "Prices are always the cheapest right before a company goes out of business." To increase cash flow, competitors slash prices and liquidate inventory. To conserve cash, competitors carry out lay-offs. These competitors are struggling, and their top customers are looking for alternates. Familiarize yourself with these competitors' customers.

The preceding list of criteria is a good place to start, but there are other considerations for tough times. How is this target affected by the current tough time? How did this target bounce back from the last downturn? These questions reaffirm the quality of the target through tough times.

Once you create a profile, select viable sales targets that fit this profile. Compare your current list of targets with your profile to ensure that they are a good fit. Not every target is a perfect fit, but they should fit relatively well. Some criteria are hard to know on the surface. Once you dig deeper, you'll find the information you need. For example, you won't know if a target is relationship oriented until you get to know that opportunity. Your target should have the right raw material. If the target starts to feel like bad business, switch your focus to more viable opportunities. Keep in mind that it's easier to switch your focus with a full pipeline of opportunity. Always be on the lookout for viable opportunities.

"How much time should I spend pursuing ideal targets?" a salesperson asked in a seminar. The response is, "All of it." There is nothing more important than pursuing ideal targets. Everything, and I mean everything, is secondary.

- Updating your customer relationship management system is secondary.
- Training is secondary.
- Weekly conference calls are secondary.
- Chipping in to help other departments is secondary.

Be ruthless with your schedule. If you're are bogged down, prune your schedule to free up more time. The minimum expectation is to focus 80 percent of your time pursuing ideal targets. Time is the currency you invest. Focusing your time, energy, and effort on ideal opportunities yields the greatest return on your investment.

Fill your pipeline with ideal targets. Identify the ideal number of targets you can manage, and dedicate at least 80 percent of your time to those opportunities. Here is what 80 percent looks like:

- Four of five sales calls dedicated to ideal opportunities
- Four of five phone calls dedicated to ideal opportunities
- 4.8 days per week dedicated to ideal opportunities
- Eight hours per day dedicated to ideal opportunities

Those are not mathematical errors in the last two bullet points. Selling through tough times is not a 40-hour-per-week endeavor. Tough timers put the time in to do what is necessary. This means at least 10-hour days and six-day workweeks. You can rest during the good times. Time is your most precious resource. Now is the time to make the most of it. Focus 80 percent of your effort pursuing ideal opportunities.

CREATE A SIREN PROFILE

In Greek mythology, Sirens are mystical creatures that lure sailors to their island with their enchanting song. Sailors are captivated and deceived by the Siren song. In Homer's *The Odyssey*, Ulysses was navigating the waters near the Sirens' island. Ulysses knew about their tempting song and ordered his men to shove beeswax in their ears so that they couldn't hear the tempting call. However, Ulysses did not. He had to hear the Sirens' call to know when his ship had passed their island. So he ordered his men to tie him to the mast of the ship. He did this for good reason. The Sirens would tempt with their song, causing ships to change course, crash into the surrounding coral, and sink. The Sirens deceived and misled the sailors from their intended path.[3]

In sales, Sirens take the form of seemingly viable prospects. Salespeople are especially vulnerable to the Siren song during tough times. Sellers succumb to their scarcity mindset and eagerly jump at any opportunity—viable or not. As with Ulysses' sailors, Siren opportunities distract sellers from their intended path. Siren opportunities appear in several misleading ways. Here are some indicators that you're dealing with a sales Siren.

Have you ever received a call from an unknown prospect for a request for information or a request for proposal (RFP)? You're excited about the opportunity, as you should be. But before investing your time, ensure that

the target fits your profile. If the target refuses to schedule a meeting to discuss its needs, it's a Siren. If the target withholds information and just wants
your price, it's a Siren. This Siren is likely using your price to drive down its
preferred provider's price. In these instances, RFP means "request for price."

Sirens express interest in hearing your presentation but refuse to schedule
a discovery meeting to discuss their needs. Before even considering a proposal, insist that you meet and discuss your targets' needs. If they agree to
meet, pursue the opportunity. If they don't want to meet, thank them for the
opportunity and politely refuse, or hand off the opportunity to an internal
quoting team.

Some Sirens try selling you on the grandeur of the opportunity. Once
you prove that you're willing to work with them (i.e., discount), they'll open
the gates, and you'll be flooded with opportunities. This could be a Siren
opportunity. If you decide to pursue this opportunity, look at their raw material makeup. If it fits the profile for good business, then pursue it. If it does
not fit, then pass.

Ask for a second opinion. When an opportunity sounds too good to
be true, talk to your sales manager or a colleague. You'll notice that Siren
opportunities initiate contact. This is common because Sirens do most of the
calling. I'm not suggesting you ignore these opportunities. Instead, discern
whether these opportunities are the right fit before investing your time. If
you're too enamored of the Siren's call, you can't objectively decide whether
it's worth pursuing. Ask your manager or colleague for advice. Only dedicate
your time to viable targets that fit your profile for good business.

Create a profile so that you can recognize these Sirens. Review previous
Siren opportunities, and determine what they have in common. What were
the red flags as you pursued these opportunities? Talk to your colleagues, and
amass a list of criteria. Create a Siren profile to clearly recognize what you are
trying to avoid.

No one has more control over your time than you. Ultimately, you decide
how to spend your time. If you do decide to invest your time, give it your full
effort. Don't pursue opportunities expecting that it's okay to lose business
and claim it's a Siren. Be bold, and take risks as you pursue this opportunity.
Be courageous in your demands, go to the high-level decision maker, take
chances with your messaging, and ask the tough questions.

DEVELOP THE PROFIT PIRANHA PROFILE

Do you have a customer who always complains? Nothing is ever good enough for him or her. This customer complains about your price and your service. This customer constantly asks for discounts and concessions. This customer is high maintenance and requires more resources. This customer pays their bills late, and the margins are razor thin. Does this sound like good business? No. Should such customers go to the competition? Yes.

In my previous book, *Value-Added Selling*, these customers are called "profit piranhas."[4] Tough times are an opportunity to identify and remove profit piranhas. Good economic times provide a cushion of tolerance. During good times, we're less concerned about these profit piranhas. It's hard to see the impact they have on the bottom line. These profit piranhas devour your resources and your time, deteriorating your profitability. Do you want these customers to be the base on which you build your business? If profit piranhas are bad business in good times, it's reckless to serve them in tough times. Thin the school of profit piranhas swimming in your pond. Tough times create a unique opportunity to unload this dead weight. In good times, you may not take this opportunity. Tough times are good!

One executive was aware of a profit piranha devouring his company's resources. This executive explained to the customer that he could no longer support the customer at the current margin. The customer wouldn't budge, so the seller stopped serving the customer. The organization now had more resources to go after higher-quality targets. After thinning his company's pond of this profit piranha, the seller posted record profits. The profit piranha he cut was the company's largest revenue customer. This takes commitment.

Identifying your profit piranhas is like identifying your ideal prospect. In this exercise, think of your aggravating, low-margin, slow-pay customers. Ask yourself, "What do these profit piranhas have in common?" Create a profile based on your profit piranhas' common characteristics.

If you have profit piranhas in your portfolio, it's time to act. Make it clear to the customer that you are no longer supporting him or her for the current price. This conversation is most effective at higher levels within the organization. Before having this conversation, accept that you might lose the customer. This is one of the most freeing experiences in sales. Responding this way completely shifts the power from the profit piranha to you. Don't be surprised if the profit piranha recognizes that you are at your walking point and accepts your terms. Often these profit piranhas realize how much they need you when they no longer have you.

There are additional measures to get rid of profit piranhas: enforce payment terms, deprioritize requests, tighten credit limits, and so on. This might sound harsh, but you cannot afford to support profit piranhas through tough times. Every ounce of energy wasted on profit piranhas could be focused on ideal customers and prospects.

The mark of a good salesperson is knowing what business to pursue, but the mark of a great seller is knowing which business to avoid. This is the power of discernment. Whether it's a Siren or profit piranha, be aware of how they fit within your ideal target profile. The stronger the fit, the more such customers are worth saving or pursuing.

PLANNING

Planning is critical all the time—especially in tough times. Planning gives us something that we desperately need—a sense of control. Planning provides a perceived sense of control in tough economic times when we need it the most. During a recession, I was training a group of salespeople and asked them, "How are you managing the current situation?" The consensus was, "I've lost my sense of control." We can all relate to this sentiment. During tough times, we lose *some* of our control, and it drives us crazy! There is one thing we fear more than losing a sale, money, or even our job—it's control. In fact, a sense of control keeps us healthy and happy.

Consider Judith Rodin and Ellen Langer's famous nursing home experiment.[5] Residents were randomly assigned to two groups. The first group didn't have to lift a finger. Their schedules were already created and rooms prearranged. This group had little perceived control. The second group was on their own to create their own schedules, select activities, and rearrange their furniture. This group had more perceived control.

After three weeks, there was a noticeable difference. The group with more control was happier, and their mental alertness improved. After 18 months, this group showed signs of improved health. Control—whether perceived or actual—is good for us.

Salespeople who feel in control are more productive. Planning adds a layer of certainty in uncertain times. Planning builds confidence in tough times.

Planning Demonstrates Commitment

Have you noticed that the more time you invest in a project, the more committed you are to the project's success? For example, suppose that you are remodeling your kitchen. You visualize the perfect kitchen—the type of lighting, the color scheme, the furniture. You research different brands and meet with contractors and designers. You are committed to the project, and the time you invest proves your commitment.

Planning evokes commitment. The more time you dedicate, the more committed you are to your success. Planning invokes the *IKEA effect*, where people place a higher value on what they build.[6] IKEA is known for selling furniture that you must piece together yourself. Researchers have found that individuals who put their furniture together place a higher value on it. You are more committed to what you create. The plan is yours; you created it. You are more likely to execute a plan that you create.

Planning Doesn't Produce Results

Have you ever met a salesperson who would rather prepare than produce? Such sellers are always getting ready to get ready. They overanalyze each situation and agonize over every detail. Their desire to create the perfect plan stifles their actual selling effort. It's better to act on a good plan than to wait until the plan is perfect. While not having a plan impedes your success, overplanning is just as damaging.

There are several routes that will lead to the same destination. Some people obsess over every detail: traffic congestion on each route, overall distance, number of stoplights, and so on. And others develop a simple plan and just go, beating everyone else there. Target planning is like just going. Develop a simple plan and act. A well-designed plan without action delivers zero results. Plan until you feel confident in your action, but don't overplan to the point where you have no time to act.

Plans Are Flexible

At the young age of 13, William decided to sell soap for his father's company. He incentivized customers with a free can of baking powder with each soap purchase. He realized that people were more interested in the baking powder than in the soap, so he developed a new plan: sell baking powder. He came up with another plan to incentivize customers. He offered customers two packs of chewing gum with each order. Again, he realized that customers were more interested in the chewing gum than in baking powder. So William Wrigley decided to sell chewing gum, and the Wrigley Company was born.[7] Imagine if Wrigley rigidly stuck with his original plan to just sell soap? It should also be noted that Wrigley's spearmint chewing gum was introduced in 1893, the same year as the panic of 1893 (the start of a four-year depression).[8]

Rigidly following a plan doesn't make sense in tough times. Like William Wrigley, adaptability is key to your success and survival. A plan provides guidance, not the detailed route. While pursuing an opportunity, you might realize that there is another path leading to a different but better result. Be open to these opportune moments of change.

CREATING YOUR TOUGH-TIMES PLAN

This section is a step-by-step guide for creating a sales plan for your ideal targets. This planning exercise applies to both prospects and customers. Your tough-times planning guide includes six sections. Each section of the plan has a list of questions to guide your effort. Target planning is a continuous process of gathering information and implementing techniques. A downloadable planning template is available at www.ToughTimer.com.

Your plan may focus on growing new business or protecting existing business. In kung fu, there is an expression that parallels the idea of offensive and defensive selling: *the hand which strikes also blocks*. Through tough times, it's critical to focus on new opportunities while protecting existing ones.

Target Summary

As you pursue a target opportunity, you'll need background information. This section includes basic information about your targets and how they are impacted by tough times. Use these questions to complete this section:

- How is the target's industry impacted by the current tough time?
- How is the company impacted by this tough time?
- How was the target positioned before the tough time?
- Does this tough time create new opportunities within this target?
- Does this opportunity align with our ideal target profile?

Small Wins (Goals)

In tough times, progress is more meaningful than performance—progress leads to performance. Small wins are concrete outcomes of moderate importance. Small wins keep you motivated, focused, and engaged. Along the path to sales success, there is a set of small wins that lead to the culmination of a sale. Use these questions to complete this section:

- What is the first small win I need to achieve?
- From contact to contract, what are the other small wins I need to achieve?
- What resistance should I expect?

Decision-Maker Profile

On average, six decision makers are involved in the process.[9] During tough times, more decision makers get involved. It's critical to understand who these key players are and how they influence the buying process. Use these questions to complete this section:

- Who is (are) the ultimate decision maker(s)?
- Who are the influencers within this opportunity?
- What lower-level decision makers (i.e., purchasing) are involved?
- Who are my advocates within this opportunity?
- What decision makers are vulnerable in this opportunity?
- What new decision makers are now involved in this opportunity?

Competitive Analysis

Who is your competition? Whether you are selling as the incumbent or the new provider, competition is always present. The goal is to identify where your competitor is vulnerable. Conduct a thorough positive comparison highlighting your solution's strengths and the competitor's weaknesses. Use these questions to complete this section:

- How does my solution align with the customer's needs?
- In a side-by-side comparison, how does my solution compare?
- Where is this competitor vulnerable?

- Where is my solution vulnerable, and how can I shore up any weaknesses?
- How does my solution stand out?

Discovery

Compelling presentations begin with a complete understanding of the buyer's needs, wants, and fears. In Chapter 9, you'll learn how to generate a dialogue centered on the customer's needs. Complete this section after your discovery call. Use these questions to complete this section:

- How has the current tough time impacted this target's needs?
- What are this target's growing concerns?
- What are this target's organizational needs?
- What potential problems is this target experiencing?
- What are the buyer's immediate and long-term needs?
- Summarize the prospect's needs from your discovery meeting.

Persuasion

Persuasion is convincing the buyer to choose your solution. Whether selling to an existing customer or a new prospect, your ability to persuade determines your success. Use these questions to complete this section:

- Why does the customer need this solution through this tough time?
- How does this target define value?
- How can I align my solution with the target's definition of value?
- What social proof can I demonstrate?
- How does my solution fit with the target's needs?

Visit www.ToughTimer.com to download your copy of the tough-times planning tool.

Planning through tough times gives you a stronger sense of control. Planning provides guidance to pursue opportunities through the fog of uncertainty. Planning gives you a broader view of the opportunity and helps you anticipate needs and challenges.

Fewer than one in four salespeople have a plan for their top opportunity. There is a good chance your competition is not planning. If you want to beat your competition in tough times, do what they won't.

Overplanning can be just as damaging as not planning. Create a clear plan, but planning shouldn't cut into your selling time. I remember coaching and training a team that was limited by its propensity to plan. This group already skewed toward the passive side and looked for any excuse not to sell. The group spent more time preparing and planning than any other team I trained. Group members forgot that their objective was to sell, not plan. Plan until you feel confident in your direction—then go out there and sell!

Abraham Lincoln said, "Give me six hours to chop down a tree, and I will spend the first four sharpening the axe."[10] This may have been true for Lincoln, but he didn't have a quota to hit.

SUMMARY

There are three takeaways from this chapter: select viable targets, avoid impractical targets, and develop a plan. These are the basics of selection. Your focus and effort in selection provide the foundation for your success. If you do this right, the rest of the process is much easier.

Develop an ideal target profile. Only pursue targets that fit this profile. Opportunities that look attractive to you also look attractive to your competition. You will win these highly sought-after targets by steadily focusing on executing your plan. The purpose of a plan is to guide your effort and build confidence. Planning stabilizes the uncertainty of tough times. Tough timers are resilient and steadfast in their approach. If you want to be a tough timer, then you must do what tough timers do: select, plan, and execute.

CHAPTER 8

Pursue

Have you ever taken a shortcut that didn't work out as planned? Think back to that shortcut. Maybe you missed a turn or a signal. Either way, you veered off course. But you kept going, thinking that you'd eventually get back on the right track. The farther you drove, the more you veered off course. To get back on track, you had to retrace your steps. The shortcut ended up taking even longer than the original route.

Sellers are constantly tempted to take shortcuts—especially in tough times. Sellers take a shortcut when they pitch product before understanding their buyers' needs. Sellers take another shortcut by pursuing easy-to-access contacts instead of higher-level decision makers. Sellers take another shortcut when they talk price before demonstrating value. There are no shortcuts when pursuing your ideal targets.

Chapter 7 focused on selecting the right targets. Now we focus on pursuing those opportunities the right way. Pursuing the right way includes getting there early in the process and talking to the right people. Our research shows that engaging the right decision maker continues to be a challenge for a myriad of reasons. Some sellers haphazardly approach opportunities with plenty of excitement but little planning. These sellers are eager to get started, but what their approach exhibits in enthusiasm it lacks in intentionality. Selling in tough times requires diligently executing a plan. Other sellers struggle to get started with an opportunity because they don't know how. They are not sure who they should approach or how to approach them in tough times. These sellers may be unfamiliar with the opportunity or the industry. So they take the path of least resistance, which usually leads right through the procurement department—the department least likely to recognize your value and most likely to focus on price.

Timing is a powerful element of sales success. Sellers get frustrated when the purchasing timeline doesn't match their sense of urgency. In tough times, there is no shortage of viable sales opportunities. There is, however, a shortage of opportunities with the ideal timeline. Just because a target opportunity is ideal doesn't mean that its timeline is ideal. Sellers face longer purchasing timelines in tough times. This is frustrating for sellers because they generate momentum with all the right people but stall out, causing them to focus on other, less viable opportunities. These quick-hit opportunities help you survive, but this message is about thriving, not merely surviving. In tough times, continue approaching opportunities despite their extended timeline. Tough times are ever changing, and so are the targets' timelines.

Sellers believe that timing is everything in sales, to the point where they'll delay pursuing an opportunity if the timing doesn't seem right. The best time to pursue your ideal target was yesterday; the second-best time is today. The greater risk is not pursuing an opportunity at the wrong time; it's waiting too long for the right timing. It's one thing to try but not succeed; it's quite another not to try. Good timing is one of many factors leading to your success.

WHAT IS DIFFERENT ABOUT PURSUING BUSINESS IN TOUGH TIMES?

Customers decide differently in tough times, so you're forced to pursue them differently. Criteria shift from the premium solutions to the bare minimum. Priorities shift from profitability to cash flow. New decision makers get involved with different needs. Be aware of these changes so that you can adjust your value proposition to align with your target's dynamic buying priorities.

Decisions are heavily scrutinized during tough times. Buyers incorporate more decision makers to spread the risk; nobody wants to make the wrong decision. Buyers organize committees and incorporate more people, spreading the risk. More people mitigate risk. The more visible the decision, the more people get involved, reducing individual risk.

Decisions in tough times require higher-level buying authority. Normally, decision makers are comfortable making buying decisions within their spending threshold. In tough times, they seek additional approval even if they are within their limit. If your key decision maker is making a tough decision, he or she wants feedback from their higher-ups. This mitigates risk, but it adds another layer of complexity and opportunity. This frustrates sellers who assumed that they were selling at the right level, only to find out that other decision makers are involved. Although frustrating, this creates an opportunity to meet higher-level decision makers. This new decision maker may be less familiar with your solution and may need information. You can fill that gap. Without tough times, you may not have had this opportunity. Tough times are good!

Sellers get frustrated when deals stall out and take longer to close. The uncertainty of tough times lengthens the decision-making timeline. This new timeline runs parallel to the anticipated recovery time of the current downturn. The longer the anticipated recovery takes, the longer the purchasing timeline will be. There is no magic formula to determine how long, but the remedy is to have a pipeline full of opportunities. With a full pipeline, you're less concerned about the longer timeline.

During tough times, you face unique objections germane to tough times. Objections are simply a break in your sales momentum. Through tough times, you experience more front-end resistance than you do in good times. It's more challenging to get your sales process started. This happens for several reasons: the buyer has other priorities, the future is uncertain, budgets are cut, and so on. Salespeople misinterpret this resistance as a signal that the buyer is not interested, and they give up. This front-end resistance fuels the misperception that "nobody is buying right now." When the buyer resists, you must persist.

Buyers lose interest when they can't see the potential outcomes. Buyers can't see the outcomes because they are too focused on what they must sacrifice. Your targets are stuck in a scarcity mindset—hoarding resources. Buyers are uncertain about the future, so they tighten their grip on the status quo because it keeps them safe. Even if there is a better alternative, buyers' emotion trumps their logic. Sellers persisting through early resistance are more likely to succeed. Early resistance can thin the competitive herd. If you persist through the resistance, there is less competition.

There are challenges specific to each tough time. For example, customers can't meet face-to-face, decision makers are furloughed, or geopolitical concerns predominate. Whatever the resistance, it's critical to understand the deeper root cause. With the right mindset, new challenges create new opportunities. If your competitors continue to sell the way they are accustomed to, they will struggle. This creates an opportunity for you. Tough times are good!

FIVE RULES FOR PURSUING YOUR TARGETS

The principles of selling are constant. Whether you are selling through tough times or good times, whether you're selling in person or over the phone, the basic process doesn't change, but the tactics do. The tactical execution is the struggle. This section is about approaching your targets the right way, with a deeper understanding. Follow these five rules as you pursue your targets.

Rule 1: Broaden Your Situational Awareness

Decisions are not made in a vacuum. Decisions are made in a dynamic and ever-changing world. That new dynamic could be uncertainty, geopolitical concerns, regulations, tough competition, a sluggish economy, or any combination of these factors. Selling through tough times requires a deeper understanding of buyers and how they make decisions through tough times. External factors influence the buying decision. Broader situational awareness familiarizes sellers with the environment in which their buyers decide. In tough times, the dynamics and context are ever changing. Decision makers react differently to these factors. Sellers must think as buyers think to understand how these factors influence the buying decision.

What if you understood buyers better than your competition? The buyers would sense your customer-focused effort. You build credibility and expertise from the first interaction. You are considered the expert, and you're in tune with your buyers' needs. Here's the challenge: salespeople already have a limited view of the world of buyers; information is available, but the real challenge is determining how that information impacts buyers.

Sellers have an inflated view of how important their solution is to customers. A seller's number-one priority is to close or advance the sale; the buyer has several other priorities that take precedent. If the buyer is not ready to move forward, sellers believe that they have the timing wrong. No, it's not the timing that's wrong, it's the seller's mindset. To position your solution as a priority, first gain a deeper understanding of your buyers' priorities.

Familiarize yourself with the broader situation of your buyers. View the world through the eyes of your buyers. Look to market leaders as a bellwether.

Market leaders set the pace in good times and provide guidance in tough times. These questions will help you gain a broader understanding of your buyers' business and the context in which they make decisions:

- What tough time is your target opportunity experiencing (technological, political, regulatory)?
- How has the current tough time impacted this specific business?
- How will current market trends affect this opportunity?
- What new growth opportunities exist in this industry?
- What are the three biggest problems facing this opportunity?
- What was this organization's trajectory before the tough time?
- How is this target opportunity performing relative to the competition?
- How are market leaders responding to this tough time?
- How is this target's financial performance (easier for publicly traded companies)?
- How has this tough time impacted the target's ability to serve their customers?

Answering these questions provides context in the decision-making process. You'll have a deeper understanding of what is important to your customers and why. You can tweak many of these questions and directly ask your customers or prospects. Developing this broader awareness forces your attention on your customers. Customer-focused sellers thrive in tough times. This deeper understanding gives you a significant advantage over your competitors.

Rule 2: Identify and Categorize the Decision Makers

Decision makers have a variety of needs determined by the prevailing situation. Therefore, the needs of buyers are constantly evolving and changing. Sellers, like buyers, must adapt to the prevailing circumstances. Yet many sellers focus on selling their way. In tough times, we are forced to blast out of our comfort zones. Tough times force us to take chances, take calculated risks, and try new approaches.

Selling through tough times means staying hyperfocused on how individual decision makers define value. This means adjusting your value proposition to the ever-changing needs of buyers. This process begins by understanding the different types of decision makers.

Procurement Decision Makers

The primary function of procurement is to handle purchasing-related activities. Procurement people source materials, manage vendor relationships, and process purchase orders. Procurement managers have transactional and logistical needs: price, delivery, availability, and terms. During tough times, procurement buyers make safe decisions. They're looking for a safe solution that is easy to justify to other decision makers. Remember, in tough times, people are concerned about layoffs. Some procurement buyers channel that concern into creating more value for their organizations, whereas others simply demand discounts.

Buyers wanting to create value for their organizations create opportunities for sellers. These new opportunities could be cost-saving ideas, new programs or products, or freeing up resources with value-added services. Buyers who demand discounts are challenging to manage. These buyers' objections force you to justify your position and quantify your value. Buyers push hard for discounts, but something always scares them more than paying your price. These buyers are concerned about making the wrong decision. During tough times, decisions are heavily scrutinized. Whatever decision you are asking them to make, be aware of their tendency to reduce risk. If you're the incumbent, highlight the risk of switching to a new provider. If you are the new competitor, highlight the greater risk of doing nothing, which creates no value.

Influencers

Influencers do not make the decision, but they impact the decision-making process with their opinions and insights. *Influencer* is a catchall term to include any individual playing a significant role in the decision-making process. Influencers include managers, operators, supervisors, installers, technical engineers, resellers, and so on. Influencers include anyone impacted by the decision, including brand owners and outside firms. Influencers focus on outcomes more than price. They take on new solutions that create value for their organizations. Your job is to ensure that the transition is easy and pain free.

Influencers focus on performance outcomes. These decision makers are concerned about layoffs, the status quo, and performance. Managers are concerned about the overall health of their departments. With a reduced workforce, supervisors must do more with less. As these influencers look for ways to increase productivity, new ideas are welcomed. This creates an opportunity for sellers. Tough times are good!

Technical influencers are steady and predictable in their needs. They want proven solutions that deliver predictable results. Technical influencers protect quality and performance. These influencers will not sacrifice standards to save a few pennies—standards above all else. As other decision makers look to cut costs in tough times, these influencers could be your greatest advocates.

Influencers serve as your eyes and ears. Influencers feed you information: information to help you sell your solution or protect your current position. These special influencers are called *internal champions*. These internal champions are sold on your partnership and advocate for your solution. Internal champions make you aware of competitive threats and sell your solution internally when you are not there. Internal champions are critical in tough times.

High-Level Decision Makers

High-level decision makers (HLDMs) can say yes to your solution without checking with anyone else, regardless of the price or the magnitude of change. Depending on the size of the company, this could be a divisional vice president, controller, owner, or executive. HLDMs take a broad, long-term view of their buying decisions. In tough times, they make difficult decisions. They are comfortable making unpopular decisions. Lower-level decision makers are concerned about getting laid off, and HLDMs are concerned about giving layoffs.

HLDMs have two primary concerns in tough times: people concerns and business concerns. People concerns include employee stress, layoffs, and company culture. HLDMs recognize that every decision impacts their people. Their challenge is to balance people concerns with business concerns. HLDMs shoulder that burdensome weight through tough times. Business concerns include profit, competitive posture, and cash flow. HLDMs make tough decisions to manage resources to produce a profit. Profit is important. It's the lifeblood of any company. HLDMs also look to protect or grow their competitive positions. Some will opportunistically view a downturn as a means to gain a competitive footing. During tough times, cash flow is king. HLDMs are concerned with keeping enough cash on hand to run their businesses. HLDMs invest in solutions that generate cash, improve competitive posture, or improve long-term health. HLDMs will take calculated risks. They are comfortable making abstract and complex decisions that impact their overall business. Demonstrate how your solution will address the HLDMs' two primary concerns: business concerns and people concerns.

Rule 3: Establish Your Point of Entry

Point of entry refers to how you choose to initiate contact at your target opportunity. Successfully pursuing an opportunity means meeting with all the right people. Unfortunately, it's easier to meet with the wrong people. The easiest decision makers to meet with aren't necessarily the ones you want to meet with.

Early in my sales career, I never had trouble meeting with procurement buyers—they always seemed available. Receptionists never hesitated to share the procurement department's contact info, but they would never give me the CEO's. On one high-profile refinery project, the procurement department was placed outside the security gates so that salespeople could easily meet with buyers. All the other decision makers were officed inside the security gates, where I needed to be. Of course, when I reviewed my progress with my sales manager, I enthusiastically told him about the opportunity and my progress. But when procurement placed orders, they called my competitor. Procurement was not interested in buying my value-added solution; they were interested in price. I quickly learned that the title of procurement indicated the ability to buy but not the willingness to buy. In retrospect, procurement managers would keep me away from other influencers. I would make several requests to meet with engineers. Each request was denied. I was in a never-ending game of keep-away. The closer I would get to making contact, the further the procurement managers would pull me away.

Why are procurement personnel so easy to meet with? Because that is where company managers want you to go. On initiating contact, procurement blocks salespeople from other key decision makers. This prevents salespeople from doing their job of understanding the total needs of customers, identifying problems, and generating buy-in for their solution, making price less relevant. Procurement managers chisel out as much margin as they can. When you gain buy-in with additional decision makers, your job gets easier, and procurement's job gets a little harder. Therefore, organizations pave a road to procurement so that it's easier to meet with them versus other decision makers. Salespeople take the paved path of least resistance to engage procurement, and then they're blocked. Salespeople spend more time with procurement-type decision makers than with any other decision maker. Thirty-four percent of salespeople admit that they spend most of their selling time with procurement buyers. Consider the irony: salespeople spend most of their time attempting to sell value to the one decision maker least likely to buy value. If you start with procurement, you're going to stay with procurement. Take the road less traveled. In tough times, new opportunities emerge, and so do points of entry.

In the preceding section, we divided decision makers into three categories. Decision makers can be categorized, using the matrix in Figure 8.1, along two axes: expertise and authority. Decision makers either have the expertise to influence buying decisions, the authority to make such decisions, or both. Decision makers influence the buying process in two ways—by having more expertise or by having ultimate authority. Expertise leads to impact. Authority leads to action. Incorporate decision makers who are knowledgeable about the decision and have the authority to say yes. Use the simple matrix in Figure 8.1 to identify the relative impact a specific decision maker has on the buying process.

FIGURE 8.1 Decision-maker impact

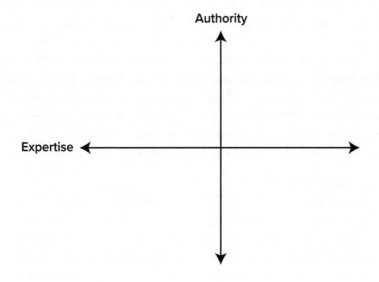

There are three points of entry when you are pursuing a target opportunity. You can move in from the top, the bottom, or the middle. How you initiate contact is critical. Initiating contact with the right decision makers significantly increases your chances of success.

Enter from the Top

Early in the decision-making process, initiate contact with an HLDM. There are several reasons to start at the top. The primary reason is that you are talking to the person who can say yes. It's also easier to navigate back to HLDMs if you initiate contact at this level first. You don't risk offending lower-level contacts if you already start at the top. HLDMs have fewer price objections. Of the three types of decision makers, HLDMs are the least concerned about price.

With your initial contact, the goal is to gather information and gain additional access. Ask questions that reveal the higher-level needs of the organization. Discuss the business and people concerns of the HLDM. You'll also want to gain access to other influencers and identify other problems and challenges. Once you gather more information, build your case for change, and report back to your HLDM.

Initiating contact at this level requires a clear and compelling message. Our research shows that decision makers are responsive to salespeople who solve problems. We asked a diverse group of buyers, "Why would you be willing to meet with a salesperson?" Fifty-five percent would meet if the salesperson could solve a business problem they were experiencing. Twenty-eight percent would meet if the salesperson shared interesting insights.[1] When you are crafting your message, reference a business problem your HLDM is experiencing. To identify common business problems, talk to your colleagues and your internal HLDMs. Have a brainstorming discussion and create a list of common problems and challenges. In your meeting request, highlight those challenges and hint at your method of solving that problem. For example:

Good morning, HLDM.
Labor shortages are one of the greatest challenges facing U.S. manufacturers. This labor shortage is costing the industry millions of dollars in lost productivity. To successfully compete, manufacturers are forced to maximize worker productivity. We recently helped an organization in your industry save more than $100,000 in

productivity. I have three insights to share with you to address this common problem. Our meeting would only last 15 to 20 minutes. Please let me know which of these three times works best.

In this example, you reference a problem, the impact of the problem, and insights to solve the problem. Also, don't request more than 20 minutes. If the HLDM is interested, he or she will give you more time. Give the HLDM three different options for your meeting rather than leaving it open-ended. It's easier for people to select from three options.

Whether a letter, email, or phone call, identify the problem you solve in the opening. This lets the HLDM know that you understand the challenges relevant to his or her business. Sellers in our training seminars mention that using a referral is an effective way to make connections with HLDMs. Leverage your existing network to see who can introduce you to the HLDM.

If you're struggling to initiate contact at this level, reach out to your manager or sales leader. Ask your vice president of sales or another high-level manager to join you on a call. Pairing your HLDM with your prospect's HLDM sends a strong message. Your sales leader's title carries more weight. Reference his or her title in your request to prompt a quicker response.

When you are meeting with the HLDM, the goal is to understand his or her needs and challenges. You want to gain an understanding of where this HLDM's business is headed. Prepare a few high-level questions to generate dialogue. In Chapter 9, there are several examples of questions to help guide your conversation.

Some sellers believe that engaging HLDMs is too risky. They're concerned about offending lower-level contacts or laying an egg in front of the top decision maker. Tough times are chock full of risk already. But the greater risk is doing nothing. Would you rather look back on an opportunity and say, "I gave it my best" or "I played it safe"? Tough times require bold action and audacious optimism.

Enter from the Bottom

Use this approach as a last resort. With this approach, you start with procurement and work your way up. This is the easiest road to start, but it becomes more arduous as you progress through the sales process. Your goal is to work your way up the decision-making ladder.

Once you initiate contact with procurement, identify the other decision makers and reach out to them. You will likely reach out to influencers and, eventually, the HLDMs. If procurement tries to block you, encourage the buyer to join you for these meetings. This helps you to understand the dynamic of the group and connect procurement with the people impacted by their decision. Help the buyer understand how his or her decision affects the rest of the organization. Continue gathering information from the influencers to build a case for change. Then initiate contact with the HLDM who can say yes.

If you are going to reach out to this decision maker, initiate contact by referencing a problem the buyer is experiencing. Use the preceding example as a template, but realize that procurement has different concerns and needs than HLDMs. Have another brainstorming session to discuss common problems and challenges facing procurement departments.

Enter from the Middle

Early in the decision-making process, initiate contact with the experts. These influencers have a wellspring of expertise and experience. These influencers are knowledgeable about their current solution, processes, or problems. Engage decision makers who are knowledgeable and considered information hubs. The more information you have, the stronger the case you can make for change. The information source doesn't make the ultimate decision, but he or she can influence the one who does. Once you gather all the information, initiate contact with the HLDM who can say yes.

Identify the common influencers involved in the decision-making process. Such influencers may be operations managers, technical influencers, or end users. Whoever you decide to reach out to, first identify the common problems the influencer is experiencing. Keep in mind that different influencers are experiencing different problems.

Now that you understand three different modes of entry, here's an example of entering from the middle:

Imagine that you're selling software that improves efficiency. You initiate contact with the process engineer (influencer). You reach out to the process engineer by highlighting a common production problem in the industry. The process engineer is the expert on the company's process and the information hub for the rest of the organization. Your goal is to gather information and further clarify the problem. Once you gather enough information, you'll initiate contact with the plant manager (HLDM). The plant manager has the authority to make the decision but relies on your and the process engineer's expertise. Your goal is to connect the common problem to the company's higher-level concerns. You demonstrate how this production problem is affecting profitability. The plant manager relies on you, the seller, and the process engineer to fill the information gap. Once you gain buy-in from the manager, the procurement manager gets involved. The procurement manager simply processes the purchase order. Procurement has little understanding of the software and even less authority to buy. Procurement is concerned about price and requests a discount. As much as procurement tries to gain a discount, you hold the line. You don't need to discount because the other decision makers have already bought into your solution.

In this example, you see why it makes sense to start with the process engineer or the plant manager but not procurement. This scenario illustrates how HLDMs get involved. The ultimate decision maker is looking to fill his or her information gap, so he or she relies on the technical influencer and the seller. During tough times, people don't want to make the wrong decision; therefore, the ultimate decision maker is eager to gather intelligence and insights. The ultimate decision maker relies on you and the influencers to fill the gap. By the time procurement gets involved, the decision is made. You just need to work out the details.

Expertise leads to impact. HLDMs expect you, the expert, to solve their problems. They expect you to deliver insights and educate them. HLDMs expect you to connect your solution to their goals and initiatives. This can only happen if you come to that meeting armed with the right information.

Rule 4: Get There Early and Stay Consistently Present

The goal is to pursue the right opportunity early in the decision-making process. The earlier the better—ideally, before buyers recognize that they have a need. To ensure that you pursue the opportunity at the right time, get there early in their buying process and maintain a consistent presence within the opportunity.

Sellers are getting involved later in the decision-making process. This is the end result of sellers waiting for buyers to initiate contact. Today's buyers have more information. They start deciding without the seller's insight. The later you get involved, the more you're selling against a competitor versus selling to the buyer's needs. The later you get involved, the less you're viewed as a partner. Why wait for the buyer to reach out to you? Selling is about initiating contact and making things happen, not waiting for the phone to ring or the inbox to ding.

In tough times, getting there early provides a significant advantage. By getting there early, you familiarize the buyer with your solution. Buyers look to mitigate risk and crave stability. A familiar solution is stable and safe. If the buyer is more familiar with you than a competitor, that provides an advantage.

In a seminar, a salesperson asked the same question you're probably thinking: "How can you get there early if you're not sure when the buying process starts?" Simple. Ask the buyer when it starts. If the target has a formal buying process, he or she will give you a time frame. Whatever the timing, initiate your sales efforts before your targets begin their process. Your goal is to be present before the need exists so that you can build familiarity. When you make your buyers aware of a need before they recognize it, you position yourself as a value creator.

Your targets may not have a start date. If you're not sure when your buyers begin their buying process, begin establishing your presence immediately. Be there often and consistently, and start the process for your buyers. Being there consistently increases your likelihood of being at the right place at the right time. Selling is not purely a numbers game, but the more you cast your line, the more fish you're likely to catch.

Increase your communication and develop a cadence. Communication is any method of engagement: in person, email, phone, letter, social media. The key is to maintain a steady presence in the minds of your buyers, not solely at their physical locations. This steady approach ensures that you are top of mind with your opportunities. Be omnipresent while using different communication channels. Your broader situational awareness means more relevant content to share with decision makers. Stay on top of trends and other external factors impacting their business. Buyers want to work with dependable and knowledgeable sellers.

Buyers crave stability and reliability in tough times. Demonstrating a steady approach provides a level of consistency and comfort. You are positioning yourself as their reliable partner. Everything you do and say impacts this position. The buyers' process begins when you expose them to an unrecognized need. Once buyers are aware of their need, build a case for change.

You're not selling; you're exposing the buyers' needs. This self-discovery activates change and positions you as an expert.

Rule 5: Pursue New Prospects and Existing Customers

Selling to a new prospect or existing customer is the same process, but there are tactical differences. "Hunters" focus on selling to new prospects, whereas "farmers" sell to existing customers. Most salespeople are a little bit of both. Some argue that you can't be good at both—but you can. Literally, some of the best hunters I know are also excellent farmers. Our research shows that top-achieving sellers grow their existing customers while pursuing new prospects.

Selling to existing customers presents opportunities and challenges. It's easier because you have a relationship. However, existing customers pigeonhole you to the products you're currently selling to them. Your organization might sell a myriad of different solutions, but the existing customer brands you as the "tool company" or the "widget company." They categorize you based on the core product you sell. However, pursuing an opportunity as the incumbent does provide advantages; you are selling as an insider. You have a deeper understanding of how the buyers' processes work. You have greater access than outsiders, but access only guarantees opportunity, not success.

Other salespeople argue that selling to a new prospect is easier. This contrarian mindset is steeped with the tough timer's attitude. Tough timers are drawn to the challenge of prospecting. Where some sellers see challenges in prospecting toward a new opportunity, tough timers simply see the opportunity. Prospecting from the outside means that you have less information, but knowing less can be an advantage. The less you know about an opportunity, the more questions you ask. You strip your preconceived notions and enter the opportunity more curious.

When you are pursuing existing customers, focus on previous successes and leverage existing relationships. Or, as one vice president of sales told me, "Infiltrate and proliferate." Leveraging your existing relationships is the easiest way to fully pursue an opportunity. Leverage your existing contacts, and go deeper and higher within the organization. Every new contact is a new opportunity to grow your business. Rather than cold-calling into additional departments, use your existing contacts as referral sources. Referrals build instant credibility.

When pursuing a prospect, focus on small wins and building familiarity. Although a new opportunity is a clean slate to build your image, you're selling an unknown and unfamiliar solution. This means that your sales process is going to take longer. Be prepared for this, and don't get too frustrated by it. To keep focused and motivated, look to achieve small wins. When pursuing a new opportunity, small wins include an initial meeting, a follow-up discovery meeting, product demonstrations, incorporating additional decision makers, and touring the buyer's facility. Small wins keep the process moving forward. As you navigate through tough times, progress is more meaningful than performance. Progress leads to performance.

Focus on building familiarity with your total solution. People like the certainty of what is familiar in tough times. The goal is to begin familiarizing the buyer with your solution as you pursue the opportunity. Chapter 10 has more ideas on building familiarity. At a basic level, raise awareness. The more buyers see your solution, your name, your face, the more familiar they become.

SUMMARY

How you pursue an opportunity determines your success. The road to that success has no shortcuts. That steady road to success includes focusing on the fundamentals of selling, which means selecting the right targets and pursuing those targets the right way. Tough timers engage the right decision makers the right way. Tough timers are visionary. Their success is all but assured. They are adventurous and willing to take the road less traveled.

Before initiating contact, broaden your situational awareness. Take a deeper dive to understand how tough times impact your target. Choose the right point of entry with the right decision maker. Authority and expertise determine influence; focus on decision makers who have both or at least one.

Pursuing prospects and existing customers follows the same process, but with tactical differences. Be aware of how you are positioned with existing customers. Prospecting for new customers is an opportunity to start fresh and build the ideal image in the buyer's mind.

Pursuing business in tough times presents new challenges and opportunities. During tough times, you'll engage high-level decision makers that you wouldn't during good times. Tough times force you to aggressively pursue new prospects that you wouldn't have pursued in good times. During tough times, your buyers' needs and concerns are ever changing, forcing you to adapt, evolve, and create a better solution. You do not have this opportunity in good times. Tough times are good!

Tough-Times Pursuit Template

Pursuing targets in tough times requires a focused approach. Use this template to ensure that you are pursuing your target opportunities the right way. Visit www.ToughTimer.com for a downloadable version of this template.

Broaden Your Situational Awareness

- Describe the tough time that your target is experiencing.
- What problems is the tough time causing the buyer?

Identify the Key Players and How They Define Value

- Procurement decision makers
- Influencers
- High-level decision makers

Initiate Contact with the Right Level of Decision Maker

- Initiate contact with influencers or high-level decision makers.
- Initiate contact with procurement as a last resort.
- Reference a business problem in your communication.

Dear HLDM:

Labor shortages are one of the greatest challenges facing today's manufacturers. This labor shortage is costing the industry millions of dollars in lost productivity. To compete successfully, manufacturers are forced to maximize worker productivity. I have three insights to share with you to address this common problem. Our meeting would only last 15 to 20 minutes. Please let me know which of these three times works best.

Get There Early in the Process and Be There Often

- Ask your contacts when their decision-making process starts.
- If there is no designated start date, ask about upcoming projects.
- Follow up regularly, and share relevant content with key decision makers.

CHAPTER 9

Discover

iscovery is an information exchange between a seller and a buyer. This information exchange reveals the buyer's needs, wants, and concerns. Discovery is an analogous term that has parallel meanings in the sales world. According to the American Bar Association, *discovery* is the formal process of exchanging information between the parties about the witnesses and evidence they will present at trial.[1] In sales, *discovery* is the open exchange of information between parties about the challenges, needs, and problems the prospect is facing.

In legal terms, discovery allows both parties to gather information before the trial. In this way, each side has all the facts and is not surprised in the trial. In sales, this is the equivalent of knowing all the information before you present. In our legal system, both parties are required, by law, to provide the information. In sales, there is no obligation. Tactful sellers focus on the customer and generate dialogue. Proper sales discovery is challenging and rewarding.

Discovery also means uncovering something new or unexpected. Your goal is to jointly discover a need, want, concern, or problem hidden to the buyer. Buyers don't know what they don't know. Uncovering a buyer's needs demonstrates your expertise. When buyers discover their needs, they are more engaged in the process and willing to act.

Proper discovery is critical in tough times. In tough times, a cloud of uncertainty looms over customers. This uncertainty creates angst, frustration, and opportunity. Some of the greatest discoveries occur because of tough times. Tough times force us to think and act differently; they activate a different mindset. The pain of tough times sparks creativity. This creates an opportunity for sellers and buyers to engage in a deeper information exchange and discuss new possibilities. Without tough times, you may not have this opportunity. Tough times are good!

A seller-focused mindset is the main obstacle to a productive discovery call. Salespeople who concentrate on closing deals focus on themselves, not their buyers. These sellers enter the discovery phase with the intent to sell versus the intent to understand and uncover. These sellers often lead with self-serving questions that cause buyers to put up their guard. Such sellers feel pressured to sell rather than discover. Other sellers believe that they already understand their buyers' needs before the discovery meeting. These sellers believe that their existing knowledge is enough to create the ideal solution. Their assumptions blind them to what their customers truly need or want. The sellers' assertions are top of mind, not their buyers' needs and wants. This limits these sellers' ability to fully discover their buyers' needs, wants, and desires. Enter the information exchange with an open mind and collectively discover something new.

Discovery is one of the most powerful persuasion tools. If you want to generate more sales, faster, and at higher margins, this is where the magic happens. The key is to remain unbiased in our thoughts and to discover new ideas with buyers. For some sellers, this is too risky. They see this as losing control of the sale. This is true, you do yield some control. True discovery may take a different path than you originally intended, but you may end up somewhere far better than you were expecting.

PREPARING FOR THE DISCOVERY MEETING

Before preparing your discovery questions, you need to prepare your mind. It's critical to enter the process with an open mind—which is harder than you think. Have you ever noticed when people say, "Don't look," the first thing you do is look? The same is true when you tell yourself, "Don't focus on selling." Once again, we look at what we should avoid. The goal is to clear your mind of seller-focused tendencies before your discovery meeting. Clear your mind. Prepare to receive the relevant information.

Preparing for the discovery meeting requires suspending your own assumptions. What if you entered the conversation thinking that you already know the buyer's needs and which solution fits? Your certainty blinds you to other possibilities. Before your meeting, clear your mind. Simply acknowledge your thoughts and put pen to paper; literally, write your assumptions out on paper. You're purging your presumptions. The act of writing clears your mind. This same exercise can be applied to negative self-talk. Pen to paper provides the vehicle to purge negative thoughts.

Imagine that you're selling capital equipment in the manufacturing industry. From your vast experience, customers want reliable equipment that produces quality parts. If you enter every meeting with this assertion, you'll likely steer the conversation toward quality and reliability. Then, during the information exchange, you'll interpret the needs of your buyers through the prism of reliability and quality. You process information to support what you believe. This is classic *confirmation bias*. Confirmation bias is seeking information—consciously or unconsciously—that supports your initial belief. It's hard to discover new ideas and insights when you are reinforcing your old assertions.

Curiosity is another way to suspend your assumptions. Curiosity leads to new ideas and innovative ways to serve customers. Before discovery meetings, develop a curious mindset. Research that appeared in the *Harvard Business Review* shows that curiosity can counteract the negative effects of confirmation bias.[2] The same study also revealed that curiosity helps people view tough situations creatively. Curiosity diminishes the effects of confirmation bias and sparks creativity. Enter discovery with a curious mindset. When facing tough problems and challenges, be curious. Ask yourself thought-provoking questions about the challenging situation. In this case, you're switching focus from achieving an outcome to real learning. Curiosity sparks creativity.

Your only motive in discovery is to learn, not sell. Learning leads to performance. Focus on your customers, not your quota. The goal of learning can be achieved only when we obtain flow in the conversation or true dialogue. In his wonderful book, *The Fifth Discipline*, Peter Senge explains the difference between dialogue and discussion.[3] Discussion is a ping-pong approach to conversation, whereas dialogue is a free flow of meaning and information exchange. In dialogue, the collective becomes curious and attains insights greater than what could be discovered individually. Dialogue is a collaborative effort leading to new insights and ideas.

The goal of this dialogue is to understand the customer at a deeper level. Our goal is to seek alignment in thought to travel the same direction with our customer, not sell the customer on what direction he or she should go. In jazz, band members riff in what seems like chaos. However, jazz musicians learn to align. They take turns riffing and build off each other's momentum.

This is known as being *in the groove*. The same is true for a proper discovery meeting. The goal is to be in the groove with your customers. You're not talking over them or under them; you are in a state of information flow with your buyers.

DURING THE DISCOVERY MEETING

You have two primary functions in a discovery meeting: generate dialogue and deeply listen. Asking the right questions and listening to your buyers determine a successful exchange. A good information exchange taps into the group's collective insights, leading to greater outcomes. Two heads are better than one, and four eyes are better than two. Tap into your full potential by fully engaging your buyers in discovery.

Dialogue

Discovery begins with dialogue. Dialogue is more than having a conversation or asking a few questions. Dialogue is assessing the other person's mindset and seeking to understand his or her position. Dialogue is not about winning a conversation or arguing a particular point; it's attempting to genuinely understand. Dialogue is complete when both parties have a clear understanding.

Effective dialogue begins with how you enter the conversation. Entering the conversation respectfully and as an equal garners a free flow of information. For example, a seller meets a business owner but believes that he or she is inferior to that decision maker. This seller is less likely to share his or her thoughts and ask tough questions. This means that the discoverable remains undiscovered. Conversely, suppose that a seller meeting with a new buyer believes that his or her experience and knowledge make that seller an expert. This mindset precludes the seller from learning anything new. Again, the discoverable remains undiscovered.

The same can be true on the other side of the table. Often customers think that they know their needs and exactly what solution is best. With so much information available, buyers develop a false sense of confidence on a given topic. With all this information, everyone is an expert. This is the equivalent of patients diagnosing themselves after googling their symptoms.

When interacting with customers, tactfully remind them to remain open to new ideas. Encourage others to be open-minded by being open-minded yourself. Acknowledge other people's ideas and insights. Establish commonalities with other people. This rapport-building technique shows buyers what you have in common with them. People are more open to another's ideas if they are like-minded. Share stories that reward open-mindedness.

For example, "Ms. Buyer, I have a customer who reminds me of this situation. This customer was reluctant to meet because he attempted to solve the same problem several times. However, we had an open discussion about the real challenges he was facing and developed a solution that uniquely solved his problem." Sharing a story is another tactful way to encourage openness.

Curiosity during the call is critical. Tell your customer that you are curious. It is common for interviewers to use the phrase "I'm curious" to preface a question. These two words could be the most powerful phrase in discovery. This simple phrase is both disarming and intriguing. You're acknowledging that the buyer knows something you don't and that you genuinely want to learn more. This encourages the buyer to be open.

Consider the last time you were talking with someone and he or she said, "I'm curious, how did you . . . ?" These two words prefacing a simple question yield a more in-depth response. You're not asking the question to elicit an intended response. Instead, you're asking because you want to know.

Deep Listening and Contemplation

"Asking questions buys you time. While the customer is responding to your question, you can think of the next question you want to ask." This advice came from an experienced salesperson early in my career. Although I did hear his advice, I never applied it.

Too many sellers listen with the intent to respond as opposed to the intent to understand. Listening is more than the awareness of sound; it's focusing with laser-like intensity on the conversation. It's more than just hearing words streamlined into sentences. It's about understanding the words and the emotions behind the words. Review these tips to become a better listener:

- **Resist the urge to start pitching as soon as the buyer mentions his or her pain.** When customers mention their challenges, sellers start pitching their solution. Discovery is understanding the problem, not solving it. Pitching during discovery hijacks the conversation. If you switch the conversation too soon, buyers can't share their needs.

- **Take notes and flesh them out later.** Focus on what you heard and what you felt. Recall the customer's emotion. For example, did the customer show frustration when talking about the current challenge? Buyers use emotions to demonstrate what is important. Recognize these emotions for a deeper understanding of what truly matters.
- **Mind your mannerisms.** Have you talked to someone and you notice that he or she can't wait to insert his or her ideas? Before you even finish your sentence, such people open their mouths, ready to insert their ideas. It happens. These mannerisms give the impression that you are not listening. These distracting mannerisms disrupt the information exchange.
- **Maintain eye contact.** Have you talked to someone who looks everywhere but right at you? This is distracting. You get the sense that the person is not paying attention. The eyes display critical emotions. In tough times, buyers are chock full of emotions: doubt, disappointment, frustration, unhappiness. Maintain eye contact to stay focused on the conversation and the emotions of the buyer.
- **Let buyers know that you are listening by validating their comments.** Buyers respond to sellers who listen. Summarizing and paraphrasing signal that you are listening. Summarize the buyer's needs, and ask the buyer if he or she agrees. For example, "Jane, it sounds like your primary need is to identify the root issue with your new equipment and provide a solution to solve the problem. Is that correct?" When the buyer agrees, you are already starting to generate buy-in. Validating prompts the buyer to share additional thoughts and insights.
- **In your dialogue, use the buyer's words to create context.** Use the buyer's words to create a window into the buyer's world. As you absorb the buyer's words, put yourself in his or her position. Empathy is critical to deep listening.

Deep listening is a prerequisite to great discovery calls. Buyers will share oodles of information. The deeper you listen, the more you discover. Use these tips to develop your listening skills.

Self-Discovery

Self-discovery involves helping buyers uncover their own insights, ideas, and understanding of their needs. People value their own insights and ideas more than those of other people. This tendency is rooted in the *endowment effect*, which is a cognitive bias that compels you to place a higher value on the things that you own—including ideas.[4] For example, when people sell their homes, they often value them above market value. People place a higher value on their own home because it is theirs: they created memories in that home, they renovated that home, and so on. Naturally, that home is more valuable to that person than it is to the market.

The same is true for ideas and insights. Rather than convincing buyers to accept your ideas, convince them to accept their own. The information buyers discover on their own is more persuasive than the information you share. It's the insights you help the buyer discover that make the difference—and make the deal.

Through tough times, buyers need an added layer of comfort to make their decisions. This comes in the form of *self-discovery*. Self-discovery occurs when a decision maker uncovers insights and information through dialogue with a salesperson. Self-discovery guides a customer down a path of enlightenment to reveal something on his or her own. Buyers are more willing to change if that change stems from their ideas, not yours. Buyers are more excited about their discovery than about *your* discovery.

For example, one seller demonstrated an innovative fastening system to replace several labor-intensive applications. Although this fastener would reduce labor costs dramatically, it was 10 times more expensive than the existing method. Rather than telling the customer all the ways he could use this system, the seller let the customer discover his own ideas. The seller introduced the product and demonstrated it but then asked the buyer a simple question, "What do you think is the best way to use this product?" The buyer shared his ideas and bought the system. Once the seller had shown the buyer how the system worked, she let the buyer discover ways to use it. The customer bought the solution because it was his idea.

In essence, you are showing buyers an idea but letting them connect the dots. Customers know what they want to accomplish. Self-discovery involves showing customers an opportunity or potential outcome and letting them decide how to get there. You're going for that *aha moment* where buyers discover something on their own. Once they discover the idea, they own it.

Discovery Questions

One question asked the right way changes everything. Questions are powerful. Questions generate dialogue and cause buyers to think and uncover new insights. The right questions generate dialogue with buyers and help you jointly discover new insights and ideas. Use these discovery topics to generate good questions during tough times.

Stretch the Time Horizon (into the Future and the Past)

Buyers have a short-term mindset that focuses more on the present than on the future. This creates two challenges. During tough times, you need to get buyers out of the present moment. The present moment is uncertain and challenging. Second, as buyers make purchasing decisions, they focus on short-term sacrifice instead of the long-term gains. Buyers are more aware of what they sacrifice in tough times because resources are scarce. Risking today's resources looms larger than what they potentially gain in the future. For buyers to bypass what they sacrifice today, focus the conversation to the future or revisit the past.

Focusing on the future puts buyers in a more optimistic state of mind. Through tough times, the future has more possibilities than the present. Here are several questions to focus a buyer's attention on a better future:

- When things start picking up, what will your priorities be?
- Where do you see your company headed in the next few years?
- A year from now, what would cause you to look back on this time and say, "I made the right decision to partner with your company?"
- Putting aside the current recession or tough time, where does your company want to be in the future?
- Long term, what additional services and support will you need?
- Once the economy turns around, how do you want to be positioned?

Each of these questions focuses on the bright future instead of the dreary present. Future-oriented questions focus a buyer's attention on outcomes, taking the focus off what the buyer sacrifices today. During tough times, buyers are hypersensitive to what they sacrifice.

Stretch the buyer's time horizon by revisiting the past. Our history is full of tough times, whether it's a tough competitor, a rolling recession, or a global crisis. When facing tough times, ask your buyers to reflect on their previous tough times. Ask your buyers questions about their decision making during past downturns.

For example, "Ms. Customer, the Great Recession was about 10 years ago. Although those times were tough, your business has flourished since. What were some of the decisions you made during the previous tough time to take full advantage of the upswing that followed?"

Once the buyer shares her thoughts, draw a parallel to the present. For example, "Ms. Customer, knowing that you will make it through this tough time, what similar action should you take today? How can we help you make the most of today's tough time so that you can take full advantage of tomorrow's upswing?"

If buyers seem uncertain on what to do, give them an out. Explain to your buyers, "Hindsight is always 20/20. Knowing what you know now, what would you do differently?" This will give your buyers a chance to share their thoughts and ideas. Once they respond, draw a parallel to the present. The key is to get buyers out of the moment. The present is filled with uncertainty. Stretching the time horizon provides buyers with hope.

Supporting Questions

In tough times, people need a show of support. They might not need the support you offer, but it's comforting to them to know it's available. These questions reveal ways to help buyers. A willingness to help and support is a powerful selling tool in tough times. This behavior builds loyalty and trust, leading to long-term meaningful partnerships. These questions stimulate dialogue around reliability, safety, and support, which is how customers define value through tough times. Use supporting questions to generate dialogue. You can reframe these questions based on whether you're meeting with a prospect or an existing customer. Here are some sample supporting questions:

- How can we better support you through these tough times?
- How can we help you support your customers during these tough times?
- What additional services do you need through these tough times?
- What can we do to make your life easier during these tough times?

- How can we be more flexible for you in these tough times?
- What's missing from our current offering?
- What do you expect from us through these tough times?
- Have these tough times revealed any service gaps in our current solution?
- On a scale of 1 to 10, how is our support during these tough times? What can we do better?
- Through these tough times, what challenges are you experiencing with our solution?

You can also use supporting statements to elicit dialogue. Here are some examples:

- Let's review where we are and discuss some ideas to better support you. Please share your thoughts on our current service level.
- Given the tough times, let's review our current solution to see if it's still a good fit.
- Given the current situation, let's discuss what has changed.

These supporting questions and statements focus on buyers' needs. Support is critical during any tough time. By making buyers a priority in tough times, you receive the reward of their loyalty. The more support you show your customers, the more they will support you.

Challenging Questions

How often do you challenge the status quo? Are you comfortable challenging the old way? Does your acceptance of the status quo blind you to new and different ways of thinking? Before responding, read this short example regarding the British military.

An American officer was visiting with the British army prior to World War II. On this trip, the American officer noticed something as he watched a British armor battery deploy from its truck. There were seven men, but it appeared that six were doing all the work, and *the seventh man just stood by the truck*. When the American asked his British escort about the seventh man, the officer admitted that armor batteries always had seven men, but he was unsure what the seventh man did. He promised to investigate it. The next day, the officer reported that the seventh man used to hold the horses.

Too often we continue down a path without questioning the direction we are headed. We stop asking *why*. We simply follow the path without questioning or challenging where it's going. As in this story, we accept the status quo, especially during tough times.

When we face tough times, change is likely to follow. But during these tough times, people cling to the status quo because it provides a sense of normalcy and stability. Tough times challenge us to change but paradoxically tempt us to preserve the status quo. This dichotomy of rapid change and clinging to the status quo creates an opportunity to ask tough questions—the *why* questions.

Sellers shy away from why questions because they challenge buyers. However, buyers are already challenging their previous decision in tough times. They'll ask, "Why do we do it this way?" or "Why did we implement this process?" These questions open the minds of buyers to change, creating opportunities for sellers. Challenging your buyers' thought processes encourages change that emanates from within. A good why question engages buyers at a deeper level, helping you understand the driving forces behind their decisions. It's not enough to understand what your buyers are doing; you must understand why they are doing it.

Tough times create opportunities for buyers to candidly assess their previous decisions. Tough times also give buyers an out. If they've made bad decisions, it's easier to change using tough times as the trigger. Such buyers save face. Here are some sample challenging questions:

- Why does your company have that process in place?
- Why did your company do it this way in the past?
- Why does your company partner with that supplier?
- Why is your company considering a change?
- Why is your company focused on this project at this time?
- Why is there an emphasis on cost cutting?
- Why are those features, benefits, or outcomes important to your company?

Notice that most of these questions begin with "Why does your company . . . ?" versus "Why do you . . . ?" The question "Why did *you* implement that process?" is too direct. Buyers may become defensive, which discourages open dialogue. This format is less direct: "Why did your company implement that process?" Preface higher-risk questions with, "I'm curious," for example, "I'm curious. Why does your company have that process in place?" The phrase "I'm curious" softens the approach and encourages open dialogue.

Why questions are great follow-up questions when buyers share information. Why questions encourage buyers to elaborate. For example, a buyer says, "In addition to quality and reliability, safety is critical." The salesperson's response is, "I understand that safety is important, but why is it more important now?" This encourages the buyer to share additional information and elaborate.

The goal of these questions is to encourage buyers to ask themselves why. In the opening example, the British officer failed to ask why. He accepted without question the fact that armor batteries always had seven men. It's easier to accept something than to challenge it. By helping your customers ask why, you are leading them to self-discovery.

What-If Questions

The what-if question is a close cousin to the why question. Imagine dialoguing with a customer who explains that he or she is having several issues with his or her current processes, and you ask a what-if question. For example, "Mr. Customer, what if there was a better way to approach this problem?" What-if questions inspire deep thought, anticipation, and curiosity. What-if questions offer a different reality, a new way of viewing a problem and finding a solution that leads to self-discovery.

What-if questions lead to self-discovery because they trigger a different response in the brain. Typically, we're asked a question and we rely on previous logic to get us there.[5] What-if questions require a new way of thinking. This is a subtle shift that leads to new discovery. These questions allow buyers to dream and think in new ways, creating new possibilities.

What-if questions generate excitement and anticipation. In tough times, people dream about a brighter future and better outcomes. What-if questions inspire buyers to translate their dreams into actions. What-if questions engage buyers' emotions as they envision a brighter future. What-if questions provide hope in tough times. Use what-if questions to trigger deeper discussion into a particular challenge or problem that buyers are experiencing. Here are some what-if questions to consider:

- What if there is a better way to approach this problem?
- What if we try a new approach that leads to a different outcome?

- What if you no longer had these issues?
- What if there was a better way to manage your resources?
- What if there was a better way to communicate with your team?
- What if you had to change or try something new?
- What if it didn't have to be this way?
- What if your company wasn't struggling with this problem?
- What if we could change that process?

The goal of the what-if question is not to elicit a direct response from a buyer; the goal is to inspire deeper thought. The what-if question is used as a transitionary statement to dive deeper into a specific challenge or issue. For example, a buyer explains, "My company is having several production problems causing delays. We have tried solving this problem with new software." Respond by asking, "What if there was a better way to solve this problem? Let's explore this problem and think of some ideas." The question triggers thought, not necessarily a direct response.

These questions pique the curiosity of customers and stimulate dialogue. Your goal is not to use such questions to segue directly into a pitch; it's to trigger deeper thought in the minds of your buyers, leading to self-discovery.

Opinion-Seeking Questions

Opinion-seeking questions elicit the thoughts and ideas of buyers to create a solution. It's easier to convince someone to accept their own ideas than to accept yours. When buyers create part of the solution, they show greater ownership. What if you could ask a question to evoke your buyers ideas? (Notice how the what-if question builds anticipation.)

The magic words are "What are your thoughts?" or "What do you think?" These powerful questions engage decision makers and evoke self-discovery. Here are some sample questions:

- What do you think the ideal solution should look like?
- What are your thoughts on how to solve this problem?
- What do you think is the core issue?
- What are your thoughts on the project?
- What are your thoughts on applying this technique?
- What are your thoughts on changing the process?
- What do you think of the current process?

- Regarding the ideal solution, what do you think it should look like?
- We have a few ideas on the ideal fix, but we'd like to hear your thoughts.
- What are your thoughts?

Opinion-seeking questions engage buyers and spur dialogue. If you feel uncomfortable asking these questions, preface each question with "I'm curious."

Discovery in tough times is slightly different from discovery in good economic times. The focus is on understanding buyers' needs, but you're also engaging buyers at a deeper level. You're helping buyers self-discover their own needs. Change in tough times requires a deeper level of commitment. Your questions generate dialogue that draws out information and ideas. These questions serve as a guide—not a script—to help generate a dialogue. A discovery call should be fluid.

AFTER THE DISCOVERY SALES CALL

The Blue Angels are arguably the most elite aviators in the world. If you have witnessed a Blue Angels performance, you can attest to their brilliant display. Blue Angels strive for perfection. Perfection is a lofty goal, but it's necessary when you're a Blue Angel. In certain formations, the Blue Angels fly only 18 inches from one another. The stakes are high, and the Blue Angels prepare, execute, and debrief as if their lives depend on it—because they do.

Blue Angels spend more time debriefing their performances than they do planning and executing them.[6] For hours, they critique every element of their performance, including the march to and from the aircraft. No detail is too small or ego too big. They strive to get better. Blue Angels know that the debrief is where the learning takes place.

What if you debriefed your discovery calls with the same intensity? You would learn more about your customers and enhance your selling skills. Debriefing a discovery call is a three-part process: review and reflect, follow up, and build your solution.

Review and Reflect

Reviewing a discovery meeting is more than thinking about the call. Reviewing is a deep reflection on your customer's needs, wants, concerns, and challenges. Sellers are quick to make the next call. They spend little time reflecting on their previous meeting. Reviewing and reflecting require vigorous note taking. You're filling in the information gaps from your notes. Review and reflection lead to further understanding and are consistent with a customer-focused approach.

Reflect on what the customer said, and think about what the customer did not say. What the customer didn't say can loom larger than what was said. Take time after the call to fill in the blanks and review your call notes. Put pen to paper to connect your memory to the moments. The minute you leave a discovery meeting, you start losing information. When you leave the meeting, review your notes and begin filling in the informational blanks. Use your customer relationship management system or put pen to paper. Whatever you use, just do it. If you don't review it, you will lose it. Use these questions to review and reflect on your discovery meetings:

- How was the dialogue?
- What were the buyer's key concerns?
- What buzzwords and phrases did the buyer use?
- What is the buyer's goal for the organization and for himself or herself?
- What did the buyer say?
- What did the buyer not say?
- What did the buyer self-discover in this meeting?
- What were the buyer's emotions?
- What were the buyer's deeper desires?
- What deeper concerns were revealed?

Follow Up with the Customer

What's more important than understanding your customers' needs? The answer is, showing customers that you understand their needs. Customers partner with sellers who understand their needs, wants, and fears. A well-thought-out follow-up note demonstrates your understanding. Shortly after your discovery meeting with a buyer, send a follow-up note. This note can take the form of an email, LinkedIn message, text message, video message, or letter.

The follow-up note has a twofold purpose: it demonstrates your understanding of the buyer's needs and reminds the buyer of his or her own needs.

Buyers have a short half-life when recalling their needs. Your buyers are busy, and they have other priorities. As soon as they leave the discovery meeting, other priorities pile on over the needs you just uncovered. The benefits of self-discovery can only last if the customer is aware of his or her needs. An effective follow-up message will highlight the customer's needs, wants, and concerns.

Begin Building Your Solution

You are the most aware of your buyers' needs when you are deeply reflecting on their needs. Start designing your solution when the information is fresh. Don't wait. You begin losing information at an exponential rate. Use your meeting notes and ideas to create a solution that aligns with your customer's definition of value. As you create your solution, don't assume that your initial ideas are going to be your best. View this rough-draft solution as an iteration of a much better solution to follow.

SUMMARY

Your discovery goal is to uncover buyers' needs and help buyers to discover their own needs. When you discover something new—together with your buyers—they feel a stronger sense of ownership of the solutions you are creating. Successful discovery begins with the right mindset. The goal is to free your mind from assumptions. The freer your mind, the more open you'll be to new insights and ideas.

Discovery calls are successful if you ask the right questions the right way, generating a dialogue with buyers. Seller-focused questions lead buyers to your solution. Buyers pick up on this seller-focused behavior and put their guard up. Once you discover your buyers' needs, reflect on the conversation, follow up with the customer, and begin building your solutions.

Persuasion begins in the discovery phase. When buyers realize that they need to change, they open their minds to your ideas and insights. Buyers are more likely to change when that change emanates from within.

Tough-Times
Discovery Template

Discovery is the information exchange that takes place between sellers and buyers. This information exchange reveals the buyers' needs, wants, and concerns. This template is your go-to guide for effective discovery sales calls. Visit www.ToughTimer.com for a downloadable version of this template.

Prepare for the Discovery Meeting

- Embrace the right mindset—you're there to learn and dialogue, not to sell.
- Suspend your assumptions prior to your meeting.

During the Discovery Meeting

- The goal is to generate dialogue, not just a response from your buyer.
- Listen intently to the customer during your exchange: take notes, maintain eye contact, summarize, and paraphrase. (Complete list available in the "Deep Listening and Contemplation" section.)

Create a List of Discovery Questions

- Stretch the buyer's time horizon into the future and the past.
- Use supporting questions to provide stability.
- Ask challenging questions to shift the buyer's mindset.
- Use what-if questions to inspire deep thought.
- Ask opinion-seeking questions to invoke self-discovery.

After the Discovery Call

- Review and reflect—fill in the blanks from your meeting notes.
- Send a follow-up note and schedule the next steps.

CHAPTER 10

Persuade

Persuasion is a dynamic process that influences internal and external factors that act on buyers. Persuasion is a set of activities you engage in to convince buyers to select your alternative versus all other options—including the status quo. Even if you're selling a one-of-a-kind solution, you have competition. Buyers tell themselves, "I shouldn't spend the money right now" or "I'm not sure if the timing is right" or "Given the circumstances, we should wait." Your biggest competitor is not another provider—it's the persuasive pull of the status quo.

In tough times, you persuade buyers on two levels: (1) to take action and (2) to purchase your solution. Buyers are tempted to pause in tough times and question whether your solution is the best use of their resources. Buyers might be sold on your solution but not sold on the timing. Persuasion in tough times involves a deeper level of commitment. Before committing to your solution, buyers must commit to the idea of investing and changing in tough times.

Although it's challenging to change, there is hope. In the long run, people are more likely to regret inaction more than taking action. If buyers feel the right amount of pressure, they're willing to act. As the pressure to act mounts, buyers weigh today's risk versus tomorrow's potential regrets. Tomorrow's regrets are more painful than the failure they risk today.

How can you get your buyers to think long term if you think short term? Sellers view their profession in a seasonal manner. They think, "I need to close this deal by the end of the month." This is a transactional view of the profession. There is no real deadline to convince buyers to change. The deadline is manufactured by you or your company. Deadlines create pressure to push and close rather than tactfully persuade and position. Persuasion in tough times is more than simply pushing your solution—it's positioning your solution.

Tough times are unpredictable. It's hard to determine when downturns end and upswings begin. Sellers get frustrated with the lack of progress in tough times, so they begin pushing harder, pitching more aggressively, and discounting deeper to close more deals. The desperation of these sellers is apparent, and buyers are turned off by this approach.

Selling is not a finite game with a finish line. The finish line doesn't exist. You're constantly jockeying for position. Start viewing your persuasion strategy as positioning versus pushing. Establish your presence as the front runner during tough times. Position your solution as the benchmark on which every other option is graded. Tough times are an opportunity to gain customer mind share and industry market share.

Persuasion through tough times is all about mitigating risk. There are two types of risk with each decision: the risk of doing something and the greater risk of doing nothing. Change how the buyer views risk. The risk associated with changing won't loom nearly as large as the risk of sticking with the status quo.

Persuasion requires commitment, not just compliance. People can be coerced to comply, but commitment requires a deeper level of persuasion. Tough times are opportune times to make long-term positive behavioral change, which requires commitment. Salespeople misinterpret compliance as commitment. Buyers will meet with you, go through a demonstration, and share information, but that doesn't mean they are committed. Buyers may be interested in an idea, but they are not ready to act. Committed buyers demonstrate their commitment in their words and actions. Committed buyers suggest next steps and provide a path moving forward. Persuasion in tough times is about shifting buyers from compliance mode to commitment mode.

Persuasion in tough times requires a layered approach to maximize commitment. Layered persuasion happens in three stages. Stage one is convincing buyers to share information with you. This is the discovery phase of the sale we discussed earlier. Chapter 9 discussed the importance of self-discovery. Persuasion begins with an exchange of information. Before buyers consider changing, they must feel comfortable with the alternative option. A fruitful exchange builds a steady foundation where buyers feel comfortable committing.

The second level of persuasion occurs by changing how buyers think. Changing the way someone thinks begins with first understanding how that person thinks. On the discovery call, you start to think as the buyer thinks. Now you will learn how to influence by surrounding the buyer with your powerful message.

The final level of persuasion is to act. The buyer only takes action if the other two layers are intact. Exchange information with the buyer, change the buyer's thoughts, and convince the buyer to act. Although action is seen on the surface, it only manifests because of a deeper belief that can only happen with deep information exchange. Persuasion is not a single event; it's a campaign. In this chapter, we'll explore the different dynamics of persuasion.

SEVEN RULES FOR PERSUADING IN TOUGH TIMES

"How do I convince customers to buy if they're struggling to keep the doors open?" This is what a seller asked in one of our training seminars during a downturn. You are likely experiencing the same challenge.

A buyer struggling to take action operates from a fearful mindset. A fearful buyer lacks the resources and the reassurance to make the decision you're asking him or her to make. This lack of resources and reassurance is a one-two punch causing buyers to pause and hoard their resources. Persuading in tough times is a two-step process. The first step is selling the buyer on the idea of taking action instead of pausing. The second step is selling the buyer on your specific solution. You can't convince buyers to invest in your solution until they're sold on the idea of investing in the first place.

Persuasion is proactively and positively affecting a buyer's perception of your solution. This means preparing your message and preparing the buyer to receive your message. Therefore, you are setting the stage and influencing the context in which the buyer decides. You are priming the buyer to act by influencing how he or she receives your message.

For example, a hotel concierge recommends a nice Italian restaurant and mentions the signature toasted ravioli. As you research online, you see that people are raving about the signature dish. When you get to the restaurant, the waiter recommends his favorite dish, toasted ravioli. You peruse the menu and order the toasted ravioli.

Although the waiter recommended the signature dish, your decision was already made. From the beginning, the concierge primed you to select the signature dish. The online reviews provided the social proof. The waiter's recommendation further solidified your decision. The constant mentioning of the dish built familiarity. By the third mention, you could almost taste the dish. Your familiarity with the signature dish coupled with the relative uncertainty of other menu items led you to order the toasted ravioli. The only way that you would not order the dish is if it were sold out.

Your decision to order the signature dish is a result of multiple influences over a period of time. Persuasion is not a single event; it's a campaign. Persuasion is a dynamic process with a myriad of activities—both face-to-face and behind the scenes—to influence buyers. It's about changing the peripherals to influence how buyers think. Persuasion is more than just a face-to-face presentation; it's everything you do to influence buyers. Use the following seven rules to guide your persuasion effort.

Rule 1: Align Your Solution with the Customer's Definition of Value

Alignment is promoting the aspects of your solution that match a buyer's definition of value. Position your solution as the front runner by demonstrating how your solution aligns with the buyer's definition of value.

Robert Cialdini posed this intriguing question in his book, *PRE-SUASION*: "Why do we typically assume that whatever we are focusing on in the moment is especially important?"[1] Cialdini explains that we give heightened attention to factors that provide us with value. This creates an opportunity for sellers to craft a narrative that aligns with buyers' definitions of value. You choose what information is focal to your buyers. Focus the attention of your buyers on the aspects of your solution that align with their definitions of value.

For example, suppose that you are selling software that promises to increase profits, enhance productivity, and improve quality. In your discovery call, you realize that your buyer genuinely cares about improving the quality of his or her solution. Quality is king for the buyer. Therefore, you need to win on quality. You and your competitors are striving to own the quality position in the buyer's mind.

If you were selling the software, how would you win that battle? Would you share case studies highlighting the quality of your solution? Would you highlight your value-added services that enhance the quality of your buyer's finished product? Would you share International Standards Organization quality certifications with your buyer? Would you share testimonials from previous customers highlighting quality-based outcomes? The answer is yes in all cases. Before presenting your quality solution, you are campaigning on quality. Your solution does other things, but your goal is to own quality. Align your solution with what is focal to your buyer.

I call this the *tip calculator phenomenon*. In one memorable *Seinfeld* episode, Jerry gave his father a gift, The Wizard. The Wizard was a personal digital assistant that had several functions. But there was only one function that Morty (Barney Martin) cared about: the tip calculating function. In fact, Morty didn't call it The Wizard, he referred to it as the "tip calculator." Throughout the episode, Jerry expresses his frustration by exclaiming, "It does other things!"[2] Your solution does other things, but it must be the best at what your customer cares about most.

Winston Churchill said, "If you have an important point to make, don't try to be subtle or clever. Use a pile driver. Hit the point once. Then come back and hit it again. Then hit it a third time—a tremendous whack." Churchill could be talking to salespeople attempting to influence buyers. Uncover the buyer's definition of value, and then align your message with that definition. You control the narrative by choosing which information to share with buyers. What is focal is deemed important to buyers. Here are some examples of how you can control the information flow:

- **Third-party endorsements or articles highlighting features, attributes, and benefits consistent with your customer's definition of value.** If the publication highlights a myriad of benefits, highlight those aligning with your buyer's definition of value.
- **Facility tours highlighting your capabilities consistent with the customer's definition of value.** These tours can happen virtually or in person. If your customer values quality, then showcase your quality on the tour.
- **Shared product information and one-sheets consistent with the customer's definition of value.** Product demonstrations emphasizing features that align with the buyer's definition of value.
- **Incorporating inner-company experts who can influence the buyer.** If the buyer values technical support, bring in your technical manager.
- **Arranging for an existing customer to meet with your prospect.** Ensure that the existing customer is similar to the prospect.

The only limit to your campaign is the edge of your imagination. The only operating premise is simple: align your message with how your buyer defines value. The tighter the alignment, the more persuasive your campaign will be.

Rule 2: Build Familiarity

Human beings are creatures of habit. We do things repeatedly. We go to the same restaurants, exercise the same way, and choose the same products. These habits ease decision-making: it takes less effort to do what is familiar. We like the familiarity of routine. The same is true when buyers are making decisions. During tough times, buyers make decisions under the cloud of uncertainty. To help clarify, buyers focus on what is familiar. This includes salespeople with whom they are familiar. Before persuading a buyer to select your alternative, build familiarity with your product, company, and you, the salesperson. Your solution is bigger than the products you sell. Our research on top-achieving salespeople shows that customers derive value from three different dimensions: the product, the company, and the salesperson. Familiarize your buyers with each dimension of value.

Unfamiliar buyers respond in different ways. Buyers put up their guard when they are forced to explore unfamiliar options. An unfamiliar buyer is unlikely to engage with you, let alone buy your solution. They won't accept your meeting requests, or they see no reason to move forward. As the seller pushes harder, the buyer raises his or her guard even further. It's not that the buyer doesn't want to buy; he or she is just unfamiliar with your solution. Familiarizing involves preventing buyers from shutting down before you start. Familiarize your buyers with each dimension of your solution.

There are several ways to familiarize buyers with your solution. One of the most powerful ways is through social proof or social learning. In her wonderful book, *Influential Mind*, Tali Sharot explains the importance of social learning: "When people perceive others' choices, the brain automatically encodes added utility to those selected options in regions that are important for signaling value. Our brains operate according to a rule that what is desired by others is likely valuable."[3]

Build familiarity through social proof. Social proof is showing that your solution is familiar to someone, even if it's not familiar to the buyer. Social proof can be inserted anywhere while attempting to persuade buyers—the sooner the better. For example, if a market leader recently purchased your solution, then having that business provides social proof to other prospects considering that decision. The prospect thinks, "If it's good enough for the market leader, it's good enough for me."

When you see a new product on a repeated basis, it's no longer new—it's familiar. Partner with your marketing team to create campaigns and collateral support pieces. The more exposures the decision maker has to you, the more familiar you become. Build familiarity by going where your decision makers go. Attend tradeshows where you are likely to meet your key decision makers and market leaders. Network where they network. Get involved in your industry's professional associations. Your presence creates familiarity.

Familiarity includes your social presence on networking sites such as LinkedIn. By connecting with your prospects, you're familiarizing yourself with them. Every time they see your name, you build familiarity. Connect with your buyers, and comment on their content. In today's world, people are hyperaware of who views their profiles and shares their content. This activity validates the other person, which, in turn, builds more familiarity.

Rule 3: Lower Resistance

What barriers are in your buyer's way? The shortest distance between two points is a straight line, but rarely in sales do we get a straight line to our goal. There are detours. It's best to identify those detours ahead of time. In sales, we call this *proactively lowering resistance* or *removing barriers*. Buyers are more easily persuaded if there are fewer obstacles in their way. You're familiar with this concept from previous chapters. This same concept can apply when persuading buyers.

In tough times, you face more barriers and front-end sales resistance. Lowering resistance means anticipating and addressing buyers' concerns. Barriers can take many forms, but the most common is an objection or buyer resistance. Sellers spend more time responding to objections than they do proactively removing them. This creates a new challenge for buyers. If a buyer makes you aware of a challenge or an objection, he or she will feel the need to defend the position. Once buyers dig their feet in to defend their position, it's harder to persuade them. There is a better way to proactively respond.

Removing barriers begins with anticipation. Jack Welch, the legendary GE executive, once referred to a leader's ability to "see around corners."[4] Although Welch is referring to the characteristic of a great leader, he could be predicting the characteristic of a great seller. Tough timers know that there are hurdles and barriers. They don't ignore them—they remove them. Begin removing barriers by identifying them. Use the following questions to help guide your barrier analysis:

- How is this selling scenario similar to previous scenarios? Based on that experience, what barriers should I look for?
- Along the path to success, what additional issues could I experience?
- How can we make it easier for this prospect to select our alternative?
- What's getting in the way of the buyer selecting our alternative?

Each of these questions forces you to peek around that corner. Once you reveal a barrier, begin removing it. For example, if you know that your prospect is suffering financially, begin formulating clever financing options or help the buyer pool different budgets. If you know that your key contacts are vulnerable, begin widening your relationship base within the opportunity. Talk to your internal champions to identify potential roadblocks. Internal champions want to see you succeed. Internal champions are transparent because they're on board with your solution.

Once you have the information, tactfully address the resistance with a supportive message. Use case studies to highlight the positive aspects of your solution that address the buyer's concerns. During the presentation, be a little more direct in acknowledging the buyer's concerns. Your message should strike a supportive and empathetic tone. The key to addressing buyer resistance is to demonstrate empathy. The key to demonstrating empathy is to use two powerful words—*I understand*. For example, "Mr. Buyer, I understand that budgets are already tight. However, our solution's proven cost savings and performance metrics will easily cover the overages."

Rule 4: Raise Expectations

"Underpromise and overdeliver" is a common mantra in business, especially in tough times. During tough times, resources are scarce, and companies make do with what is available. Many sellers abide by this mantra without knowing how damaging it can be. First, what buyer would get excited about underpromising? Are you trying to underwhelm the buyer to the point where he or she can't help but be satisfied? Would you begin your meeting by saying, "I know you have several options, but we are by far the most mediocre"? No buyer (or salesperson) would get excited about that.

Raising expectations means promising a lot and delivering more even when times are tough. It's making big promises, not unrealistic ones. As you raise your buyers' expectations, you become the benchmark on which everyone else is rated. Set the new benchmark with your promises, and reach higher with your performance.

There is a more insidious reason why it's dangerous to underpromise. People rise or fall to the expectations that are placed on them. Therefore, constantly underpromising means that you eventually live down to those low expectations. Because you set no challenging benchmarks, you never reach your full potential. Set a high performance bar. Make your competition reach for you instead of bending down to reach them.

Confirmation bias plays a role in satisfaction. Raising expectations invokes the self-fulfilling prophecy mentioned earlier. Big promises program your buyers' expectations. Buyers are primed to look for information and examples that confirm what they are programmed to expect. This creates an opportunity to further influence your buyers' expectations and their level of satisfaction. Here are ways to raise the buyer's expectations:

- Promise shorter lead times or quicker turnaround times.
- Commit to additional technical support or post-sale support.
- Offer extended warranties or service-level guarantees.
- Dedicate internal resources.
- Detail your implementation or transition plan.
- Present a list of complimentary value-added services.
- Offer flexible payment terms and ordering options.

Tough times are growth opportunities. Tough times demand your absolute best and a little bit more. You must push yourself beyond what you think is possible. In *Greatest Salesman in the World*, Og Mandino highlights the importance of stretching to reach your full potential with this line: "I ask not for gold or garments or even opportunities equal to my ability; instead, guide me so that I may acquire ability equal to my opportunities."[5] In tough times, let your capabilities and effort stretch with the opportunities that present themselves. Keep stretching in tough times, and your ability will catch up with the expectations you set.

Building perceived value raises buyers' expectations. Perceived value is mainly sensory. It's the way something looks, sounds, feels, and even smells.

For example, gift wrapping influences expectations. It generates excitement. It sets a high benchmark. The packaging should be consistent with the overall image of your solution. You wouldn't wrap a Rolex in an old newspaper. Packaging invokes the self-fulfilling prophecy. The higher the quality of the packaging, proposal, or presentation, the higher the product's quality.

Think of how this concept applies to your marketing information. Use high-end paper to print your collateral pieces. Meticulously edit your correspondence and proposals. Review samples to ensure that they are presented perfectly. Every element of your solution (including you as the salesperson) is an opportunity to build perceived value. Position your solution as the benchmark on which every other alternative is graded.

Rule 5: Use Analogies

The mind operates like a lawyer arguing a case. Lawyers spend significant time looking at similar previous cases with the desired outcome. Once a suitable case is found, they don't argue the merits of the current case. Instead, they argue the fundamental similarities to the previous case, establishing a legal precedent. This expedites the judge's decision-making process. Your buyers fundamentally do the same thing.

In *Surfaces and Essences: Analogy as the Fuel and Fire of Thinking*, Douglas Hofstadter and Emanuel Sander explain that we judge and make current decisions based on previous experiences.[6] We rely on precedent and previous know-how to decide today. This is especially true when we face uncertainty. When buyers are uncertain, they rely on the past to guide them through the present.

Humans make decisions based on precedent. We analyze previous experiences, and if the structure is similar, then we'll apply that previous logic to what we experience today. We look at unfamiliar situations and try to piece together data that are familiar based on previous experience. Then we try to make this new decision using that familiar data. Right, wrong, or indifferent, this is how we make decisions. We use logic and reason to further justify our current decisions. Although we are not always the best model for logic and reason, hindsight provides the clarity we need to make consistent decisions.

When buyers are deciding, there is a constant tug-of-war between their emotion and their logic. Your analogy is likely running contrary to the narrative in the buyer's head. The buyer is experiencing tough times and is fearful. Such a buyer is operating from a scarcity mindset, so the logical thing to do is to hoard resources. Fear has hijacked this buyer's attention, and he or she cannot see past the pain. Your analogy must tell a different story that triggers a different emotion. Rather than stoking the emotions of fear, emphasize courage, optimism, and belief. These emotions are more aligned with the buyer taking action. Your analogy must emotionally appeal to the buyer and be consistent with what you are persuading the buyer to do.

Use analogies that call attention to the benefits of taking action during tough times. Position the downturn as an opportunity to invest. Analogies are effective when they are familiar to the person you are persuading. Use the investment analogy to highlight the importance of investing in a downturn.

For example, "Mr. Customer, I understand that there is a lot of uncertainty. However, what we're experiencing now is an opportunity similar to a dip in the stock market. When the market is down, that's the time to invest. This is when you gain the greatest return. Imagine how much more you will gain by acting now."

Use the market-leader analogy. Draw a comparison between the market leader's activities and your buyer's activity. Market leaders set the pace in good times and provide guidance during tough times. Review your target's industry, and find examples. Every industry has market leaders. Drawing a comparison with those industries can help drive decision-making.

For example, "Ms. Customer, I noticed that your industry market leader recently invested in new equipment to expand its operations. If your goal is to gain market share, then it's critical for you to keep moving forward and investing, even in the midst of a downturn. In fact, this could be an opportunity to gain an edge on your competitors."

Use a broader-market analogy. Draw an analogy to the broader market not specific to any industry. Provide your buyers with research or examples highlighting how companies can not only survive but thrive after a recession. In a *Harvard Business Review* article titled, "Roaring Out of Recession,"[7] researchers found that companies that improve operational efficiency and, at the same time, invest in growth areas are more likely to outperform their rivals. You could use an analogy referencing broad economic studies such as this one.

For example, "Mr. Customer, I understand that things are tough right now, but this is the opportune time to gain a significant competitive advantage. This study indicates that investing right now positions you to outperform your competitors when times get better. Now is the time to invest in your business."

The most powerful analogy is to draw a parallel to the buyer's previous downturn. Drawing an analogy is about connecting buyers to the past so that they act consistently in the present. This process requires stretching the buyer's time horizon to a previous tough time. Like the lawyer analyzing preceding court cases, once buyers are reminded of their previous decision, they begin connecting the dots. Reviewing the previous tough time also highlights the economic boom that followed. Greater economic expansion follows every tough time.

As buyers reflect on the tough time, they acknowledge the challenges, but they also remember the expansion that followed. Looking back reassures buyers that their previous tough time eventually passed, as will the current one. All of this generates a better mindset to persuade buyers. Here's an example of that conversation:

> **Situation:** You meet with a high-level decision maker facing tough times. Your solution could significantly impact the buyer's business, but the buyer is hesitant to move forward given the current economic uncertainty. Review a previous tough time, and draw a parallel to the present. Here's how you set up this conversation:

> **Salesperson:** I understand that your industry is facing tough times. This reminds me of the previous recession. What's most noticeable is the amount of success your company has experienced since that recession. Your company has nearly doubled revenue and market share. You positioned yourself during the tough time to take advantage of the opportunities that followed. Looking back, what strategic decisions better positioned your company for recovery?

> **Buyer:** In the previous downturn, we made a decision to keep our foot on the gas and make investments our competition wasn't willing to make, which included investing in our infrastructure, updating software, training our employees, etc.

> **Salesperson:** Knowing that this current tough time represents a similar opportunity, wouldn't it make sense to apply that same logic to this decision?

Notice how the seller is drawing a parallel from the past to the present. The seller is highlighting the buyer's previous action and showing how the current situation is like the previous one. The goal is to make a connection from the past to the present to take full advantage of a future opportunity.

Rule 6: Quantify the Impact of Your Solution

In tough times, buyers want a sure thing. Buyers analyze what they sacrifice and what they gain to ensure that what they are risking is worth the reward. It's easier for a buyer to compare the prices of two options because price is straightforward, but impact is not. Too few sellers can demonstrate with certainty the dollar impact their solution has on customers. The greatest challenge in tough times is not communicating the value you deliver—it's quantifying the impact.

Think of three ways your solution adds value, such as customer service, quick response, and quality. The customer would agree that these three benefits bring real value. It's not a question if those benefits are valuable—it's a question of how valuable. Most companies do a superior job of creating value but are unable to quantify the impact on buyers. Through tough times, it's not enough to present your value; you must quantify the impact. Unquantifiable value is less relevant and less impactful. The less tangible the cost savings, the less perceived impact on the buyers. The key is to quantify the value you deliver.

During tough times, buyers make decisions under a microscope. Decisions are scrutinized and must be justified. Imagine that you are an operations manager deciding to switch providers. As you onboard the new provider, other decision makers want to know why you switched. When this decision is questioned, there must be proof to justify the decision. Tangible impact provides buyers with the necessary justification.

Most of the value you deliver is implied, but it may not be perceived by buyers. Because value is implied and less tangible, buyers don't think much of it. For example, suppose that you sell a solution that reduces labor costs. You demonstrate the solution, and the cost savings are implied in your solution. Your solution reduces labor costs, but you have no hard data showing the dollar amount. Your promise to reduce labor costs blends in with other competitors promising to do the same.

What if you quantified the impact of your solution? Suppose that you research your solution and calculate an expected labor savings of 10 percent. If the customer budgeted $100,000 for labor on this project, your solution saves the customer $10,000. Your implied value is now tangible and real. That $10,000 is like pure profit to the buyer's bottom line.

In other instances, your value is less tangible. For example, suppose that you offer complimentary training to help workers become more productive, but no data show the specific labor savings. Although the customer agrees that your training is a benefit, there is no hard figure to make it tangible. The same is true with customer support or any number of value-added extras. In your presentation, the goal is to quantify your value and make the impact tangible. Use the following tips to quantify your value.

Conduct an Impact Audit

Through tough times, buyers scramble for ways to cut costs, streamline processes, and gain efficiencies. Tough times are the catalyst for many buyers to cut costs. During tough times, buyers become painfully aware of their processes as they scrounge for ways to eliminate waste. The timing could not be better to conduct an impact audit. This process involves analyzing the buyer's business and quantifying the potential impact of your solution. Your request to conduct an impact audit is timely and relevant to the buyer's needs. In tough times, every dollar counts, including the dollars you help the company save. The dollar impact of your value provides the proof and certainty buyers need to take on the risk of changing in tough times. Lead with what is tangible.

Begin this process by identifying all the ways your solution impacts the buyer. This requires an in-depth understanding of the customer's business. There are two ways to quantify the impact of your solution: the cost that you help save and the profit that you help gain. Below are two examples demonstrating both.

Let's say that you are selling automation equipment to a consumer-products company. Your solution can reduce the time to market for a new-product launch. This new product is expected to generate $12 million in revenue its first year ($1 million per month). Your automation software package would decrease the time to market by three months. This means that your solution would enable the buyer to earn an additional $3 million in revenue. That $3 million gain is the impact.

During tough times, buyers are keenly aware of what they sacrifice. In many cases, what a buyer gives up or sacrifices is more compelling than what he or she gains. In tough times, your impact audit can reveal what the buyer is truly sacrificing. Consider the following example.

During the Great Recession of 2008, a seller was encouraging a buyer to replace his current tool fleet with cordless tools. The seller told the business owner that the company was wasting too much money on extension cords, but the owner was not convinced. The seller then quantified the true cost of the current tools. The seller used a stopwatch to calculate the time laborers spent looking for extension cords and open outlets. The results were compelling. In one instance, it took more than 30 minutes to find a cord and drill a hole. The brutal part was that two other workers were waiting around for the laborer to drill the hole. In total, that was 1.5 labor hours. At a dollar per minute, this one instance cost the customer $90 in productivity. Once the seller quantified what the tools were costing the business owner, he was ready to switch. Losing that $90 in productivity was more painful than investing in cordless tools.

Regardless of whether it's a potential gain or reducing a loss, the key is to quantify. A tangible loss or gain is more compelling than the unknown gain. Use these questions to help you conduct a thorough impact audit:

How does your solution enhance the customer's profitability or cash flow? In tough times, your customers look for ways to conserve resources. Their mindset shifts from long-term success to weathering the short-term storm. The following questions help you identify the short-term, immediate benefits to your customer:

- Does your solution enhance the quality or performance of the buyer's current solution? If so, quantify how this impacts the business.
- If the buyer uses a substandard solution and experiences issues, quantify the cost to the business.
- Does your solution improve productivity allowing the buyer to do more with less?
- Does your solution enhance the customer's image? If so, quantify the dollar impact on the business.
- Do you offer flexible terms or financing options to improve the buyer's cash flow? If so, quantify the impact on the business.

How does your solution reduce overall cost? In tough times, buyers are more open to cost-cutting ideas. Buyers look for any opportunity to save on costs. Every dollar saved contributes to the buyer's profit or cash flow. The buyer's tough time sparks creativity to explore new cost-cutting opportunities. You might not otherwise have this opportunity.

The following questions help you quantify the short- and long-term gains buyers experience from your cost-saving effort. The more immediate and tangible the gain, the more compelling it is to the buyer. The longer the buyer waits and the less tangible the gain, the less compelling it becomes.

Short-Term Gain Questions

- Does your solution reduce labor costs?
  - Reduce operator hours to produce the same result.
  - Reduce engineering costs.
  - Reduce internal administrative costs (i.e., processing invoices).
  - Reduce customer-complaint handling costs.
  - Reduce total installed cost.
  - Reduce seasonal labor costs.
- Does your solution reduce energy costs?
- Does your solution reduce scrap or rework?
- Does your solution reduce logistical costs?
  - Delivery costs
  - Warehousing costs
  - Inventory costs
- Does your solution reduce raw material costs?

Long-Term Gain Questions

- Does your solution reduce financing costs?
- Are you reducing facilities costs?
- Are you reducing maintenance costs?
- Are you reducing training costs?
- Are you reducing warranty costs on the solution to customers?
- Are you reducing conversion costs?

Every time you answer yes to these questions, follow up with this question, "How much?" The how-much question quantifies the impact; some impacts are easier to quantify. Get creative in how you quantify your solution. You might provide an educated guess in lieu of concrete analytics. Although an educated guess is not as tangible, it's still meaningful. During tough times, buyers focus on your price, but this exercise quantifies the real costs. As you reveal the cost of the buyer's current or competitive option, the buyer starts to realize that it's too costly to bear.

How does your solution create new opportunities for the customer?

In tough times, companies are desperately looking for ways to grow their business. Identify the ways your solution helps the buyer grow the business, and quantify that value.

- Can the buyer go after new markets because of your solution?
- Can the buyer ramp up production to better serve customers?
- Can the buyer broaden the product portfolio to existing customers?
- Does your solution provide opportunities for the buyer to grow the business with existing customers?

During the discovery phase of the sales call, you identified the buyer's key success metrics and how the buyer defines value. For example, the buyer must reduce labor hours and scrap rate. Make the customer's metrics the focal point of your impact audit. This is another way to align your solution with how the buyer defines value.

Impact is more persuasive than your opinion. When you promise a benefit to a buyer without making it tangible, it's just that, a promise. Substantiate your promises with proof. Buyers value proof more than your promise. Quantify the impact of your solution.

Rule 7: Influence the Reference Point

Influence the buyer's reference point by establishing a benchmark on cost savings. Buyers are skeptical when you provide documented cost savings. A skeptical buyer may downplay the actual number from your original reference point, so you need to proactively influence the buyer's reference point using an anchor.

Before moving on, consider the following experiment adapted from Daniel Kahneman's *Thinking, Fast and Slow*.[8] Without consulting Google, answer these two questions:

- Are there more or less than 16 member countries of the United Nations?
- How many member countries are there in the United Nations?

You might be wondering, "What does this have to do with selling through tough times?" Just bear with me and you'll see.

Whether you know it or not, you were primed to answer the first question a certain way, all because of that number 16. This randomly selected number set an anchor in your mind. Your reference point (or anchor) is 16 countries. You know that there are more than 16 member countries of the United Nations, but how many are there?

The magic happens with the second question. Without consulting Google, few of you could answer this question correctly, but you made an educated guess. Or did you? Because I have anchored you to the low number of 16, you were more likely to guess a lower number than a higher number (40–80). The reference point was intentionally low to influence your guess to be a lower number.

What if I had anchored a separate group to a higher number, such as 210? Ask a friend or colleague to answer these two questions:

- Are there more or less than 210 member countries of the United Nations?
- How many member countries are there in the United Nations?

I'm guessing your friend responds by saying that there are fewer than 210 members. But when your friend guesses the actual number, he or she is more likely to guess a higher number (150–180) than a lower number. The response was influenced by the higher anchor.

The *anchoring effect* is a common cognitive bias. We rely too much on the primary or first information as a benchmark, influencing subsequent decisions. Anchoring is seen all around us. You can use the impact audit as an anchoring tool in your presentation. Establish the reference point by setting the anchor.

Imagine meeting with a buyer and saying, "Our audit shows that we can save your company $80,000 this year by incorporating a different solution." Initially, the buyer might be suspicious of your number. You would then follow up your statement by saying, "Why don't I walk you through the specific cost savings and you can share your thoughts."

The decision maker might challenge you on your calculation, and he or she rightfully should. Bear in mind that your estimated cost saving established an anchor in the buyer's mind. The buyer might think, "This solution doesn't bring $80,000 in cost savings; it's more like $50,000. But that's a significant number." A higher anchor point raises the buyer's expected cost savings. Be prepared to explain and justify your results to the buyer.

This is an effective tool for setting yourself up as the benchmark in the negotiation. Imagine that a buyer is analyzing a few different proposals and believes that your solution saves the company $50,000. However, the competition did not bother to set an expectation. Your value-added impact becomes the standard on which every other option is graded. You immediately separate yourself from the pack. The goal is not to set an unrealistic expectation—set the right expectation. The deeper you dig, the more value you can quantify.

Anchoring also applies to pricing your solution. Flexibility is critical in tough times—flexibility in support, service, and the packages you offer customers. Customers like options. Use a good-better-best model to present your solution. If you anticipate pricing pushback on your recommended solution, begin with a premium option to set the anchor. Place your recommended option in the middle. Offer a chopped-down version as the least expensive option. Chances are the buyer will choose the middle. The goal is to provide buyers with three options to satisfy their needs. Recommend the option that is the best fit relative to the buyer's needs.

SUMMARY

Persuading in tough times requires a deeper commitment for buyers to act. Buyers are tempted to hit the pause button during tough times and tighten their grip on the status quo. Persuasion is a proactive effort to surround buyers with the right information as they make their decision. Craft a narrative that aligns your value with the buyer's definition of value.

Buyers are more likely to accept a change in the status quo if that change is familiar to them. Familiarize your buyers with your total solution, including yourself. Buyers make decisions based on precedent. Use parallels to demonstrate the familiarity of the buyer's decision.

Buyers are more likely to change when they see tangible results. Many of your value-added extras are implied in your solution but may not be perceived by buyers. Quantify the value of your solution, and highlight the impact it has on customers. Quantified value is more impactful and persuasive.

Tough-Times Persuasion Template

This persuasion template provides you with seven tips to be more persuasive in your next presentation. Use this template to prepare and persuade your buyers more effectively. Visit www.ToughTimer.com for a downloadable template.

Build Familiarity

- Connect and comment on social media.
- Create and share content.
- Participate in professional associations.
- Share social proof.

Align Your Solution with the Customer's Definition of Value

- How does this customer define value (quality, performance, service, etc.)?
- How does your solution align with the customer's definition of value?
- What specific action will you take to promote your alignment? (Refer to the "Align Your Solution with the Customer's Definition of Value" section of this chapter for a complete list of ideas.)

Remove Barriers that May Impede Your Progress

- How can you make it easier for buyers to select your alternative?
- Identify what barriers get in the way of persuading buyers.

- What action will you take to remove those barriers? (Refer to the "Lower Resistance" section of this chapter for some ideas.)

Raise the Buyer's Expectations

- What big promises will you make to your customers?
- What additional services and support can you offer?

Use an Analogy to Inspire Buyers to Act

- Broader economic analogy
- Market-leader analogy
- Investment analogy
- Previous-downturn analogy

Quantify the Value of Your Solution Through an Impact Audit

- Detail how your solution improves profitability or cash flow.
- Detail how your solution reduces costs.
- Explain how your solution creates new opportunities.

Influence Your Buyer's Reference Point

- Set the anchor.
- Offer a good-better-best option.

CHAPTER 11

Partner

Old wooden ships sail using basic design principles. The massive sails catch the wind. A sail is connected to a vertical pole called a *mast*. There could be several masts depending on the size of the ship. A mast attaches through the deck to the base of the ship. It's mind-boggling that wooden ships could withstand the tumultuous oceans and turbulent storms. Imagine the strain placed on a mast as the wind howls. What keeps the mast in place? Well, it turns out that ships are designed to withstand howling winds because of a partner. In nautical terms, a *partner* is a timber framework secured to and strengthening the deck of a wooden ship around a hole through which a mast passes. The partner strengthens and reinforces the deck hole where the mast passes through. If there were no partner, the mast would rip open the deck when under strain. The partner keeps the mast intact, enabling the ship to move forward. It's easy to partner in good times, just like it's easier to sail in calm waters. Partners are only tested in the storm of tough times.

In the business world, sellers and buyers partner by working together toward a common goal. In tough times, customers need your support and strength, acting as partners on a ship, keeping their mast intact.

Tough times create a unique opportunity to bond deeper with your customers. The pain of tough times pulls people apart or brings them closer together. Those who experience tough times together develop a camaraderie—a feeling of "we made it through this." Consider a tough time in your life. There were people with whom you developed a closeness. You personally grow through tough times, and so do your relationships. You don't have these opportunities in good times. Tough times are good!

Have you noticed that some sellers have deeply rooted, unflappable relationships? These sellers develop an unshakeable bond with their customers.

New sellers are eager to build those strong relationships and ask, "How do I do it?" Relationships require integrity, empathy, follow-through, putting others first, and time. Strong, unshakeable relationships also require one more element—tough times.

Take an inventory of your current relationships: friends, family members, colleagues, spouse. Ask yourself, "Which relationships are the strongest?" This significantly trims the list. Analyze the list and ask yourself, "What do all these strong bonds have in common?" There are several factors, such as trust, loyalty, integrity, and so on. But you will notice another factor—tough times. When you are at your worst, someone on that list is at their best for you. Just as you grow through tough times, your relationships grow through tough times.

On the surface, many sellers have good relationships with their customers. Buyers and sellers are cordial and enjoy doing business with one another. These are not bad relationships; they just lack depth. Tough times force us to remove the facade and create a level of authenticity. Through tough times, sellers and buyers appear more human and vulnerable. Connecting at that depth creates a unique bond bolstered by trust and authenticity.

You'll notice, after any tough time, that people demonstrate a stronger sense of community and caring. Consider the devastating events of September 11, 2001. Typically, the streets of Manhattan are hustling and bustling; keep your head up and keep moving, rarely acknowledging anyone. It was reported, after 9-11, that New Yorkers showed a stronger sense of community and caring for one another. New Yorkers were greeting and acknowledging each other. There was an authentic level of concern among those who experienced the event. It's because they made it through something together.

Although tough times are unwelcome, they create relationship-building opportunities. Tough times tap into our need for social connection. We crave it. This survival technique is deeply imprinted in our psyche. We need each other. This was most evident during the COVID-19 pandemic. Social distancing protected our physical health but deteriorated our mental health. People would sing from balconies, organize drive-by celebrations, host virtual happy hours, and applaud frontline health workers. These events underscore what we genuinely need through tough times—people.

As you navigate tough times, build deeper bonds with your customers. Once you bleed with your brothers and sisters, you become stronger together.

Tough times are deeply imprinted in our memories, and so are the selfless acts we experience in tough times. Your customers will remember the tough times. What will they remember about you in those tough times? In this chapter, we'll explore the two key dynamics of partnering with customers through tough times: protecting and deepening the customer relationship. Protecting and deepening your customer relationships generate loyalty well past the present tough times.

PROTECT

There's an old expression, "the wolf at the bottom of the hill is hungrier than the wolf already on top." The wolf at the bottom is scratching, clawing, and climbing its way to the top, whereas the wolf at the top can rest and enjoy the view. So when the hungry wolf climbs to the top of the hill, who do you think is better prepared to fight? The wolf that has been resting or the battle-hardened wolf that has been climbing? Your competitors are like the hungry wolf climbing the hill. As hard as you worked to win your customers' business, there is a competitor scratching and clawing to steal that business from you.

During good times, sellers get complacent. Complacency can egregiously appear as neglect or mildly appear as indifference. Some sellers take their top customers for granted. They stop looking for ways to create value, thinking, "Why do I need to create more value? They are happy with my service. They're not complaining." Why should the seller change if everything is working? Complacency creates vulnerability, not value. Compare your effort and eagerness to those of your top competitors. Customers also compare your effort and eagerness to those of your competitors. Buyers may challenge your commitment, wondering, "Why isn't my current provider working this hard to keep my business?"

As times get tougher, your competition pursues your customers more aggressively. These competitors may offer similar value at deeply discounted prices. Whether that value is real or perceived, buyers begin to question your solution's fairness to what the competition is offering. Price is only an issue in the absence of value. Fairness is relative to the price paid and value received. However, competitors disrupt the balance. They offer similar value at cheaper prices, making your solution seem less fair. This is called the *equity gap*—the gap between your price and the value the buyer receives. A new competitor offering a cheaper price widens that gap. A wider gap creates a window of opportunity for your competition. As the gap widens, your customers become more open to your competitors' solutions. Even the most loyal customers cannot restrain a wandering eye when the deal looks so attractive.

Protection is about blocking out the competition and closing that equity gap. Protection is about eagerly and earnestly looking for ways to create more value for your customers—like when you were a hungry wolf. Imagine if you treated your best customer like they were your best prospect? You would tap into the hunger that initially drove you to the top of the hill. Find that motivation and use these techniques to protect your strong customer relationships.

Regenerate Value

What if the only way to regenerate is through a path of destruction? Destruction creates opportunities to grow. Nature is filled with parallels that provide hope during tough times. Consider a lodgepole pine. This persistent tree can grow in some harsh environments. However, lodgepole pines have trouble reproducing because their seeds are sealed in a thick, hard cone. The cone is so thick it does not break down enough for the seeds to take root. The seed is only exposed when there is extremely high heat—like a forest fire. Lodgepole pines require devastation to reproduce. Similar to lodgepole pines, the devastation of tough times provides fertile ground for sellers to regenerate value. The more value you generate, the more you protect and strengthen customer relationships.

Regenerating value for existing customers is more challenging than you think. When you regularly interact with the same customers, opportunities to improve hide in plain sight. You'd like to create more value, but you're unsure how to do it. Because you cannot change the customer's environment, you must change the way you view it. View your existing customers with a fresh set of eyes.

To gain a new perspective, sell against yourself. Selling against yourself means approaching an existing customer as if you were the competition. If you are selling against yourself, you're more likely to find gaps in your solution. You would look for weaknesses and present new offerings. You would uncover new ways to serve the customer. Here is a list of questions to consider as you sell against yourself:

- What additional value-added support can we offer this customer?
- What weaknesses will our competitor find in this solution?

- What are the common challenges/problems the customer is experiencing?
- Is there a better solution that we should be offering?
- How can we make it easier to do business with our company?
- What does our customer dislike doing that we can do for them?
- What is missing from our current solution?

If you're still struggling to find ideas, trade places with a colleague or manager. Fresh eyes have a better chance of uncovering an overlooked opportunity. Conduct a joint call with one of your colleagues or managers. Let the customer know that your colleague will serve as a fresh set of eyes. For example, "Mr. Customer, I have managed your account for several years. I value our partnership. I'm looking for ways to improve our level of service, but because I call on you frequently, those opportunities might hide in plain sight. So I'd like to invite in a colleague of mine to bring a fresh perspective. I'm still your main contact, but I would like her to identify some ways we can create more value. What are your thoughts?"

Customers welcome and appreciate these opportunities to grow. This demonstrates both humility and professionalism. This team-selling approach further demonstrates your commitment to the partnership.

Rediscover

Discovery is a dynamic process of uncovering and understanding your buyers' needs. Your customers' needs will change with the prevailing times. Your competitors are looking for any trigger event to open a discussion around the buyers' needs. Tough times force us to adapt, evolve, and enrich the partnership with our customers. The longer your customers use your solution, the more likely it is that their needs have changed. Use the prevailing times to trigger your discovery, not your competitors'. "Ms. Customer, you've been a valued partner of ours for several years. Needs change over time based on the dynamics of your industry. Let's have a discussion on what has changed." Here are some sample rediscovery questions to generate a discussion.

- What are the three most significant trends impacting your business right now?
- How has the new economic environment impacted your business (goals, initiatives)?

- What are your new priorities moving forward?
- If we started from scratch, what would the ideal solution look like?
- What significant changes have you experienced over the past six months?

Rediscovery creates an opportunity to unearth new needs your buyers didn't know existed. A true partner keeps pressing until he or she is confident that the partner is taken care of. Remember, if you provide your customers with the best solution (not just your previous one), you effectively lock out the competition.

Complimentary Services

Customers look for the greatest value in tough times. They want the biggest bang for their buck. Buyers are now more open to your services. Even if customers are familiar with your value-added services, reeducate them. Buyers forget about offerings if there is no immediate need. As their value-added partner, it's your duty to familiarize your buyers with your complimentary services in tough times. You're simply reminding your customers of what you promised them on the front end.

In tough times, customers have more time on their hands. We all have that "someday" list. Customers tell you, "*Someday*, we'll have enough time to get started on that project, or that training, or that _____." Well, in tough times, someday is today. During tough times, buyers are looking to take advantage of services that require only time as an investment. Make a list of all the complimentary products and services you have available, and present that list to your buyers. The buyers will appreciate your support and remember your offer when times are good.

When offering your complimentary, value-added services, don't use the word *free*. *Free* is the worst four-letter F-word you can say in sales. Whatever follows the word *free* cheapens it. People place less value on free things. The words *complimentary* and *no-charge* evoke a different response and build perceived value.

Prioritize

Do your customers feel like they are a priority? Tough times disrupt supply chains and create shortages. There are countless examples of shortages throughout history, whether it's coins, metals, rubber, oil, and so on. The most notable example is the recent shortages from the COVID-19 pandemic: toilet paper, paper towels, hand sanitizer, disinfectant spray. In the business-to-business setting, many customers were looking to their suppliers for face masks, shields, hand sanitizer, and other personal protective equipment (PPE). It seemed like every company was selling face masks and sanitizer.

One seller was flooded with calls from prospects that previously turned him down. This seller decided to demonstrate how he prioritized customers in a public way. The seller posed and then answered this question on LinkedIn: "Why buy from my company?"

In his post, he explained that all his customers who bought their disinfectants, PPE, and paper products will continue getting their products. He mentioned that his phone was ringing off the hook from companies that previously turned him down to go with national suppliers because they were less expensive. The same companies that turned him down because his solution was 5 percent higher were now begging him to fill their orders. The seller could've shuffled around inventory and charged a premium. He could have leveraged the new situation to create significant growth opportunities. But doing this would have jeopardized his ability to serve his existing customers. So he chose to take care of his existing customers first.

In this one post, the seller demonstrated who the priority was—his partners. In tough times, customers won't remember every detail, but they'll remember how you made them feel. If you made them feel like they were a priority, they'll reward you with continued loyalty. Never sacrifice long-term partnerships for short-term profit. Those tempting moments are the true tests of a partnership.

Value Remind

Even the most loyal buyers question their buying decisions—especially during tough times. Other stakeholders scrutinize and question the buyer's previous decisions. Buyers must justify their decisions to anyone in doubt, including themselves. Through tough times, buyers' preferences focus on what they must have versus what is nice to have. Your challenge is to convince your buyers—and everyone else—that your value is a necessity, not just a nicety.

When buyers make big decisions, there is a higher risk of buyer's remorse. The risk of buyer's remorse is even greater during tough times, especially when buyers must choose between several viable options. *Value reminding* is an effective way to mitigate buyer's remorse. This technique has been widely used in the automobile industry. Much of the advertising dollars spent are to reinforce the new car owner's previous buying decision. Satisfied car owners tell their friends.

There are several ways to reinforce the value you deliver. For example, send your customer a thank-you letter and highlight the value-added extras you offer. The letter is one way to surround the buyer with all the value you deliver. With your value top of mind, the buyer feels justified in the decision to partner with you. You can also conduct a thorough business review. In this exercise, you simply review your value-added extras with your customers and ask them to deliver feedback on your performance. As your buyers share glowing feedback, they are reminding themselves of your value. Organize a tour of your facility, and introduce your customers to the behind-the-scenes team. Connect your customers to the team that creates the value they receive. Buyers learn to appreciate the effort behind the value you deliver. This further justifies their decision and the fairness of your solution.

The grass isn't greener on the other side, but buyers are curious about what they are missing. This curiosity creates a new interest in the competition. Buyers may meet with the competition or even try their solution. They're not dissatisfied with your solution; they're just accustomed to it. The value you deliver is expected, and your buyers start to take your value for granted. To prevent a wandering eye, remind your customers of your value.

Proactive

During tough times, you are overwhelmed with fires to extinguish. We love using the analogy of a firefighter responding to the situation. We extinguish the biggest fires and then move to the next. It's like we're always playing catch-up. It doesn't have to be this way; even firefighters take proactive measures to contain wildfires. In a wildfire, firefighters start backfires, which are small, contained fires to burn the trees and brush in advance, depriving the advancing fire of fuel. This proactive measure controls what many think is uncontrollable. How can you more proactively fight fires in your business?

During tough times, buyers are more passive and defensive, waiting to see what happens and then responding. This natural response to tough times is temporary, but it can create a domino effect up and down the value chain. For example, suppose that you have a customer who requires shorter turn-around times so that he or she can reduce inventory costs. This means that you'll have to respond quicker, using more of your resources and leaning on your providers. As different stakeholders are more passive and responsive, it creates more pressure on sellers. With all that pressure, eventually someone is going to fold. There is a better way to manage this pressure.

What if you proactively anticipate your customers' needs before they surface? This creates a symbiotic relationship where buyers and sellers work together. This proactive approach is about making things happen, not waiting for things to happen. Proactive sellers anticipate needs by leveraging their expertise and empathizing with their buyers. Ask yourself, "How can I take this project or request one step further for my customer?"

One of the most visited pages on any website is the "Frequently Asked Questions (FAQ)" page. Buyers have the same questions running through their minds. Your website might not have an FAQ page, but what if you use the concept to proactively support your customers? Make a list that addresses the most common questions buyers ask. Then share that list with your customers. You're answering questions before they even ask. What could be more proactive?

DEEPEN AND BROADEN

When trees experience a drought, their roots grow deeper into the ground to find water. The root-to-shoot ratio increases. With a deeper root system, the tree fares better in the long run. Hence the phrase, "Strong roots bear good fruits." How strong are your roots with your customers?

Like trees facing a drought, you too can deepen your relationship roots in tough times. Tough times strip down the superficial aspects of any relationship. They cut to the core of what it means to be human, creating an opportunity to authentically bond with customers. Our research shows that more and more people get involved during tough times. This means more opportunities to build deeper, genuine relationships with customers. More decision makers present a unique opportunity to permanently create deeper roots. You won't get this opportunity in good times. Tough times are good!

Create More Internal Champions

In Chapter 8, we mentioned internal champions. Internal champions are your raving fans. Internal champions do not have buying authority; their clout stems from their high opinion of you and your solution. These internal champions create an opportunity to protect and deepen your partnership with your customers.

Internal champions are most affected by change. They might be end users giving feedback to their boss or supervisors managing a group of workers. Internal champions feel the pain of tough times and are filled with uncertainty. Your ability to provide stability goes a long way.

Do your best to make internal champions look like heroes to their bosses or their teams. This builds a deep and personal loyalty. When your internal champions feel like heroes, they navigate tough times with more hope and certainty. Publicly praise your internal champions. Highlight their role in any success. Brag about them to their supervisors. However, you do it, make them look like heroes. Make your internal champions look like heroes to their bosses, and they'll make you look like a hero to yours.

Level-Adjacent Relationships

"How big is your relationship with your best customer?" Early in my career, my sales manager asked me this question. At first, I didn't understand, so I started describing my relationships in the account. My manager could tell that I was struggling to understand the question, let alone answer it.

He explained, "When I say *how big*, I want to know how broadly you have connected the customer to our company. I'm sure you have good relationships with the right people, but what about our inside sales team or our technical department? Have you connected your contacts to them?"

Now it made sense. It wasn't about me connecting with customers; it was about connecting my customer to other contacts within my company—creating a bigger relationship. Every customer has needs extending beyond the ability of the salesperson. This is why you have a team in place to support you. The more contacts your customer has, the stronger the bond between your companies. A true partnership means marrying the customer to the entire company, not just the salesperson.

During tough times, your customers are tasked to do more with less. They need a stronger show of support from you and your company. They need direct access to the support network. In tough times, customers don't have the patience for you to be the conduit for all requests. The solution is simple: connect your contacts to your team.

Wouldn't it make sense to have your tech people talk to their tech people? Wouldn't it make sense to have your inside sales team coordinate logistics with their procurement team? Wouldn't it make sense for your quality control people to work with their quality control people? The answer is yes. *Level-adjacent relationships* create value and build partnerships. Facilitating level-adjacent relationships grows your influence exponentially and strengthens the bond between your organizations. As you map out your relationship with your existing customer, identify the level-adjacent counterpart within your organization. Ask yourself, "How can I make a stronger connection between these individuals?"

Every seller has a natural communication style. Some sellers are better at detail work and problem solving; other sellers are better at selling abstract ideas and motivating buyers. Some sellers are better at selling to a business owner than to a technical engineer. In sales, you are a chameleon. However, it's challenging to change what feels natural. Instead of changing, adopt a team approach that plays to everyone's strengths. Engineers communicate more effectively with other engineers. Operations managers communicate more effectively with other operations managers. When building bigger relationships, you don't have to change your personality—simply change the level-adjacent contact.

Level-adjacent relationships create a stickiness factor. Consider how consumers develop a stickiness factor with certain brands. The more products or services you buy from one provider, the less likely you are to leave. For example, if you have an iPhone, iWatch, AirPods, and several chargers, you're less likely to leave Apple. In relationship building, there is a similar stickiness factor. The more level-adjacent relationships you create, the stickier the bond.

Higher-Level Relationships
Tough times are filled with uncertainty. In uncertain times, leaders look for clarity. They are seeking information and processing different emotions in the vacuum of their own organization. This creates a narrow view of the future and their industry at large. Strong leaders recognize their tunnel vision and seek outside information. This means that they like talking to other business leaders.

Tough times are your greatest opportunity to partner at the highest level within your customers' organizations. High-level leaders meet with other high-level leaders. These leaders want to exchange their thoughts, insights, and ideas. Now is the time to coordinate this effort with your leaders and your customers.

In Chapter 8, we mentioned connecting your internal HLDM to your customer's HLDM. During tough times, these high-level decision makers are more willing to meet with your higher-level decision makers. These high-level contacts want to share their insights, ideas, and outlook. Also, your customers want reassurance that your company is there to support them. Who better to reassure your customers than your high-level leaders? Your customers' high-level decision makers may want to share candid feedback about what they need. High-level contacts want to deliver feedback directly to the individual who can implement the change.

Consider other ways to engage your high-level decision makers. Organize panel discussions, focus groups, or open-house events to engage HLDMs. This is an opportunity to connect your higher-level decision makers with a few of your customers, creating a platform to share insights. However you do it, now is the time to deepen your roots by engaging HLDMs.

Building high-level relationships is the final step to deeply root yourself within the opportunity. In developing this relationship, you build an unshakeable bond that will stand the test of tough times and thrive in the future.

SUMMARY

Tough times are unique opportunities to partner with customers and generate long-lasting bonds. Buyers and sellers who struggle together stay together. Tough times provide the opportunity to transition from a solid relationship to an unshakeable partnership.

Relationships are easier in tough times. It's easy to act in the customer's best interest when his or her interests align with yours. Tough times challenge sellers to put the customer first. Like partners on a ship, the true test of strength is through tough times. When you demonstrate your unwavering commitment to your customers, your customers demonstrate their commitment to you.

In tough times, customers may question their purchasing decisions. They are bombarded with competitive promises that seem more attractive. View such times as an opportunity to protect and regenerate value to enhance your customers' experience and strengthen your bond. Keeping it fresh keeps your customers interested.

Use these tough times to broaden your reach. Engage other decision makers by building level-adjacent relationships. Be the matchmaker between your organization and your customers. Every new relationship fortifies the foundation and provides growth opportunities.

The formula for building partnerships in tough times: support your customers, protect the relationship, and deepen your roots. Tough times are deeply challenging and forever imprinted on our minds. Your customers will remember the tough times you experience together. What will they remember about you? Your actions today become tomorrow's memories.

APPENDIX

Tough-Times Partnering Template

Sellers and buyers partner by working together toward a common goal. Through tough times, your customers rely on you to weather the storm. Tough times test the strength of any partnership. Use this template to guide your partnering activities during tough times. Visit www.ToughTimer .com for a downloadable version of this template.

Embrace the Right Mindset Before a Partnering Call

- The purpose of a partnering call is to support and serve, not to sell.
- Be open-minded to new ways to create value.

Regenerate Value for Your Customers

- Create a list of value-regeneration questions. (Review the "Regenerate Value" section for a complete list.)
- Fresh eyes see new opportunities. Schedule a joint call with a colleague or peer.

Rediscover Your Customers' Needs

- Review your customers' needs to see what has changed.
- Create a list of rediscovery questions to uncover your buyers' needs. (Review the "Rediscover" section for a list of questions.)

Remind Your Customers of the Value You Deliver

- Connect your contacts with your internal team.
- Document your value in a thank-you letter.

Proactively Create More Value

- Anticipate your buyers' needs.
- How can you take this project or request one step further for your customer?

Create Bigger Relationships with Your Partners

- Broadly connect your customers to your company.
- Build level-adjacent relationships with your influencers, internal champions, and high-level decision makers.

CHAPTER 12

Leverage

Gravity is the force by which a planet or other heavenly body draws objects toward its center. An object with more mass attracts more objects. When objects are closer to a planet or heavenly body, there is a stronger gravitational pull toward the planet or body. Are your customers gravitating toward you or the competition? Who is likely to attract more opportunities, you or the competition? To keep your prospects within your orbit and not the competitor's, increase your mass by expanding your offerings with your existing customers.

Sales organizations obsess over growth. Growth is a two-part process: acquiring new customers and growing existing customers. Why do some sellers prioritize new-account revenue over existing-customer revenue? A dollar earned from a new prospect or an existing customer might look the same, but it impacts the bottom line differently. So which is better, a dollar from a prospect or from an existing customer?

During training seminars, I'll ask salespeople, "Is it easier to sell more to existing customers or to brand-new prospects?" An overwhelming majority agrees that it's easier to sell to existing customers. I'll then ask, "Is it more profitable to sell to existing customers or to new prospects?" Again, an overwhelming majority agrees that existing customers are more profitable. Bottom line: it's easier and more profitable to sell to existing customers. The cost to serve an existing customer is relatively constant while your margins increase. You have a successful track record and established relationships, and you know how the company decides. You are familiar with the customer and how to efficiently serve him or her. You're selling from the inside, not the outside.

In tough times, success does not have to be as hard as we make it. Use your resources to efficiently grow your business, and expand your offerings to existing customers. For the sake of clarity, *prospecting for new customers is just as critical as selling to existing customers!* However, in the short term, selling to new prospects is less profitable than selling to existing customers. Tough times create unique prospecting opportunities. Your prospecting effort is like buying stocks when the market is down. You'll cash that stock in at a later date for the payday. Selling to existing customers is like a stable annuity that provides cash today.

Leveraging our existing customers provides profit to weather tough times. Jack Welch famously said, "You can't grow long term if you can't eat short term. Anybody can manage short. Anybody can manage long. Balancing those two things is what management is."[1] Although Welch is referring to managers, he could be talking about salespeople. Leveraging existing customers provides the fuel needed today so that you can prospect for future growth. Pursue prospects today who create tomorrow's leveraging opportunities.

Leverage is growing your business with your existing customer base. This means selling to multiple locations and multiple departments, expanding your product mix, or raising prices. Leveraging is a growth and protection strategy. Every additional product you sell is one less opportunity for competitors to weasel their way in. Your competitors are just as eager to sell into your accounts and eventually expand their offerings. Every additional product you sell is like nailing shut the back door to ensure that your customers do not leave and your competitors do not enter.

There are several ways to protect and grow your existing customer base. The purpose of this chapter is not to talk you out of prospecting—it's to talk you into leveraging. Any successful seller must balance his or her approach of pursuing new business and leveraging existing business.

IDENTIFY LEVERAGING TARGETS

Have you ever passed an opportunity and thought, "Why are we not doing more business with that company?" This happens more than you think. As salespeople, we are obsessed with finding the next opportunity, sometimes forgetting that our best growth opportunities are right in front of us—existing customers.

Some sellers unknowingly become satisfied and complacent. In *Good to Great*, Jim Collins writes, "Good is the enemy of great. And that is one of the key reasons why we have so little that becomes great."[2] The same is true for sellers. Good sellers become satisfied with what they are getting.

These sellers are doing well. Why risk it? These salespeople think, "Well, I'm already selling a decent amount here and don't want to appear too greedy." These sellers are satisfied after eating the appetizer and no longer desire the main course. Other sellers simply get too familiar with a customer and miss growth opportunities. They need fresh eyes to see the opportunity. As you get closer to an opportunity, you no longer need binoculars. Instead, you need a microscope to see deeper. Either way, the result is the same: there is untapped potential in your existing customer base. Leverage is about going deeper to uncover new opportunities.

Begin your leveraging campaigns by identifying leveraging opportunities. Develop criteria to identify those opportunities. Here are some sample criteria:

- **Identify customers for whom you have created immense value.** It's easier selling to a customer who has had a positive experience. Build off the success you created for your customer, and look for ways to grow.
- **Identify under-penetrated customers.** Look for large opportunities where you have a fraction of the business. Perhaps you are only selling to one department or selling a smaller part of a much broader solution.
- **Identify customers where you have access to other decision makers.** Every new contact is an opportunity. Depending on your solution, multiple decision makers are involved. The greater your access, the easier it is to sell.

When selecting an opportunity, think in terms of ease and impact. Which customers are easy to grow, and where will you have the greatest impact? Time is the currency you invest. Invest it wisely.

Next, use leveraging questions to uncover growth opportunities. Leveraging requires planning and execution. There are questions you can ask yourself and your customers to identify further growth opportunities. Ask yourself, or your internal team, the following questions to gain a better understanding of your solution:

- What hidden products or services can we offer this customer?
- How can we further customize our solution?

- What new product lines or services can we offer this customer?
- What new solutions could we create for this customer?

The following questions generate a discussion with the customer and reveal additional opportunities. Here are some sample leveraging questions to ask your customers:

- What additional products or services do you need from us?
- What additional problems or challenges are you currently facing?
- What is missing from our offering?
- How could we further customize our solution for you?
- What additional services would you like us to create (training, consulting, implementation services)?

Conduct a capabilities presentation with your customer. This simple presentation is an overview of what your company can do. This presentation should only happen once you have a clear sense of the buyer's needs and have built a strong relationship with the customer. The goal is to educate the customer, not throw things at the wall to see what sticks.

Too often sellers are unaware of the full suite of products and services available. What if there were hidden ways you could create more value and impact your customer's business? To fully leverage an opportunity, you must understand all the ways you create value. Use the previous questions to uncover your full range of capabilities and leverage your opportunities.

STEPPING OUTSIDE YOUR CORE

Don't be afraid to step outside your core. Management gurus and thought leaders emphasize the importance of staying within your core products and services, which is a good strategy, by the way. It's important to stay in your lane, stick with what you know, and fully capitalize on your strengths. What if the market for your core business suddenly becomes less viable?

Tough times create an ever-changing environment, forcing organizations to be nimble and flexible. Be flexible in your value proposition. In our training seminars, one equipment salesperson explained her strategy for selling in tough times. This seller focuses on six-figure deals. However, during recessions, deal sizes shrink, and customers focus on fixing equipment instead of replacing it. The seller was forced to change. Instead of selling new equipment, she focused on selling maintenance packages. This was a far cry from her typical six-figure deal, but it was profitable. The seller acknowledged that every sale she made was one less her competitor could make. She had to temporarily shift focus. While the competition was starving, she still found a way to eat. If you want to stay relevant in tough times, sell what is relevant in tough times.

In tough times, cash flow is critical. Look for products and services that spur quick cash, including old inventory, spare parts, solution upgrades, or additional services. Additional services carry no inventory cost. Talk to your top customers, and identify additional services you can provide these customers. Value-added services are a great way to boost your profits and level of service.

"There is no small part, just small actors." This theatrical mantra emphasizes the importance of each role in a play. The same is true about selling through tough times. Never believe that your role is too small, and neither are the orders you provide. Every order you generate creates positive momentum. Some sellers argue that small opportunities are too big of a hassle. It can either be your small opportunity or your competitor's. Your competition is eagerly trying to infiltrate your best customers; they'll take any window of opportunity. A mouse can fit through a hole the size of a no. 2 pencil. Like a mouse, your competition can weasel its way in through the tiniest hole. By passing on an opportunity (no matter how small), you create an opening for the competition.

Step out of your core by repurposing your products and services. Many solutions can be repurposed and tweaked to go after new segments. Stay light on your feet, and look for those opportunities during tough times. Partner with your management team and product team to discuss opportunities. In every crisis and tough time, there are still companies and industries that are thriving. How can you tweak your solution to target those segments?

Nimble companies thrive through tough times. Be flexible in how you serve customers and your employees. Stanley Black & Decker (SBD) looked for ways to keep its factories going during the Great Depression.[3] As the construction market softened, so did demand for SBD's tools. SBD was flexible and looked for opportunities to keep its manufacturing lines running. So the company converted its factories to make a new toy, Stanlo. It was a building set for kids. SBD made a leap from construction tools to construction toys. This flexibility allowed SBD to profit, pay a dividend, and save jobs. Consider taking a leap in your industry.

LEVERAGE CUSTOMER PROBLEMS

Whenever there are problems to solve, there is profit to gain—for you and for your customers. Tough times create problems. These problems create leveraging opportunities. But to solve a problem, you first need to find it. Unrecognized problems tend to hide in plain sight. Customers (and sellers) don't know what they don't know. Discovering new problems goes beyond simply asking questions—it involves a deep dive into the customer's business.

Solving customers' problems requires understanding their problems. We cannot understand a problem until we first identify that problem. To identify the problem, immerse yourself in the customer's world. This requires assimilation of the business. Identifying problems to solve begins with observing. The deeper you dig into your customer's business, the more value you create. One way to dig deep is through a *problem-solving assessment* (PSA).

A PSA is an investigative tool to identify problems in your customer's business. Once identified, you create a complete solution to solve this problem. This assessment occurs as a result of a series of interviews, project walk-throughs, and observations. Along the way, you will naturally discover opportunities to improve and solve additional problems. Ask your customers these questions while conducting your PSA:

- What are the three most common problems you experience on a weekly/daily basis?
- What common problems have you accepted as unsolvable?
- How have you have attempted to solve these common problems?
- What common complaints do you hear from your management or frontline employees?
- What common complaints do you hear from your customers?
- What new problems or challenges have these tough times created?

Use these questions to interview different levels of decision makers. Also observe the customers and use your expertise to identify problems the customers didn't even know they had.

For example, a salesperson conducted a PSA and determined his customer wasted too much time locating fasteners in the production process. The installer was wasting five additional minutes looking for a five-cent fastener. The installer's loaded wage was close to $30 per hour, or $0.50 per minute. This customer had a problem. The customer was losing $2.50 in productivity looking for a five-cent fastener. The seller realized that this same problem was happening at several other stations. This seller identified the problem and presented a better-organized solution to solve their problem. The seller leveraged his existing business by solving a problem, leading to an increase in profit for the salesperson and the customer.

Once you identify the problem, the key is getting the information to the right people. Large consultancies have mastered this process with executive briefings. Consulting firms generate a report that identifies problems and improvement opportunities. The consultancy then creates solutions to solve the client's problems. This report is then delivered to the executive team—the key decision makers. What if you could create something similar for your customer? Effectively, you are showing the customer a problem and then offering a solution to that problem. Highlight the problem before presenting your solution. You can't sell aspirin until the buyer has a headache.

LEVERAGE PRICE INCREASES

Leverage is about growth—growing your revenue and profit. One way to grow profits is to raise prices. Every dollar increase is pure profit to your company's bottom line. As your price increases, so does your risk. *Price elasticity* refers to how pricing affects the demand of a product. In general, as prices go up, demand goes down. If you raise your prices too high, you could lose some business. But that's not necessarily a bad thing.

Use price increases to weed out your price-shopping customers. Analyze your least profitable customers—the bottom 15 to 20 percent. How much more profitable could you be without those customers? If your business is more profitable without those price shoppers, then increase their price. These profit piranhas chew away at your bottom line. Profit piranhas already pay lower prices, pay their bills later, complain more, strain your resources, and never appreciate all the value you deliver. There is one way to fix this problem: significantly increase the price they pay.

At what price would this business be worthwhile? Look at the profit-piranha customer and ask yourself, "How much more profit would I have to generate to make this customer worth it?" For the right amount of profit, any customer looks better. Raise your price so that the exchange is equitable. Make it clear to the customer that you cannot serve him or her at the current price. Then explain the value you deliver and present new pricing. The buyer might object to the new price, but demonstrate your commitment by holding the line.

Start charging customers for your complimentary value-added services. When buyers have to start paying for these services, they'll be more apprecia-tive. There are two ways to charge for this level of service: raise the price or charge for the à la carte service. Document and analyze the cost and expected margin on these services, and present your customer with a new pricing model. The customer can either pay for the individual services or receive a price increase.

Another way to increase your profit is to make fewer concessions. This includes terms, delivery, order priority, and so on. Stop performing favors for profit piranhas at the expense of serving more viable customers. Some buy-ers call this *funny money* because it's hard to pinpoint the profit impact. Rest assured, late payments, delivery services, and lenient terms cost your com-pany something. There's nothing funny about losing money.

It's okay if you lose this business. Serving too many profit piranhas could force you to lose your own business. Leverage them up with a price increase or leverage them out to the competition. One disclaimer: never resort to this technique unless you are comfortable losing the customer. We are supposed to be empathetic and supportive in tough times, but the relationship must be equitable. Tough times are filled with tough decisions. Consider the long-term implications of serving these customers to the detri-ment of your business. The longer you serve these profit piranhas, the more money you lose. Would you rather trim your bad customers or have to trim your own employees?

LEVERAGE EXISTING RELATIONSHIPS

Every individual is an opportunity to expand your network. Your growth opportunities are only limited by your existing business relationships. Each relationship represents a growth opportunity. If you want to expand your business, expand your relationships.

There are at least five individuals involved in most business decision-making processes. However, it's common for sellers to have only one or two key contacts. You might have great relationships with those decision makers, but that is not enough. The only limit to your growth potential is your relationship network. Build your network and grow your sales. Set a relationship target, not just a growth target. You might have two solid relationships within an opportunity. Challenge yourself to double that number to increase sales.

Salespeople get comfortable calling on the same people. Only meeting with familiar contacts creates a narrow view of the organization's needs. Just imagine the opportunities you could be missing. Some sellers are reluctant to expand their network for fear of offending their main contact. This reluctance is unwarranted. Leveraging relationships means growing laterally into other departments, not necessarily vertically. A true partner wants to see you succeed and should help you expand your network. Meeting with additional contacts poses no threat to your existing contacts.

Each new relationship is an opportunity to grow and protect your business. You will cross paths with many people in your career. Treat people with the respect they deserve. On my podcast, *The Q and A Sales Podcast*,[4] I encourage sellers to treat everyone twice as important as their title suggests. Today's internal champion (advocate) may be tomorrow's high-level decision maker.

The easiest way to grow your network is to ask for referrals. In training seminars, I ask sellers how often they ask existing customers for referrals. Shockingly, more than half rarely or never ask customers for referrals. What a missed opportunity! Getting a referral is like starting on second base. Your referral generates trust and opens doors for you. Referral-based business also reduces the amount and intensity of price objections.

Request referrals from your strongest advocates. These individuals have experienced the value you deliver. These advocates want to help you succeed. During tough times, people want certainty. What could be more certain than a glowing referral from a colleague? Your internal champions provide an unbiased perspective and proof of success. From the beginning, their referral positions your solution as the go-to solution.

Leave your referral request open-ended. The customer knows his or her company and who decides what. Explain what you are trying to accomplish, and ask your referring customer for his or her thoughts. If needed, provide your contact with an overview of additional solutions. Once your contact understands your goal, he or she will connect you with the right people.

There is one more referral source that is often overlooked by salespeople—other salespeople. Reach out to your customers' salespeople. It's easier to ask for their help because they understand your position. They know what it's like trying to meet new contacts and find opportunities. Reach out and build a relationship.

Referrals are an easy way to grow your network. Each relationship you build is another opportunity to grow your business. Referrals don't always happen on their own; they begin with a great customer experience and building solid relationships. A referral is one of the greatest compliments you receive in business.

SUMMARY

It's critical to sell to prospects and existing customers. However, in the short term, selling to existing customers is easier and more profitable. During tough times, this additional profit helps you to thrive, not just survive. Leveraging begins by identifying viable sales targets. Use the criteria from this chapter to identify growth opportunities. Selling through tough times requires stepping outside your core products and solutions. Your fringe products and services are important revenue sources in tough times. Use tough times as a trigger to sell the ancillary items or create new products and services to support your customers.

Any time the customer experiences a problem, there is an opportunity to gain profit—for you and the customer. Schedule a PSA to identify problems the customer is experiencing. Talk to multiple decision makers, and observe the customer. Sometimes problems hide in plain sight, so begin your PSA with a fresh perspective.

Raising prices is another growth avenue in tough times. First, raise prices on your profit piranhas. You cannot afford to serve these customers at the expense of other customers or your business. Identify which customers you can live without, and raise their prices to make the business worthwhile. It's okay to lose some business in tough times; shed the deadweight.

Leverage your existing relationships. Ask your customers for referrals into other departments, divisions, or locations. Referrals open the buyer's mind and lower buyer resistance. Succeeding through tough times is easier than we make it. Reach out to your existing customers, and capture those growth opportunities.

Tough-Times Leveraging Template

L everaging is growing and protecting your business with existing customers. It's easier and more profitable to sell to your existing customers. Every sale to an existing customer is one less opportunity for your competition. Visit www.ToughTimer.com for a downloadable version of this template.

Identify Leveraging Targets

- Create a list of customers where you have opportunity and access and for whom you created value.
- Create a list of leveraging questions to ask these customers. (Sample questions are located in the "Identify Leveraging Targets" section.)

Leverage Customer Problems

- Observe your customers and their processes.
- Interview multiple decision makers for a diverse perspective.
- Review the PSA questions from this chapter.

Leverage Price Increases

- Identify your least profitable customers.
- Increase their prices, charge for value-added services, or minimize concessions.

Leverage Existing Relationships

- Develop a minimum of five good relationships within your top customers.
- Ask for referrals from your existing contacts.

PART III

SELLING AND LEADERSHIP TACTICS

W hat you do daily determines your success—whether you're a leader or a sales professional. Salespeople and sales leaders operate in the tactical world, wanting to know how to achieve their desired success. This final section is a collection of tips for leading and selling more effectively through tough times. In this section, you'll learn to maintain a balanced pipeline, create a precall plan, craft a compelling message, and sell in a virtual environment. In this section, leaders will learn the basic principles of leading through tough times and fundamental tactics to guide their daily effort.

Generating luck through tough times is a wishful title given the lack of conventional luck we experience in tough times. However, luck is not purely coincidental: you have more control over luck than you think. In Chapter 13, you'll learn the two dynamics that generate more luck through tough times: pipeline management and precall planning.

Crafting the right message requires the right words and the right tone. A scripted message falls flat and doesn't work. Messaging principles deeply rooted in empathy will guide the tone of your message. In Chapter 14, you'll learn the two techniques to craft the right words compellingly.

Virtual selling is still selling. Familiar virtual selling tools include phone, email, texting, video conferencing, and social media. Sellers begin their careers selling virtually. These tools aren't new, but their prominence is new. Chapter 15 is a practical guide to selling effectively in a virtual setting.

Leadership is critical through any downturn. The challenging moments you experience are defining moments in your career. Through tough times, salespeople need leaders, not just managers. There is no exact playbook for leading a team through tough times. Each tough time is unique. In Chapter 16, you'll learn three leadership principles that will guide your effort.

The final chapter is a hope-filled message to navigate the uncertainty, fear, pain, and struggle of the tough time you are experiencing. Your tough time may linger after you turn the last page, but the final chapter provides the hope you need to endure the ongoing tough time you face.

CHAPTER 13

Generating Luck in Tough Times

The Roman philosopher Seneca said, "Luck is what happens when preparation meets opportunity." Think of how lucky some sellers get in tough times. These sellers seemingly manufacture opportunities out of thin air. They find ways to crush their quota, while other sellers struggle mightily. Some of these sellers attribute their performance to luck, but their luck stems from preparation and finding opportunities.

In working with world-class sales organizations and their best salespeople, I've noticed a common thread—and it's not luck. The common thread is *activity and preparedness.* When sellers struggle, it's because they are missing one or both of these common threads. If you're not putting in the effort, you have fewer opportunities. No matter how prepared you are to swing the bat, if you take fewer at-bats, you're less likely to hit the ball. Other sellers prospect at a blistering pace but don't prepare. They're more focused on making calls rather than making sales.

Through tough times, there is circumstantial poor performance and avoidable poor performance. There is no excuse for the latter. Highly active and prepared sellers prevail in tough times. The best way to get lucky in sales is to increase your opportunities and prepare for those opportunities. This chapter focuses on filling your pipeline with the right opportunities.

FILLING YOUR PIPELINE

Researchers Shay O'Farrell, James Sanchirico, and Orr Spiegel analyzed 2,494 commercial fishing trips over two years.[1] They classified fishermen into two categories: exploiters and explorers. Exploiters consistently fished the same locations. Explorers, on the other hand, fished a wider range of locations, exploring new opportunities. After their exhaustive study, these researchers concluded that explorers generated more fishing revenue than exploiters, but not during stable, good times. Explorers only had an advantage during tough, uncertain times.

As with other industries, the commercial fishing industry faces tough times. During this experiment, several popular fishing spots were closed to protect an endangered species. During this tough time, exploiters were not sure what to do. It took them longer to find new spots. The explorers, however, had more experience fishing in multiple spots. Explorers are better positioned and outperform exploiters in tough times.

Are you willing to explore new opportunities? Tough times are an ideal time to increase your selling activity and pursue new opportunities. Even in tough times, opportunity is abundant. Tough times are filled with peaks and valleys. We aim to minimize the valleys and extend our peaks. To succeed in tough times, create a steady inflow of new opportunities. New opportunities are critical to maintain balance. Your existing customers won't be enough to carry you through tough times. You must explore new opportunities.

The difference between a full pipeline and an empty pipeline is balance. Selling through tough times requires more activity to achieve that balance. You work twice as hard to get half as much. You need a steady inflow of new opportunities to replace those that stall or fall out. There is no magic number as to how many calls to maintain this balance. However, there is a magic ratio.

A balanced pipeline consists of potential opportunities, qualified opportunities, and red-hot opportunities. To fill your pipeline, qualify your potential sales opportunities, and then convert your qualified opportunities into a red-hot opportunity. The ratio to stay balanced is 6:2:1. You need six potential opportunities, two qualified opportunities, and one red-hot opportunity. Maintain this balance to ensure that you have a steady inflow of opportunities.

A *potential opportunity* is an unqualified lead. It is a lead from your sales manager or colleague. It's a new opportunity that you spot while covering your territory. On the surface, these potential opportunities look like a good fit. You haven't had an in-depth conversation with this prospect yet.

A *qualified opportunity* means that there is a reasonable chance that you will convert the prospect to a customer. You are 50 percent certain the opportunity will buy from you. You have met with various decision makers and believe the opportunity is viable. As you qualify opportunities, some will turn out to be unfeasible. As you weed out less viable opportunities, backfill with new potentials.

A *red-hot opportunity* is likely to buy soon. You are 90 percent confident that you will win the business. These opportunities demonstrate a strong interest in buying your solution. These opportunities demonstrate their willingness by reviewing terms, filling out credit applications, discussing timelines, and making verbal commitments.

This ratio of red-hots to potentials is applicable whether you are managing the number of prospects or sales dollars. For example, if your monthly goal is to generate $100,000 in revenue, every month you'll need $600,000 in potential opportunities and $200,000 in qualified opportunities to create that $100,000 red-hot opportunity.

Once you fill the pipeline, the key is to maintain balance. Balance means that you continuously assess and purge your pipeline. Analyze your opportunities weekly. Determine which opportunities are viable and which are not. Too many sellers hesitate to call a deal dead. They would rather have their pipeline appear healthy and vibrant than honestly assess their reality. These sellers try to convince everyone that their deals are still alive. Their review sessions are eerily familiar to a scene from *Weekend at Bernie's* (Gladden Entertainment, 1989). If a deal is dead, move it out—and move on.

You also purge your pipeline when you win a deal. In tough times, it's important to celebrate your success, but you need to get back to work. It took six potentials and two qualified opportunities to generate that red-hot opportunity. When you do close that red-hot opportunity, you'll need to increase your activity to rebalance your pipeline. Enjoy your success, then find two more qualified opportunities and six more potentials.

Control what you can control in tough times. Control your activity level. Control your effort. You cannot control the buyer's decision, but you can control giving the buyer a choice.

PRECALL PLANNING

Our research shows fewer than 10 percent of salespeople regularly plan their calls.[2] Consider this for a moment: 90 percent of salespeople don't routinely plan. This is an extremely low bar. Before you say, "No. That's not me. I plan my calls," keep in mind that planning is more than thinking about the call. Planning is establishing an objective and detailing how you will achieve that objective. If you kind-of-sort-of know what you want to accomplish on a call but fail to formally prepare, you're not planning.

There are several bogus excuses salespeople use for not planning. Salespeople think, "I don't need to plan. I already know the customer's needs." Assuming that you know the customer's needs asserts that the customer's needs never change. Customer needs are constantly changing, especially in tough times. This mindset precludes you from learning anything new.

Salespeople say, "I don't have time to plan." Think of the irony: salespeople claim that there is not enough time to plan, yet there is time to make another call when your unplanned call is ineffective. Time is the currency you invest. Planning every call ensures the greatest return on your time investment. Other sellers believe that their vast sales experience diminishes their need to plan. These are the salespeople who try to wing it. These salespeople believe that experience trumps preparation and planning. They are wrong.

Some sellers believe that the significance of the call doesn't merit a plan. One seller asked in a seminar, "It's just a drop-in. Do I really need to take 10 minutes to plan this call?" You don't need to plan every call—just the calls you want to be successful.

If any of these excuses sound familiar, stop using them. Precall planning will dramatically increase your success. Our research shows that 95 percent of top achievers routinely plan every sales call.[3] If you want to be a top achiever, do what top achievers do.

The tough-times sales call looks a little different from selling in good times. In tough times, there are additional factors to consider. You must consider how the industry is impacted and how the opportunity is positioned. A tough-times sales call requires extra attention and effort.

Planning is a habit, just as not planning is a habit. Tough times require discipline. Make it a habit to plan every call, and you will be successful. There are several legitimate reasons to lose a sale in tough times, but being unprepared isn't one of them. Precall planning requires zero talent on your part. You do not have to be good at it—just do it. Not planning a sales call demonstrates arrogance or pure laziness. You either think you are so talented that you don't need to plan or you are just too lazy.

Plan every call, and you will be successful. Preparing for a sales call is a simple process, but it requires time. Ask yourself these precall planning questions, and set yourself apart from 90 percent of the general sales population. Many of these planning questions apply equally whether you're selling in good times or in tough times. Download the call planning template at www.ToughTimer.com.

Question 1: What Is My Call Objective?

This question is first because it is the most important question in precall planning. A sales call with no objective is defective. There must be a purpose to your call. A well-thought-out call objective is the foundation for any successful customer interaction.

In sales, the ultimate objective is to sell. However, along the path to success, there is a series of outcomes that culminates in a sale. Identify the small wins leading to the sale. These small wins are your immediate call objectives. Today's small win could be gathering information. Tomorrow's objective may be scheduling a demo. Eventually, your objective is to close the sale. Your primary call objectives are determined by where the buyer is in the decision-making process.

On every sales call, there is a primary objective and a standing objective. The standing objective is to create value for the person you are meeting. Buyers have little patience for sellers who create no value—especially in tough times. Every interaction is an opportunity to create value and stand out from the crowd.

Question 2: How Will I Demonstrate Support on This Call?

During tough times, it's critical to support your customers and prospects. You can demonstrate support in several ways. Review the value-added services you make available to your buyers. Educate your customers on new services that you have available. You may have previously shared this information, but during tough times, customers are more open to your support calls.

Question 3: How Can I Be a Merchant of Hope on This Call?

During tough times, people need hope. Your buyers are surrounded by negativity and uncertainty. Be a positive information source. Before you call or meet with a customer, find good news to share with him or her. It could be an article showing something positive about the industry or the economy at large.

There's an old expression in the media, "If it bleeds, it leads!" The most traumatic, shocking, and negative story is the headline. Negative stories are abundant through tough times, but there is still good news to find. Find an article that provides hope. Scour newspapers and media sources for positive stories.

During tough times, people are hungry for hope. Hope helps you see a brighter future, even when dark days are upon us. You have an opportunity to lift people up. Share a helping of what people are hungry for—hope.

Question 4: How Will I Stretch This Decision Maker's Time Horizon?

Stretch the buyer's time horizon forward and backward. Transporting the buyer into the future enables you to bypass today's negativity. Ask future-oriented questions so that the buyer takes a longer-term view. Stretch the buyer's time horizon backward. Reflect on a previous tough time with the buyer. This reflection highlights how the buyer emerged stronger from a previous tough time. This reflection reminds buyers of their resilience and their progress from the previous tough time. Refer to Chapter 9 for a list of questions and ideas.

Question 5: What Is My Probing Objective?

Often sellers focus more on what to pitch the customer versus ask the customer. This is a seller-focused approach that leads to a pitch-style meeting. Customer-focused sellers center the conversation on the customer by asking the right questions.

The types of questions you ask vary depending on your call objective. Refer to your call objective, and determine what questions you need to ask. Create a list of questions to generate dialogue. Again, you are not reading from a script. Scripted questions seem forced, and buyers put up their guard. Use the questions to generate discussion, not to elicit a certain response from customers. Be flexible as the conversation flows in different directions.

Question 6: What Is My Presentation Objective?

What you present is determined by the buyer's needs. Those needs can change. Be flexible in your presentation. You don't need to sell your entire solution to the buyer; introduce the buyer to your solution in small doses. Organize your thoughts by creating talking points to persuade the buyer.

Think of how your solution impacts the buyer—what is the buyer going to gain from it? Your presentation objective includes highlighting the impact, not just utility. Impact is more compelling than utility. Utility is what your solution will do. Impact is how your solution deeply affects the buyer. Whatever you present, be sure to include the impact.

Question 7: What Obstacles Do I Anticipate?

Obstacles appear at any stage of the selling process. If you're in sales, you're going to hear objections. Buyers might say, "The timing just isn't right" or "We just don't have a budget right now." These objections are common as cash-strapped buyers wait out the tough time. Be prepared to respond to these objections. You can anticipate this resistance without creating an objection.

What common objections are you experiencing? Is it about timing, budget, price? Prepare for these objections before they surface. For example, several buyers tell you that the "timing isn't right." Craft a go-to response like, "I understand that the timing is not ideal, but let's discuss this option while we have some downtime. You might not decide today, but at least we can open up the conversation. At a minimum, we'll review different ideas."

If you regularly experience the same resistance, there is no excuse for surrendering to it. A prepared seller anticipates resistance and gets past it.

Question 8: How Was the Overall Health of This Business Before the Tough Time?

Some companies are better prepared to handle tough times. Financially sound companies see tough times as opportunities. They invest in their business and look for growth opportunities. They might invest in more inventory, expand their operation, or hire more people. Identify these targets, and add them to your list of viable opportunities.

Read industry trade journals, and search a company's news section on their website. Highlight positive and negative news. Companies that were struggling before a tough time are likely to fare worse than more stable companies.

Question 9: How Is This Specific Industry Impacted by Tough Times?

One person's pain is another's pleasure. Tough times affect each industry differently. For example, during the Great Recession of 2008–2009, discount retailers such as Walmart and Dollar Tree did well. Just because some companies are suffering doesn't mean all companies are suffering. Analyze your customer base to determine what industries are performing better. Increase your activity in these industries.

Regarding the two previous questions, staying up-to-date on current economic events helps you gauge how industries are performing—positively or negatively. Read and research daily to answer these questions. Your knowledge helps identify opportunities and neutralize threats.

Question 10: What Action Do I Want from the Buyer at the End of This Call?

There has to be a call-to-action. The call-to-action is what you want the buyer to do at the end of the call, for example, sending information, scheduling a follow-up meeting, or signing a contract. Clearly state the customer call-to-action.

The call-to-action is as important as the call objective. Your sales activity must lead somewhere. In sales, there is no success in standstills. You are progressing forward or stalling out and going backward. Establishing next steps keeps your momentum moving forward.

Before your meeting, write down your customer call-to-action. Before leaving, share the call-to-action with the customer. It's easier to gain a commitment in person rather than via email.

Remember to visit www.ToughTimer.com to download your call-planning template. Commit to planning every sales call. Every call means every cold call, phone call, virtual call, or face-to-face meeting. Precall planning will make you more successful.

SUMMARY

The harder you work and the more you prepare, the luckier you get. This chapter is about maintaining a balanced pipeline of sales opportunities. Achieving balance requires a high level of activity, especially in tough times. Through tough times, you'll have to make more calls to generate the same results. There is no magic number of calls you need to make, but there is a magic ratio: 6:2:1.

As you increase your activity level, increase your planning effort as well. Our research shows that 95 percent of top achievers routinely plan every call, while only 10 percent of the general sales population plan their calls. Plan every call, and you will be more successful. It's really that simple. Precall planning is the closest thing there is to a silver bullet in sales. If you want to be a top achiever, then do what top achievers do.

CHAPTER 14

Crafting Your Customer Message

On April 20, 2010, the Deepwater Horizon oil rig exploded, killing 11 people and releasing oil into the ocean off the coast of Louisiana. It took nearly 90 days to seal off the well and stop the flow of oil. This event was the largest marine oil spill in the history of the petroleum industry. It's estimated that 3.19 million barrels of oil were released into the ocean.[1] During this crisis, hundreds of thousands of seabirds were killed, countless fish died, and ecosystems were destroyed. Thousands of miles of shoreline were impacted. Commercial fishing operations hemorrhaged money. After a rigorous cleanup effort, the environmental impact remains.

One of the most memorable moments in this event was the ill-timed comments of BP's CEO, Tony Hayward. When Hayward apologized for the disruption and devastation, he said, "[T]here's no one who wants this thing over more than I do. I'd like my life back."[2] His comments were tone deaf to the suffering of those impacted by this disaster. Hayward faced immediate backlash. After a few more missteps, BP replaced Hayward as CEO.

In tough times, messaging matters—not only the words but also the tone. People are emotional in tough times, which affects how messages are processed. Salespeople might send the right message with the wrong tone. Or they might have the right tone but cannot find the right words. A compelling message has the right tone and structure.

During tough times, sellers reduce their messaging activity. These sellers are unsure of what to communicate. This lack of communication divides the seller and the customer, creating an opportunity for the competition. Tough times force sellers to tweak their messages. Customers define value differently through tough times. Adjust your message accordingly. Customers still need value in tough times—it's up to you to deliver. This chapter focuses on customer messaging principles and tactics.

CUSTOMER MESSAGING PRINCIPLES

Customer messaging is the initial and ongoing conversation sellers have with customers. How you act, what you say, and how you say it influence the message. Each message is unique based on the seller, buyer, and situation. Given the uniqueness of every situation, you cannot rely on a script. Selling scripts only work if the buyer is following the same script. The following messaging principles provide a general framework to communicate your message in tough times. Messaging tactics help you craft the right words, whereas messaging principles help you strike the right tone.

Communicate with Empathy

Plato wrote, "Be kind, for everyone you meet is fighting a hard battle." This thought is especially relevant in tough times. Every person experiences tough times with a varying degree of pain. Tough times are relative. Tough times also pile up on people. Your message is created from the perspective of buyers. A compelling message must be filtered through an empathetic lens. Empathy is the key to powerful and persuasive messages. Empathy is viewing the world through the eyes of another. It's seeing as they see and feeling as they feel. Empathy provides a customer-focused view. Empathy allows you to deliver your message with the right tone.

Salespeople fight battles in tough times just like customers. Through tough times, you have more in common with your customers than you think. Viewing the world through the eyes of customers is your foolproof way to communicate your message of value. Before sending any message, empathetically proof that message.

In our training seminars, participants imagine what it's like to be a customer. These sellers enter almost a meditative state and imagine their customers' world. The purpose is for sellers to create the right mindset before reaching out to their buyers. You can do the same exercise. It only takes a few minutes.

- **Step 1.** Close your eyes and think of a customer. Write the person's name on a piece of paper.

- **Step 2.** Imagine what it's like to be that person. Use the following questions:
  - What are the person's daily activities?
  - How is this person impacted by these tough times?
  - What are this person's struggles, fears, and concerns?
  - What motivates this person?
- **Step 3.** Now that you have a better understanding of this buyer, how does he or she define value?

This three-step exercise is simple yet powerful. These questions filter your message to remove the seller-focused undertones. Before sending any message, empathize with your customers. Imagine what it's like to be them. Viewing the world through their eyes delivers a deeper understanding of how they define value.

Communicate Impact

As mentioned in Chapter 3, value is calculated using four different variables: price, cost, utility, and impact. Utility is what your product or service does. Impact is how your solution affects the buyer. Buyers care more about the impact of your solution than its utility. Yet, too often, messaging campaigns focus more on utility than on impact. Utility-focused messaging blends in with the competition—further commoditizing your solution. Communicating utility makes you sound like every other salesperson. Customers define value based on your solution's impact, not its utility. Translate the utility of your solution into meaningful impact for the customer.

Imagine sitting across the table from your toughest buyer. You know who I mean—that one buyer who is direct and doesn't mince words. Imagine making a presentation to that customer. When you mention one of your value-added extras, the buyer says, "So what?" This is a simple but powerful question. It is the key to unlocking your solution's impact on the customer. This question cuts through the noise to clarify how your solution affects the buyer. For example:

Salesperson: Mr. Customer, our new ABC 3000 system automates your manufacturing process while enhancing the quality of your widget.
Buyer: So what?

Salesperson: This will lead to greater profitability and increased
     market share. By implementing this system now, you'll gain a
     significant competitive advantage.

The so-what question clarifies the impact on the buyer. The utility is auto-
mating and enhancing quality. Impact is greater profitability and increased
market share.

Your so-what response differs based on the prevailing times. Your solution
impacts buyers differently through tough times. The utility of your solution
remains constant, but the impact changes. In the preceding example, the
ABC 3000 still automates processes and enhances quality in good times
and tough times, but the impact changes. Adjust your message to reflect the
impact that buyers care about in tough times. In tough times, buyers care
about resources, cash flow, and protection.

Continuing with the same example, your so-what response should be
adjusted for tough times. For example, "Our solution will protect cash flow
and reduce labor costs, freeing up resources to invest in other areas of your
business." The first example focuses on growth and profit. In the second
example, the focus is reduced labor cost and protecting cash.

During tough times, utility remains the same, but impact changes. The
impact changes because the customer's mind shifts from an abundance
mindset to a scarcity mindset. In good economic times, customers seek to
grow what they already have. In tough times, those same customers seek to
protect what they have. With a scarcity mindset, customers focus on allocat-
ing resources without waste. Customers are fearful of misusing their scarce
resources. We are reducing loss instead of enhancing gain. In good times,
focus on enhancing gains; in tough times, focus on reducing loss.

Mitigate Risk

In the Great Recession, the auto industry faced a tsunami of change and
tough times. The top American auto manufacturers required a bailout to
keep the doors open. It was not a good time to be in the auto industry. But,
as with any tough time, both winners and losers emerged from the crisis.

Hyundai was one of the winners. Like other auto manufacturers,
Hyundai managers scratched their heads wondering why their traditional
promotions were not working. These incentives had worked for decades.
Why were they not working?

The company researched the issue and realized that people had money and motivation, but they also had fear. Customers could afford the vehicles but were fearful of committing to long-term payments when the future looked so uncertain. Hyundai made a bold move to mitigate risk: they created the Job Loss Protection Program.[3] If a person were laid off within one year of signing this deal, he or she could return the car to the dealership without having to make any more payments. This eased buyers' fear, and Hyundai won. All it took was a little reassurance. Hyundai mitigated risk and enticed customers to buy. Hyundai's market share increased by 40 percent.

In tough times, customers value different aspects of your solution. They have different emotions that drive behavior. Tweak your value proposition to address buyers' concerns. Tough times force you to get creative and adjust your company's value proposition as your customers see fit.

In customer messaging, there are two simultaneous conversations: the conversation you are generating and the conversation in the customer's head. You are sending the buyer a message, but the buyer is receiving that message through a filter of fear, uncertainty, and doubt. A compelling message mitigates the effects of that filter.

TOUGH-TIMES MESSAGING TACTICS

Selling during tough times requires communicating the right message with the right words. These messaging tactics help you find the right words, and the above-mentioned principles help you strike the right tone. This message can be formalized as a leave-behind or one-sheet and also informally as talking points on a sales call. The first tool is the tough-times proposition, and the second tool is the tough-times value audit.

Tough-Times Proposition

The tough-times proposition is a statement emphasizing what the buyer stands to gain while concurrently emphasizing the urgency to act now. Timing is critical in sales, and tough times are no exception to this rule. Buyers are more likely to hit the pause button in tough times. This is why it is critical to establish urgency with the tough-times proposition. This statement establishes relevancy and emphasizes outcomes while at the same time explaining why there is a compelling need right now. Answer these questions to build your tough-times proposition:

- What current problems is the buyer experiencing?
- What potential outcomes could the buyer gain by partnering with me?
- Why is there a need right now for my solution?

Be aware of the tone of your message in your communication. Craft your message with an empathetic response to the tough times your buyer is experiencing. Here's an example of the tough-times proposition:

Seller explaining the tough-times proposition: Today's manufacturers face a unique problem. Increased demand coupled with current labor shortages is forcing companies like yours to do more with less. As the labor market thins, this problem will continue to affect profitability. We partner with organizations like yours to increase productivity and fully leverage your resources.

Tough-Times Value Audit

Who is the best resource to explain what is important to customers? Your customers, of course. The best way to understand how buyers define value is through a value audit. Value audits help you uncover all the ways you add value to your customer's business. In tough times, you bring value in ways you never would have considered.

A value audit is simply a review of all the ways you add value to your buyer's business. This includes all the value your company, your products, and you—the seller—provide the customer. This list serves as a complete menu of value-added extras you provide the customer. As you list your value-added extras, talk to other departments within your company. Thoroughly review the ancillary products and services—especially the hidden or unadvertised products. Create a list of 30 value-added extras. Once the list is completed, review it with your top customers. You're not reviewing this list to try to sell anything. Instead, you're getting feedback on what really matters to customers through tough times. This is a basic voice-of-the-customer (VOC) study. Show your buyers your list and ask them, "Which of these value-added extras are most important to you?"

Here's an example of how you can mention the exercise to your customer: "Given the current tough times, we are gathering feedback to ensure that we are providing the right level of service. Here is a list of 30 value-added extras my company offers. Through these tough times, what are the most important value-added extras on this list?"

Take note of the customer's selections. Leave some blanks for the buyer to share what is missing. Then reach out to your other top customers for their thoughts. As you review your notes, you'll notice some overlapping themes. This overlap provides a deeper understanding of how customers define value. Because your best customers think like your best prospects, you'll know what value-added extras to communicate to your prospects.

For clarity's sake, this list is not a script to sell your value. This list of value-added extras guides a discussion around the buyer's needs and how to satisfy those needs. This list of value-added extras is a collection of talking points to support your tough-times proposition. The following scenario will help explain how the information can be used:

Seller explaining the tough-times proposition: Today's manufacturers face a unique problem. Increased demand coupled with the current labor shortages forces companies like yours to do more with less. As the labor market thins, this problem will continue to affect profitability. We partner with organizations like yours to increase productivity and fully leverage your resources.

Buyer: We are experiencing some of those challenges. We've been trying to solve this problem for several months and have heard the same thing from other providers. So how do you propose to make that happen?

Seller explaining the value-added extras: There are several ways that we help solve this problem, beginning with our technical support team. Our team has more combined experience than any other provider in their area. They will get involved early in the process to identify bottlenecks. Our depth and breadth of products cover a broad range of industries. So it appears that we'll have a solution specific to your industry. Finally, our technical design team will customize a solution around your objectives. Before I can fully explain our value, let's have a more in-depth discussion about your needs.

In the tough-times proposition, the seller explained the problem, the urgency to address the problem, and the outcome the buyer receives. The buyer expressed some interest and challenged the seller to explain how. The buyer wanted to know how you can do it. The list of value-added extras explains the how.

The so-what question explains the impact on the buyer. The so-how question explains how you deliver the outcome you proposed. By answering those two questions, so what and so how, you generate a compelling message. The most persuasive message through tough times identifies the problem to solve, communicates the outcome, and explains how you make that happen.

SUMMARY

Your message matters in tough times, both the words and the tone. There are countless scenarios and dynamics influencing how your buyers receive your message. Therefore, creating a rigid script to communicate your message will not work. Instead of relying on a script, rely on messaging principles to guide your effort. Filter your message through empathy to ensure that your message mitigates the buyer's risk.

Communicating the right words begins with understanding the buyer's problems and challenges. Communicate what the buyer gains when he or she experiences your solution, and establish urgency by explaining why there is a need now. Use a value audit to support your tough-times proposition. Buyers want to know what they gain and how you make that happen.

CHAPTER 15

Virtual Selling

Tough times bring change. The latest tough time has ushered in a way for sellers to connect with customers. "How do I sell virtually?" seems to be the most common question asked by salespeople. Sellers are forced to use new technology to stay connected as they work remotely and socially distanced from customers. This recent pandemic was unlike any other tough time in our history. The tectonic shift to virtual selling was a rough transition for many sellers. Although the virtual environment is different, the principles of selling remain the same whether you're in front of a screen or a person. The transition has been tough, but it's also created opportunity.

Throughout this book, I have highlighted the importance of a customer-focused versus seller-focused approach. Asking, "How do I sell virtually?" is seller-focused thinking. Instead of focusing on selling virtually, focus on how the customer buys virtually. Ask yourself, "How does the customer's decision-making process differ in a virtual setting?" or "What do customers need from us to make better decisions?" These are better questions because they focus on the buyer, not yourself. Whether it's in person or virtual, the customer defines value, and the customer's definition is the one that matters.

Virtual selling is here to stay. One McKinsey study found that 70 to 80 percent of buyers prefer remote (virtual) human interaction or digital self-service.[1] Through the global COVID-19 pandemic, sellers demonstrated their ability to sell virtually. This impacts how we sell during future tough times. During tough times, organizations cut spending in several categories: travel, conferences, and marketing expenditures. Sellers have proven their productivity in a virtual environment.

My training company has tracked face-to-face selling activity for the past 40 years. Over that time, face-to-face selling activity has dropped 60 percent.

People have been selling virtually for decades; it's nothing new. It's just new to a few sellers.

Take comfort in knowing that the selling principles are the same whether face-to-face or screen-to-screen. The selling skills generating your previous success also generate virtual success. For example, world-class chefs such as Gordon Ramsay have home kitchens. Ramsay feels comfortable in his kitchen as he serves world-class cuisine. In Gordon Ramsay's show, *Uncharted*, he travels the world exploring different cultures and cooking methods.[2] Ramsay often prepares meals outdoors over an open flame. He's forced to use different tools and techniques but still creates a delicious meal. Water still boils at 212 degrees Fahrenheit whether cooking at home or over an open flame. The cooking fundamentals—like the selling fundamentals—remain the same.

Although virtual selling is new to many sellers, it has created more opportunity than struggle. Sellers use the virtual selling environment to stand out from the competition by leveraging technology to differentiate the virtual experience. Other sellers take advantage of less windshield time, becoming more productive. Sellers are engaging additional decision makers and involving them earlier in the selling process. A new selling environment coupled with new technology has created new opportunities. Tough times are good!

This chapter is a collection of tips for selling effectively and persuasively in a virtual environment. Focus on the fundamentals, and familiarize yourself with this new virtual environment. The more you apply these techniques, the more comfortable you will be. Happy virtual selling!

CONTROL YOUR PROCESS

Control what you can control; don't let what you can't control distract you. The same is true for virtual selling. Sellers were forced into this new environment, triggering an emotional response. Sellers lamented, "How can I sell my solution if I cannot meet face-to-face? I'll *never* be able to sell this complex solution virtually." Or "The customer will *never* buy if we cannot meet face-to-face." This is more reflective of a poor attitude than a skills gap. Your attitude toward virtually selling drives behavior. Virtual selling is an equalizer event. You face the same challenges your competitors face.

Answer these two questions to objectively view your selling process:

- What selling activities can I accomplish virtually?
- What selling activities must happen in person?

The list of what you can accomplish will be longer than the list of what you can't accomplish. Focus on what you can control; don't lose sleep over what you cannot control. Besides, you were already selling virtually before this shift. Most of your touchpoints were already virtual: your initial emails, a LinkedIn message, sending information, scheduling a meeting, follow-up phone calls, and sending follow-up information. All of this happens virtually. Control what you can control, and get creative on what you cannot.

CREATE A PROFESSIONAL VIRTUAL EXPERIENCE

Tough timers are resilient and adventurous. They take chances and channel their adventuresome spirit to try new things and take on new challenges. This includes creating a standout virtual experience for buyers. Buyers want to work with professional sellers. The virtual selling environment creates another outlet to demonstrate your professionalism. Take full advantage of this outlet.

Curating a space is like setting up the scene in a play. The background matters, the lighting matters, and so does the sound. Background, lighting, sound, and internet connection are the four main ingredients of creating a professional virtual environment.

Background

A simple, organized background goes a long way. View the world through the eyes of your customers and their screens. Set up your workspace, and be aware of what the customer can see in the periphery. Your workspace should be organized and professional.

Proceed with caution when selecting virtual backgrounds. Busy backgrounds are distracting. The same is true for novelty backgrounds of the beach, ocean, or *Tiger King*. The green-screen tech is okay; just keep it professional, simple, and organized. A blank background with your logo or your customer's logo is suitable.

Equally important is the camera angle. Adjust your camera to produce a flattering camera angle. Keep the camera at or slightly above eye level. The lower the camera, the more chins your viewers see. There are several ways to keep it eye level. Use a stack of books, or even purchase a laptop stand. However you do it, just keep it eye level. Also, consider investing in a new 4K video camera. Older laptops have outdated cameras. Create a better visual experience than your competition by investing in a better camera.

Lighting

Lighting is important. Natural light works great to keep your face illuminated. However, avoid placing your back to a window. This blacks out your face, giving the impression that you are in the witness protection program. Direct a light source to your face. Illuminating your face makes the video more realistic. With your face illuminated, the buyer can see your emotions. Record a video conference and tweak your lighting to determine the best setup.

Sound

The right sound is critical on a video call. A well-orchestrated background doesn't matter if the buyer can't hear you. What you say looms larger than what your buyer sees. Nothing frustrates a buyer more than poor audio, whether your audio is scratchy, breaks in and out, or is drowned out by background noise. Quality sound begins with a quality microphone. Invest in the right tools. Then try reducing background noise. Hang soundproofing material (something as simple as a sheet) behind your equipment to dampen background noise and echoes.

Internet Connection

"Can you hear me now?"—the most despised words on any call. How frustrating is it when you're talking on your mobile device, the conversation breaks up, and you lose your signal? It's just as frustrating when your screen freezes or you lose your internet connection. If you're working from home, reach out to your provider for upgrade options. Consider where you set up your virtual space or your wireless router. The closer you are to the router, the better the signal. It's also important to minimize the number of devices connected to your Wi-Fi. The more devices, the slower your speed.

Creating the right space is an opportunity to differentiate your solution and gain a competitive advantage. Do what other sellers deem as too time-consuming or too expensive. Investing in your space creates a better environment. Request the right equipment from your company. If the company won't supply it, invest in the equipment yourself. Use this as an opportunity to stand out and be different. Your professionalism builds perceived value and establishes you as the benchmark on which all other competitors are graded. The more perceived value you create, the higher the benchmark you set for your competition.

PREPARATION

If you have ever conducted a product demonstration, you understand the value of preparation. Before demoing a product, familiarize yourself with it. The same applies when using technology to sell your solution. Repetition generates confidence and competence for sellers. It might be the first time the customer experiences your virtual presentation, but it shouldn't be the first time you experience it. Professionals prepare.

A successful virtual call begins with confidence in your tools. Get comfortable with the technology. The novelty of virtual meetings has worn off. It's no longer funny when you unintentionally mute yourself, show up late, wear your pajamas, accidentally share your screen, or cannot get the tech to work. Familiarize yourself with the technology before the meeting. Create an experience that stands out from your competition.

Before any virtual meeting, send the buyer a basic agenda. An agenda sets the stage for good information exchange. Sending an agenda demonstrates professionalism. One salesperson used video software to send the customer a premeeting welcome. She sent a simple one- to two-minute video introducing herself to the buyer and shared the agenda. This preparation creates a positive image in the mind of the buyer and demonstrates your professionalism.

Most video conferencing services have the option to record the meeting. Record a practice call, and role-play with your sales manager or colleague. This is the equivalent of a pro sports team watching game film to improve. Work with your colleagues to prepare and improve.

Nothing says more about your professionalism than your appearance. The first impression is not created through your words but through your appearance. Dress for the results you desire. Dress how you would normally appear to your customers. If you wear a suit, then wear a suit. If you dress casually, then dress casually. Just be professional. Regarding clothes on camera, busy patterns look blurry and are distracting. Focus on simple, solid colors. Professional sellers take pride in their appearance. Being well groomed and well dressed demonstrates professionalism. Perceivably, individuals who care about their appearance care about their customers as well. When you demonstrate professionalism in one area, it spills over to other areas of your business. Let your competition fumble around and make mistakes. You can be the benchmark.

VIRTUAL GROUP MEETINGS

Have you been on one of those calls where you constantly "hear crickets"? You ask a question to the group but get no response. It is uncomfortable. Not only are these types of calls awkward, but they are also unproductive, packing no persuasive punch.

Virtual selling creates an opportunity to engage multiple decision makers across different parts of the world. This added level of engagement generates broader buy-in and momentum. The key is to control and moderate the process. During tough times, more people get involved in the process. Engaging multiple decision makers means opening your process to more opinions and ideas. Your goal is to generate consensus among the group—on their needs and a direction moving forward.

Maintain control of the group; be direct and clear. Have an agenda, and moderate the conversation. This new, direct style may be uncomfortable to some, but it's necessary. When meeting multiple decision makers, directly call on individuals to answer questions. When the conversation pauses, encourage others to share feedback. When the group gets off topic, focus on generating consensus and buy-in. On a discovery call, encourage an open exchange by sending questions ahead of time. Give participants a chance to think about the topics and prepare. Control the conversational flow, control the group.

ENGAGE

Virtual fatigue is real. When people are fatigued, they mentally check out. Checked-out buyers are not going to buy. To engage your buyers, you need to be engaging. The goal is to create intrigue, not fatigue. Here are some ideas to make your virtual meetings more engaging.

Dale Carnegie said, "Remember that a person's name is to that person the sweetest and most important sound in any language."[3] Use the customer's name frequently. Everyone loves the sound of their own name. When engaging multiple buyers, it's critical to use their names. When people hear their name, it grabs their attention and sparks interest. It's easier to prompt a response face-to-face: you simply look at the person. In a virtual setting, simply mention his or her name.

Don't just look at the screen; look your customer in the eye . . . of your camera. In a virtual setting, let the other person know that you are listening to them. In a live setting, it is easier for buyers to determine whether you are listening or not. They can see your eye contact and watch you take notes. But what about in a virtual setting? Even if you are looking at the screen, it's not the same as direct eye contact.

Look at your camera when you and your customers are speaking. This gives buyers the impression that you are maintaining eye contact with them. If a buyer believes that you are looking at him or her, he or she will remain engaged. If you can, move the gallery screen as close to your camera as possible. In this way, you can still see the buyer. The same is true when you are speaking. Naturally, you'll glance at the screen to gauge the buyer's reactions, but also look into the camera when you are presenting. Buyers believe that you are looking at them, keeping them engaged.

Visually engage buyers with your presentation. People love pictures and videos. If your buyers can read the presentation, there is no reason to meet. Take a minimalist approach when creating presentation slides. Use as few words as possible. If you can replace a slide with a picture, even better. You are the salesperson, not your presentation slides. Those tools support you, not the other way around.

In a conversation, have you ever noticed that when one person leans in, the other person also leans in? This technique also works in a virtual setting. It's called the *lean-in*. As you lean in toward the camera, the listener believes that what you are saying is important. Leaning in alerts the buyer to listen. It's a way to keep the buyer engaged. Highlight the critical points in your presentation. At these points, lean in toward the camera. Be aware of getting too close. If the buyer can smell your breath or you're fogging up the camera, you're too close.

Have you ever noticed that most TV marketers stand instead of sit? Standing creates more motion, and motion creates emotion. The more exciting your presentation, the more your buyers will engage. Consider standing versus sitting during your next video sales call.

If you're in a group setting, use virtual breakout rooms, polling tools, or gamification software to drive engagement. Turn your meeting into a gaming event. This might sound a little hokey, but gamification of any event drives engagement. One seller demonstrated how he conducts product demonstrations with multiple decision makers. He decided to use gamification software to quiz participants after the meeting. Whoever scored the most points won the game. This is a unique way to tap into peoples' competitive spirit and increase engagement.

Decision makers may hesitate to hear feedback in a large virtual group. Use breakout rooms or polling software to gather feedback. If you are presenting to a group of 10 decision makers, ask polling questions to gather feedback or create smaller breakout rooms to keep the group engaged.

Finally, shorten the meeting. Brevity is key on calls. If meetings drag on, people disengage. It's easier to keep people engaged in shorter meetings. Meetings don't need to be long to be effective. When you send a meeting request, only ask for the time you need. Resist the urge to plan in 30- or 60-minute blocks. If you believe that a meeting will only last 20 minutes, then request 20 minutes. Work expands to the time allotted. Keep the meeting short and engaging.

SUMMARY

Tough times create new opportunities. Virtual selling is one of those opportunities. This shift allows sellers to connect with multiple decision makers more efficiently and in multiple locations. Sellers embracing this temporary shift have packed their tool chest with more ways to sell effectively. This new shift has created new opportunities, but the principles of selling and persuasion remain constant. Approach this new shift with the right mindset and the right tools.

CHAPTER 16

Leadership Through Tough Times

I really believe that when 2020 gets here we're gonna
look back and this is gonna have been the best decade
in Clemson football history. That's what I believe.

—DABO SWINNEY, Clemson head coach[1]

Clemson head coach Dabo Swinney was commenting on his vision for Clemson football. The content of this quote is not overly inspiring, but the timing is. He didn't say this after Clemson won its first National title in 2016 or its second National title in 2018. This comment was made during the 2010 season—his *worst* year as Clemson's head coach. Despite the media and all the negativity circling Swinney, he committed to his vision and achieved it.

Imagine that you were a player on Swinney's 2010 team. What would that comment mean to you? How inspired would you feel?

Tough moments are defining moments in your career. Similar to Swinney, you experience tough seasons. Whether it's a recession, a tough competitor, or a tough team, you experience tough times. The tough moments you face as a leader are defining moments in your career and those of your team members.

Great leaders create other great leaders. As you lead through tough times, you look to previous great leaders for learning points. You glean all you can from leaders who prevailed in tough times. The past offers a window to the future. What you learn from previous leaders serves you well as you lead. Your leadership through this tough time serves as future memories for those you are grooming to lead.

Leaders set the tone in any organization—positively or negatively. The same way that sellers lead customers through tough times, you lead your sellers through tough times. Tough times are a great leadership and coaching opportunity. Tough times represent an opportunity for teams to come together. Tough times open your salespeople to coaching and feedback.

For many leaders reading this book, you are experiencing your first tough time. You don't have previous experience on which to rely. This is not a bad thing. Out of necessity, you'll become stronger. You'll become more curious about your potential. Tough times reveal skills and traits that you never knew you had. Tough times are good!

Hopefully, you will have only a few of these tough times through which to form, rebuild, and develop your team. This chapter aims to help you uncover your inner strength as a leader and further provide basic leadership principles through the tough times you face.

LEADERSHIP PRINCIPLES

In his book, *The Hard Things about Hard Things*,[2] Ben Horowitz accurately describes the problem with many business books. These books focus on running a business in good times. This book echoes that theme in selling through tough times. It's hard to know what to do until you experience tough times. This chapter focuses on three basic principles to guide you through tough times. These principles are timeless and global. Regardless of the industry or the depth of your tough times, these principles will keep you on track or get you back on track.

Principle 1: Put Others First

Where is your focus? Are you focused on yourself or the team? Sales leaders, like sellers, can easily succumb to the pressure and focus on themselves. Sales leaders also operate from a scarcity mindset. With a scarcity mindset, self-preservation instincts kick in. Through tough times, the focus must be team preservation not self-preservation. As the leader, you drive the focus. You determine where to focus your team's attention.

Leaders face unique challenges in tough times. You face pressure at several different levels: pressure from senior leadership, Wall Street, your team, or your customers. This pressure piles up. Strong leaders try shielding their team from this pressure—doing more harm than good. The pressure you experience creates the context for your sellers to understand the actions you take as a leader.

Instead of shielding your team, keep the team informed through tough times. Tough timers rise to the occasion when more is at stake. Transparency creates authenticity. Shielding your team creates another problem. In some ways, you internalize the pressure, bringing your focus inward. While looking inward, you can't look outward. Keep your focus outside of yourself. View the world through your team's eyes. This view provides a deeper understanding of your team. Pontificating about your "good ol' days" as a seller and how you sold through struggle doesn't help. Resist the temptation to lead until you have listened and learned.

The best sales leaders focus on serving others. They humbly view their role as a servant and view serving as a privilege. In working with great sales leaders, I've experienced this service-minded leadership firsthand. One client in the construction industry continuously demonstrated his service-minded leadership. This company's values are deeply rooted in service—to the team, to customers, and to the community. The sales leaders demonstrated this on several occasions with some small gestures.

For example, when I would set up the training room, one of the sales leaders always helped. He would pass out learning materials when needed. The sales leaders were always last in line to get their meal, fill their coffee, and use the facilities on breaks. They were there first and always the last to leave. On the final day of training, the sales leaders even picked up the trash from the day. This humble act proved their authenticity because there were no employees around to see them do it. These leaders continuously humbled themselves whether their team saw it or not. Simple acts send strong messages.

Most leaders know the importance of focusing on others and not themselves. However, the higher you go in an organization, the greater you risk looking inward versus outward. Your vantage point must extend to the furthest employee. The greater the distance between you and your team, the higher you risk focusing on yourself. In tough times, close the distance between you and your team.

Throughout tough times, you experience challenges. These challenges tempt you to focus on yourself versus others. Those tough moments are defining moments. Step outside your comfort zone; let yourself be vulnerable. The further you get from your comfort zone, the closer you get to your next breakthrough.

Principle 2: You Get What You Expect

"This is our most difficult service to sell. Customers have trouble understanding this service because it's brand new to the industry. There is nothing out there like it." This is what my sales manager told me at a regional sales meeting. We were tasked with selling a new service. And as you likely guessed, we struggled. A month after this meeting, a new salesperson was promoted to join our team. He had no problem selling the new service. He sold more than the rest of the team combined. At our monthly review, the same sales manager said to the new seller, "It's hard to sell this new service. Everyone is struggling. How are you doing it?" The new seller responded, "I didn't know it was supposed to be difficult." The sales manager set the expectation that it was difficult, and for those who attended the meeting, it was. Expectations are a funny thing—you get what you expect.

As a sales leader, think of the times when you inherited a team. The previous manager identified the top performers and the underperformers, setting an expectation in your mind. That newly set expectation inadvertently influenced your behavior. You treated the top performers one way and the underperformers another way. Your expectations influenced their behavior.

In tough times, there is a dangerous precedent many managers accept: it's okay to expect less during tough times. It's not. If you expect less, that is precisely what you will get. Never let your team believe that it's okay not to perform. Expect your team to perform at its best. The team's best may not deliver the desired result, but expect the best anyway. People rise or fall to the expectations you set.

If your sellers are in a tough spot, don't let them off the hook. Help them believe. If your sellers feel helpless and hopeless, believe in them deeper than they believe in themselves. Sales leaders realize the powerful and pivotal role high expectations have on a team.

What if you genuinely believed that all your salespeople were talented and gifted in their profession? What if you believed that each seller was a top achiever? Would you behave differently toward them? Before answering, consider the following experiment.

In the 1960s, Robert Rosenthal and Kermit Fode conducted a series of experiments on rats.[3] Participants trained rats to run through a maze. Rat trainers were told that they were training smart rats or dumb rats. The researchers told the rat trainers that they ran genetic testing to determine which rats were smart and which were dumb.

As expected, the smart rats performed better on the maze, and the dumb rats performed poorly. But not for the reasons you may suspect. The researchers weren't observing the rats. Instead, they were observing the rat trainers. There was no real difference between the rats. The only difference was the behavior of the rat trainers.

The smart-rat trainers expected better performance from their rats, which influenced their behavior toward the rats. The dumb-rat trainers expected poor performance, which negatively influenced their behavior. The expectation drove behavior. This study has been duplicated on humans with similar results. This effect is known as the *Rosenthal effect*.

During tough times, leaders tend to expect less. This is a dangerous proposition considering that you get what you expect. Expect the best, and that is what you get. Set a higher expectation to elevate your team further. People rise or fall to the expectations given. Never burden your sales team or yourself with low expectations.

Principle 3: You Set the Tone

I started my first business during the summer of 2002, a franchise painting company. The business concept was simple. As a college student, I learned how to run a business and make a little money. It was an incredible experience. I learned several valuable business lessons, but one leadership lesson stands out the most.

Before the busy summer season, my colleagues and I attended franchisee training. Our trainer taught us how to manage our employees and paint. He repeatedly said throughout the training, "You set the tone!" While rapidly shimmying up the ladder, he'd say, "You set the tone!" While cleaning the equipment, he'd say, "You set the tone!" While painting a hard-to-reach spot, he'd say, "Remember, you set the tone!"

Eventually, our trainer explained what he meant by setting the tone: "Your employees meticulously watch everything you do and how you do it. If you confidently climb the ladder, they will be confident. If you courageously paint a hard-to-reach spot, they will be courageous. If you sloppily clean the brushes, your painters will be sloppy. You set the tone!"

As sales leaders, you set the tone. Your salespeople study your every move, observing your pace and attitude. You are always on display. During tough times, your team faces setbacks and failures. As the sales leader, you also face setbacks and failures. If you're not happy with your team's response to failure, then look in the mirror. How are you responding to failures and setbacks? If your sellers witness the slightest glimpse of self-pity in your reaction, that is bona fide permission for them to react the same way.

In the critically acclaimed documentary, *The Last Dance*,[4] Michael Jordan discussed the price of leadership and winning. This documentary provided a different view of Michael Jordan and revealed Jordan's intense leadership style. Jordan set the tone for the team. He explained, "[I'd] challenge people when they didn't want to be challenged and pulled them along when they didn't want to be pulled." Jordan would push his teammates to the edge of their capabilities, and then he would push them a little more. Jordan was never considered a nice guy by his teammates, but his teammates would also say, "He never asked me to do something that he didn't do himself." Jordan could push them because he pushed himself harder.

Do as you say, and say as you do. Check your actions before you check your words. Your attitude and behavior drive your team. Therefore, before checking your team's attitude, check your own attitude. View yourself through your team's eyes. What is their perception of how you act? Are your words and actions consistently aligned? Stepping outside of your comfort zone and pushing yourself encourage your team to do the same. Demonstrate the qualities you expect, and your team will rise to your level. Your behavior either motivates the team to extend beyond its boundaries or provides the excuse team members need to stay within them.

Your team's performance directly relates to your belief. You are the beacon of hope for your team. Your hope and belief must be deeper than the doubt your team experiences. Hope may not be a strategy, but it is a philosophy. Believing in your team encourages your team to believe in themselves. If you act in a certain way, your team will follow suit.

These leadership principles are just as relevant in good times, but tough times test your commitment to these principles. Your actions and attitude indelibly leave a mark on your team's memory. Your salespeople will remember the tough times. What will they remember about you from those tough times?

DAILY LEADERSHIP TIPS

What you do daily determines your success. The leadership principles from the preceding section will guide your success. This section aims to translate those three leadership principles into daily action. This is where the rubber meets the road. Use these seven leadership tips to help your team prevail through tough times.

Merchant of Hope

Through tough times, sellers are a positive information source for customers. Just as your customers are hungry for hope, so are your salespeople. Find positive news to share with your team throughout the week. Begin each meeting by sharing positive news or insights. Help your team find positive news to share with their customers. Spreading positive news provides your sellers with the hope they need to sell confidently. Serve up an extra helping of what your team is hungry for—hope.

Get in the Field

You need an unfiltered version of what your team is facing. You need to hear from customers and prospects. You cannot help your team through their struggles if you don't understand their struggles. You can't lead your troops while hunkering down in a bunker. Immerse yourself in your sellers' world. Your presence builds customer confidence and commitment. During tough times, your customers and prospects need reassurance. Field rides strengthen your relationship with your sellers and your customers.

Tough times create a unique coaching opportunity. As salespeople experience tough times, they are more open to coaching and feedback. Think of athletes in a slump. They'll do what they can to break free. This includes listening to their leader. Get out in the field more, and coach your team up. Tough times open their minds.

Accept Progress

Expect your team to perform; accept their progress as positive momentum. When salespeople struggle, they lose confidence in their performance. Salespeople are used to achieving outcomes. During tough times, outcomes are harder to achieve. Help your team achieve, and they will believe. Focus your team's effort on achieving small wins. A small win is a concrete outcome of moderate importance. A small win could be securing an appointment with a new prospect. Small wins provide sellers with a sense of accomplishment. That sense of accomplishment transforms into confidence, creating momentum. Through tough times, sellers must believe that they're creating progress toward their goals.

Celebrate Success

How do you feel after celebrating success? Think about those times you celebrated success. It could be a record-breaking year or you won the big deal. You felt motivated. You wanted to keep going. That feeling of success is addicting. This is why it's important to celebrate success through tough times. Big or small, celebrate them all. Tough times are filled with negativity. Find a way for your team to celebrate success. Celebrating success can be a shout-out to a salesperson at a meeting or a backyard gathering. However you do it, just find a way to celebrate success.

Seek Your Team's Ideas

Through tough times, everyone has skin in the game, including your salespeople. They have earned the right to share their ideas, thoughts, and constructive feedback. Too often leaders dismiss their team's feedback as incessant complaining. This is a mistake. Also, people who complain still care. I'd be more concerned about a sales team that doesn't occasionally complain.

Tough times are opportune moments to embrace new ideas and review feedback. The pain of tough times sparks creativity and acts as a catalyst for change. Tough times are good! Give your team a chance to share their feedback. They will feel a deeper connection to you and your company. Welcome feedback through brainstorming sessions. Discuss ideas at company meetings. Encourage your team to send you their ideas. Encourage your team to share their feedback.

Challenge Your Team and Yourself

People are highly motivated if their goals are achievable but not guaranteed. The Yerkes-Dodson law suggests that if a goal is unattainable, it can actually de-motivate.[5] During tough times, your team may experience large performance gaps. This is the brutal reality. Expect your team to perform at their best. However, their best will not always deliver the desired results. In these instances, find additional challenges beyond their forecasted goals. Challenge your team to make a certain number of quality calls per day. Challenge your team to plan every sales call or go after a select group of prospects. Find a way to keep challenging your team. Every new challenge allows your sellers the opportunity to achieve and succeed.

Prune Negativity

In his book, *The Energy Bus*,[6] Jon Gordon highlights the importance of surrounding yourself with positive people. There are people who give you energy and people who drain your energy. Gordon calls negative people who drain your energy "energy vampires."

Prune negativity the same way your salespeople prune profit piranhas. Through tough times, your positive energy is a resource. Don't waste that resource on negative people who drag the team down. If you have especially negative people on your team, confront them about their attitude. Give them specific examples of their negative behaviors and explain the impact on the team. Tell them that they need to change their attitude or they will no longer be part of the team. If they don't change, you need to make the tough decision to prune them from the team. Tough times require tough decisions. Don't let negative people drain your team's energy. It's not fair to the team.

SUMMARY

As the leader, you set the tone. Your team is constantly assessing your attitude and behavior. Your team is a mirror reflecting what you display. Carry yourself in a manner that reflects the type of team you want to lead. Put your team above yourself. It's about them, not you. If you're not happy with your team's performance, look at the expectations you set. People rise or fall to the expectations we place on them. Never burden anyone with low expectations.

As the leader, maintain an unwavering belief that you and your team will prevail through this tough time. Tough times are not pain free, but they create opportunities to improve and bond with your team at a deeper level. Tough times reveal your character and strengthen your leadership skills beyond what you thought was possible. Tough times are good!

CHAPTER 17

Final Thoughts

Remember Red, hope is a good thing, maybe the
best of things, and no good thing ever dies.
—ANDY DUFRESNE, *The Shawshank Redemption*[1]

*T*he Sawshank Redemption is widely considered one of the greatest movies
of all time. I can't think of a better movie to watch as you experience
tough times. It's a wonderful story of tragedy and triumph. If you need
a mental boost, watch it today.

Andy Dufresne (Tim Robbins) is wrongfully imprisoned for murdering
his wife. Although Andy faces many dark moments, he remains hopeful.
Red (Morgan Freeman) told his friend Andy that hope has no place in a
prison. He proclaims, "Hope is a dangerous thing." It's clear that Red is full
of despair—he is broken. In some ways, Red *learned* to be hopeless.

One day Andy made Red promise that if he ever made it out, Red would
go find a tin box Andy left for him in a nearby field. It turns out that promise
was the only thing that kept Red going.

Eventually, Andy escaped prison and fled to Mexico. Red made it out of
Shawshank on parole and found that box. In it was some money along with
a note from Andy. In the note, Andy reminded Red, "Hope is a good thing,
maybe the best of things, and no good thing ever dies." So Red began a
hope-filled journey to find his friend in Mexico.

Red narrates the end of his journey with this thought, "I hope I can make
it across the border. I hope to see my friend and shake his hand. I hope the
Pacific is as blue as it has been in my dreams. I hope." The final scene shows
Red embracing Andy on a beach in Mexico. The once-broken man is filled
with hope.

Hope is a deep desire for something *to* happen coupled with an unwavering belief it *will* happen. To Dufresne's point, "hope is a good thing, maybe the best of things." This is especially true through tough times. Hope isn't a given. Hope doesn't magically appear. Hope is the hardest to find when it's needed the most. This is why hope is valuable; it's not easily attained when it matters the most. During those especially tough moments, you must endure. Hope means that you never give up.

As you reflect on this iconic scene, consider the toughest moments in your life. Think of the hardship and despair that followed. This hopelessness appears because of the brokenness we face at those tough moments. The failures, the pain, the anguish we experience wear us down, eventually breaking us down. However, brokenness either destroys hope or acts as the catalyst to find hope.

Eventually, everyone feels broken through tough times. At those broken moments, find the motivation to piece things back together. Your mental strength is not determined by your optimism in tough times; it's measured by your perseverance when you feel hopeless. Those are the moments that matter. At those broken moments, *keep going*!

A few years ago, my family attended a party at my wife's grandfather's home. While there, my daughter accidentally broke a small but highly regarded statue. My mother-in-law quickly glued it back together. Thankfully, it kind of worked. The cracks were hardly noticeable, and the statue was intact.

Have you tried supergluing something back together? You glue the broken pieces to conceal the cracks. You don't want anyone to notice the broken pieces. Those unsightly cracks ruin the image. This is a typical response to brokenness: we all try to hide it. Broken is weak. Broken is embarrassing. Broken is ugly. We conceal brokenness from everyone—even ourselves. By concealing our broken pieces, we internalize brokenness and accept it, telling ourselves, "What is broken stays broken." By accepting brokenness, we miss an opportunity.

What if there's a better way to piece together what is broken?

In Japanese culture, repairing what is broken is not embarrassing or ugly; it's an art form. Kintsugi is the Japanese art of repairing broken pottery.[2] In Kintsugi, the cracks are not concealed; they are illuminated with gold, silver, or platinum. The broken pieces are treated as a beautiful part of the story rather than being disguised or discarded. Some collectors prefer Kintsugi pots over unbroken pots. The beauty is in the broken places.

Through tough times, everyone feels broken. Those broken moments are defining moments that determine your true strength. These broken moments illuminate your story, not destroy it. It's only in being broken that we become better versions of ourselves. Don't conceal brokenness. Don't hopelessly accept it either! Embrace brokenness with the belief that you will emerge stronger.

Our career (and life) is not defined by what happens to us; it's defined by our response to what happens to us. Everyone is broken through tough times. We may be broken mentally, financially, physically, or spiritually. At times, it seems impossible to piece things back together. Although the cracks are visible, like the broken pottery, you're made whole again.

These broken moments are defining moments that illuminate your story. Don't conceal your brokenness—let it show. Like a fighter knocked down, your scars prove that you are willing to fight. Let it show. Your brokenness will surprisingly attract others; collectively, you will find more strength. As you navigate tough times, you don't have to navigate alone.

In closing, I want to share my hope for you: I hope that you'll forge your broken pieces back together with determination, resilience, and humility. Complete your comeback story by letting those bonded joints shine like gold, platinum, and silver. I hope that your tough times last long enough for you to learn and grow but no longer. I hope that the depth of this tough time uncovers your hidden strength. I hope that strength provides solid footing for your next tough time—helping you navigate it with greater ease and confidence.

I hope that your tough time extends your capacity to create more value in this world. I hope that you lift people up during this tough time. Be a hope merchant for your customers and colleagues—spreading optimism wherever you go. Sometimes the best way to feel hopeful is to fill others with hope. Be a merchant of hope.

I hope that this deep valley provides perspective for you to fully appreciate your next peak. The journey may be tougher than expected, but the steeper the climb, the more spectacular the view.

I hope that you can fully appreciate that life is not fair. And we have God to thank for that. If life were fair, we would only get what we deserve and nothing more. May this tough time remind you of how fortunate you are.

Finally, I hope that your tough time is just painful enough to create the positive change you need in your life. I hope that you reflect on these tough times soon in the comfort of brighter days. I hope that your reflection is filled with joy and not regrets. What you learned through tough times propels you even further in good times. Without tough times, you may not have had this opportunity. Tough times are good!

The 30-Day
Tough-Timer Challenge

The great pleasure in life is doing what people say you cannot do.
—WALTER BAGEHOT[1]

Have you ever been told that you cannot do something? A colleague may tell you, "Don't bother pursuing that prospect; they'll never buy from you" or "You'll never get a meeting with that prospect." Like me, you've heard these skeptical remarks from colleagues over the years. How do you respond to these doubtful statements? Did you give in or push even harder? Although these words are meant to discourage your effort, they encourage you even more. The more you are doubted, the harder you should push.

In that vein, you need to know something about The 30-Day Tough-Timer Challenge. A vast majority of sellers attempting this challenge will fail. I don't say this to frustrate you. I want you to succeed. However, our research shows that a vast majority of sellers who attempt this challenge will not complete it successfully. Are your competitive juices starting to flow? Good. Prove me wrong and prove yourself right by completing the 30-day challenge.

Achievement and progress are critical in tough times. The 30-Day Tough-Timer Challenge provides an opportunity for you to experience both. The rules are simple. For 30 consecutive days (including weekends), complete the Daily Mental Flex®, and plan every sales call. Our research shows that only 10 percent of sellers routinely plan their sales calls. There's a good chance that precall planning will be the greatest challenge over this 30-day period. This is where a majority of sellers will fail. Tough timers use precall planning to gain a significant advantage over the competition. Precall planning was addressed in Chapter 13. The Tough-Time Call Planner and Daily Mental Flex® are available for download at www.ToughTimer.com. Prove me wrong and complete this challenge.

You might be wondering, "Why should I attempt this challenge?" This is a good question. After all, time is your greatest currency. So here is what you stand to gain:

- You will be more successful at the end of these 30 days. By rigorously completing this challenge, you will be more successful than you were before. Track your progress and you will see.
- Your newly built mental strength and preparedness will spill over into other areas of your life. You will notice other positive outcomes—personally and professionally—because of your commitment to this challenge.
- You will build a more resilient foundation as you face adversity. Your tough time may last longer than these 30 days, but your resilient foundation can become permanent.
- You will be more disciplined in your sales approach. The simple act of planning every sales call forces you to apply the process you learned in this book. Adherence to the process will create more success well after you complete this challenge.
- You will feel more fulfilled and notice a deeper commitment to your goals. Commitment breeds passion and fulfillment. Throughout this process, you will tap into a deeper motivation to drive your effort.

Complete the challenge, and success will be yours. You must put in the work. Your tough times may last longer than this 30-day challenge. But your resilient foundation will outlast the tough times you experience. Once you hit 30 days, continue this challenge. Keep going, and watch your success grow.

As you embark on this tough-timer challenge, use the following tips to improve your odds of success.

RECRUIT OTHER TOUGH TIMERS TO JOIN YOU

Partner up with colleagues and friends to keep you motivated. Schedule weekly accountability calls. Share your progress with each other, and challenge each other to keep going. Many organizations I partner with start book clubs and self-development clubs within their company. These clubs meet weekly to build each other up. Make the tough-timer challenge part of your development club. If you're a sales leader, challenge your team to complete this 30-day challenge. Team challenges build camaraderie and provide a common goal. During tough times, you're looking for ways to keep your team motivated. This challenge taps into that competitive team spirit.

SHARE YOUR PROGRESS AND SUCCESS

Sharing your progress increases your likelihood of success.[2] As you begin The 30-Day Tough-Timer Challenge, update your network on your progress. Share your progress on social media using #toughtimer. Build and support the tough-timer community. Share your story, your successes, and your struggles. Read other people's stories, and share some encouraging words. Tag me. I'd love to hear your progress. I'm most active on LinkedIn. You can also find me on twitter, @PaulReillyVAS.

NOMINATE A FRIEND OR COLLEAGUE

Over this 30-day challenge, you will notice positive change in your life. You will naturally want your friends and colleagues to experience the same benefits. Once you complete the 30-day challenge successfully, you will have earned the right to nominate a friend or colleague to attempt the challenge. Nominate anyone in sales or sales leadership or a colleague experiencing tough times in his or her industry or personal life. Support your nominee as he or she attempts this challenge. Share your successes. If you really want to prompt a response, nominate the person on social media. He or she will be more likely to accept if you make it public. Direct your nominee to www.ToughTimer.com for the details.

DEVELOP A ROUTINE

Once you start the process, you'll develop a natural rhythm. You might complete the gratitude exercise and the discipline exercise first thing in the morning, the continuous improvement exercise over lunch, and the positive reframing exercise in the evening. However you do it, just develop a routine.

Print several copies of the Daily Mental Flex® and Tough-Time Call Planner for easy access.

Once you complete The 30-Day Tough-Timer Challenge, you will be joining an elite group of sellers—the top 10 percent. I hope that you will continue the tough-timer journey well after the 30 days. Permanently embrace this positive change in your life. Once you complete this tough-timer challenge, visit www.ToughTimer.com for your certificate and tough-timer gear. Do you have what it takes to be a tough timer? Give it 30 days and find out.

Notes

Chapter 1

1. Nancy Mann Jackson, "How Long Do Downturns Last?" Acorns, updated March 10, 2020, www.acorns.com/money-basics/the-economy/how-long-do-downturns-last/#:~:text=Generally%2C%20economic%20recessions%20don't,decline%20since%20World%20War%20II.
2. Derek Thompson, "Warren Buffett to American CEOs: Please Stop Complaining About Uncertainty," *The Atlantic*, March 1, 2013.
3. Wikipedia, "List of Recessions in the United States," updated February 14, 2021, https://en.wikipedia.org/wiki/List_of_recessions_in_the_United_States.
4. Jenny Medeiros, "Walt Disney's Life Story: A Mouse, Eternal Life, and a Stolen Rabbit," *Goalcast*, January 17, 2018, www.goalcast.com/2018/01/17/walt-disneys-life-story/.
5. Catherine Clifford, "When Microsoft Saved Apple: Steve Jobs and Bill Gates Show Eliminating Competition Isn't the Only Way to Win," *The Entrepreneurs*, CNBC, August 29, 2017.
6. Steve Liesman, "Can the Markets Predict Recessions? What We Found Out," *US Economy*, CNBC, February 4, 2016, www.cnbc.com/2016/02/04/can-the-markets-predict-recessions-what-we-found-out.html.
7. John Pollack, *Shortcut* (New York: Avery/Penguin Random House, 2015), pp. 87–90.
8. *Newton's First Law*, Physics Tutorial, The Physics Classroom, www.physicsclassroom.com/class/newtlaws/Lesson-1/Newton-s-First-Law.

Chapter 2

1. *Newton's Third Law*, Physics Tutorial, The Physics Classroom, www.physicsclassroom.com/class/newtlaws/Lesson-4/Newton-s-Third-Law.
2. Tom Reilly and Paul Reilly, *Value-Added Selling*, 4th ed. (New York: McGraw-Hill, 2018), p. 48.
3. Jack Rosenthal, "A Terrible Thing to Waste," *New York Times Magazine*, July 31, 2009, www.nytimes.com/2009/08/02/magazine/02FOB-onlanguage-t.html.
4. Kate O'Brien, "How Did These Famous Investors Deal with Market Meltdowns?" MSN/Money: The Motley Fool, March 16, 2020, www.msn.com/en-us/money/markets/how-did-these-famous-investors-deal-with-market-meltdowns/ar-BB1leyWc.
5. Guinness World Records, https://www.guinnessworldrecords.com/world-records/best-selling-book-of-non-fiction.

6. Taylor Locke, "Mark Cuban's 'No. 1 Rule of Investing' When You Don't Know What to Do About the Market," CNBC, March 9, 2020, www.cnbc.com/2020/03/09/mark-cubans-no-1-rule-of-investing-when-you-dont-know-what-to-do.html.

7. Francis Galton, *Vox Populi, Nature* 75:450–451, March 7, 1907, https://doi.org/10.1038/075450a0.

8. Carl Zimmer, "The Wisdom of (Little) Crowds," *National Geographic*, April 22, 2014, www.nationalgeographic.com/science/article/the-wisdom-of-little-crowds.

9. Native American Proverb, "The Tale of Two Wolves," www.nanticokeindians.org/page/tale-of-two-wolves.

10. Mike Jones, "J. J. Watt Amazes His Texans Teammates, but a Simple Approach Is the Key to His Comeback," *USA Today*, August 22, 2018, www.usatoday.com/story/sports/nfl/columnist/mike-jones/2018/08/22/jj-watt-houston-texans-comeback-injury/1057611002/.

11. National Archives, Franklin D. Roosevelt Presidential Library and Museum, www.fdrlibrary.org/eleanor-roosevelt.

Chapter 3

1. Reilly and Reilly, *Value-Added Selling*, p. 18.

2. Sean Szymkowski, "Vintage Ad Break: Chevrolet Trucks Are 'Like A Rock,'" GM Authority, October 16, 2017, https://gmauthority.com/blog/2017/10/vintage-ad-break-chevrolet-trucks-are-like-a-rock/#:~:text=However%2C%20we're%20here%20to,Like%20a%20Rock%E2%80%9D%20in%201991.

3. Ethan Trex, "Five Great Depression Success Stories," February 10, 2009, www.mentalfloss.com; *Wall Street Journal*, May 5, 2009, www.wsj.com/articles/SB124145607475383935.

4. Melissa Ignasiak, "Flashback Friday: 'Have It Your Way,'" Baer Performance Marketing, blog post, December 14, 2012, https://baerpm.com/2012/12/14/flashback-friday-have-it-your-way-2/#:~:text=The%20campaign%20was%20launched%20in,%E2%80%9CHave%20it%20your%20way%E2%80%9D.

5. Shep Hyken, *The Convenience Revolution* (Shippensburg, PA: Sound Wisdom Publishing, 2008), p. 41.

6. "Keeping Our Promises," 19-0126 Historical Brochure, http://media.nmfn.com/mutual-experience/_media/docs/accolades/19-0126-NM_History.pdf.

7. Jon Byman, "How to Find the Best Whole Life Insurance Policy," June 17, 2019, https://www.northwesternmutual.com/life-and-money/how-to-find-the-best-whole-life-insurance-policy/.

8. "The PC: Personal Computing Comes of Age: In Their words," IBM 100: Icons of Progress, 2011, www.ibm.com/ibm/history/ibm100/us/en/icons/personalcomputer/words/.

9. Reilly and Reilly, *Value-Added Selling*, p. 20.

10. www.goodreads.com/quotes/34690-people-don-t-care-how-much-you-know-until-they-know.

11. Reilly and Reilly, *Value-Added Selling*, p. 27.

12. Michele Gorman, "Yogi Berra's Most Memorable Sayings," *Newsweek*, September 23, 2015, www.newsweek.com/most-memorable-yogi-isms-375661.

13. www.azquotes.com/quote/519610.

14. www.goodreads.com/quotes/37815-the-mind-once-stretched-by-a-new-idea-never
     -returns.

Chapter 4

1. J. L. Nolen, "Learned Helplessness," *Encyclopedia Britannica*, December 28, 2017.
2. D. H. Lawrence, "Self-Pity," All Poetry, https://allpoetry.com/Self-Pity.
3. James R. Sherman, *Rejection* (Golden Valley, MN: Pathway Books, 1982), p. 45.

Chapter 5

1. Viktor Frankl, *Man's Search for Meaning* (Boston: Beacon Press, 2006), p. 75.
2. Jocko Willink, "Jocko Motivation 'Good,'" *Jocko Podcast*, https://youtu.be/IdTMD
    pizis8.
3. Alex Forsythe, "Fred Rogers: Look for the Helpers," YouTube, April 15, 2013,
    www.youtube.com/watch?v=-LGHtc_D328.
4. "Gratitude Is Good Medicine," UC Davis Health, November 25, 2015, https://health
    .ucdavis.edu/medicalcenter/features/2015-2016/11/20151125_gratitude.html.
5. Harvard Medical School, "Giving Thanks Can Make You Happier," Harvard Health
    Publishing, November 2011, www.health.harvard.edu/healthbeat/giving-thanks
    -can-make-you-happier.
6. Summer Allen, "The Science of Gratitude," Greater Good Science Center, May 2018,
    https://ggsc.berkeley.edu/images/uploads/GGSC-JTF_White_Paper-Gratitude
    -FINAL.pdf.
7. Tushar Soubhari and Yathish Kumar, "The Crab-Bucket Effect and Its Impact on
    Job Stress," *International Journal on Recent and Innovation Trends in Computing
    and Communication* 2(10), October 2014, https://web.archive.org/web/
    20160304134124/http://www.ijritcc.org/download/1413605078.pdf.
8. Simon Spacey, "Crab Mentality, Cyberbullying and 'Name and Shame'
    Rankings," New Zealand, April 19, 2015, http://www.srl.to/u5e2dNha/Crab%20
    Mentality,%20Cyberbullying%20and%20Name%20and%20Shame%20
    Rankings.pdf.
9. Chris Widener, *Jim Rohn's 8 Best Success Lessons* (Issaquah, WA: Made for Success, Inc.
    2014), www.google.com/books/edition/Jim_Rohn_s_8_Best_Success_Lessons/8P
    -lBAAAQBAJ?hl=en&gbpv=1&dq=jim-rohn-you+are-the-average-of-the-five
    -people-you-spend-the-most-time-with&pg=PP11&printsec=frontcover.
10. www.goodreads.com/quotes/720920-every-battle-is-won-before-it-s-ever-fought.

Chapter 6

1. Sreechinth, C., *Powerful Quotes of Winston Churchill* (Scotts Valley, CA:
    CreateSpace, 2016).
2. Jim Collins, *Good to Great* (New York: HarperCollins, 2001).
3. Greg Daugherty, "Dr. John Kellogg Invented Cereal: Some of His Other Wellness
    Ideas Were Much Weirder," History Channel, August 7, 2019, https://history.com/
    news/dr-john-kellogg-cereal-wellness-wacky-sanitarium-treatments.
4. Laura Siciliano-Rosen, "French Dip," *Encyclopedia Britannica*, October 3, 2019,
    www.britannica.com/topic/French-dip.

5. Alison Spiegel, "The Caesar Salad Was Invented in Mexico. Surprised?" *Huffington Post*, March 11, 2015, www.huffpost.com/entry/where-was-the-caesar -salad-invented_n_6839542.

6. www.menshealth.com/fitness/a31280130/julius-maddox-bench-press-world -record-770-pounds-arnold-classic-2020/.

7. www.mensjournal.com/health-fitness/watch-powerlifter-squats-1036-pounds -breaks-world-record/.

8. https://time.com/5324940/americans-exercise-physical-activity-guidelines/.

9. www.brainyquote.com/quotes/mike_tyson_382439.

Part II

1. Marcus Lemonis, *The Profit*, CNBC, www.cnbc.com/the-profit/.

2. James M. Mattis and Francis J. West, *Call Sign Chaos* (New York: Random House, 2019).

Chapter 7

1. Reilly and Reilly, *Value-Added Selling*, p. 107.

2. www.brainyquote.com/authors/zig-ziglar-quotes.

3. "Siren," *Encyclopedia Britannica*, May 7, 2020, www.britannica.com/topic/Siren -Greek-mythology.

4. Reilly and Reilly, *Value-Added Selling*, p. 101.

5. M. H. Mallers, M. Claver, and L. A. Lares, "Perceived Control in the Lives of Older Adults: The Influence of Langer and Rodin's Work on Gerontological Theory, Policy, and Practice," *Gerontologist* 54(1):67–74, 2014, doi:10.1093/geront/ gnt051.

6. Lily Bernheimer, "The IKEA Effect," *Psychology Today*, October 1, 2019, www .psychologytoday.com/us/blog/the-shaping-us/201910/the-ikea-effect.

7. "William Wrigley, Jr.," *Encyclopedia Britannica*, January 22, 2021, www.britannica .com/biography/William-Wrigley-Jr.

8. "Panic of 1893," Encyclopedia.com, www.encyclopedia.com/history/united-states -and-canada/us-history/panic-1893.

9. Reilly and Reilly, *Value-Added Selling*, p. 285.

10. www.brainyquote.com/authors/abraham-lincoln-quotes.

Chapter 8

1. Reilly and Reilly, *Value-Added Selling*.

Chapter 9

1. "How Courts Work," American Bar Association, Washington, DC, September 9, 2019, www.americanbar.org/groups/public_education/resources/law_related _education_network/how_courts_work/discovery/#:~:text=This%20is%20the %20formal%20process,what%20evidence%20may%20be%20presented.&text =One%20of%20the%20most%20common%20methods%20of%20 discovery%20is%20to%20take%20depositions.

2. Francesca Gino, "The Business Case for Curiosity," *Harvard Business Review*, September–October 2018, https://hbr.org/2018/09/the-business-case-for-curiosity.

3. Peter Senge, *The Fifth Discipline* (New York: Random House/Doubleday, 1990), p. 220.

4. Daniel Kahneman, Jack L. Knetsch, and Richard H. Thaler, "Anomalies: The Endowment Effect, Loss Aversion, and Status Quo Bias," *Journal of Economic Perspectives* 5(1):193–206, 1991.

5. John Hittler, "The Genius of Asking 'What If?' Questions," *Forbes Coaches Council*, May 16, 2018, www.forbes.com/sites/forbescoachescouncil/2018/05/16/the-genius-of-asking-what-if-questions/?sh=2a8454b822ef.

6. "Blue Angels Debriefing," YouTube, April 6, 2017, www.youtube.com/watch?v=bFGL04LiMgc.

Chapter 10

1. Robert Cialdini, *PRE-SUASION: A Revolutionary Way to Influence and Persuade* (New York: Simon & Schuster, 2018).

2. "The Wizard," *Seinfeld*, season 9, episode 15, NBC, New York, February 26, 1998.

3. Tali Sharot, *The Influential Mind* (New York: Holt & Company, 2017), p. 157.

4. Jack Welch, *Winning* (New York: HarperCollins, 2005).

5. Og Mandino, *Greatest Salesman in the World* (New York: Bantam Books, 1981), p. 100.

6. Douglas Hofstadter and Emanuel Sander, *Surfaces and Essences: Analogy as the Fuel and Fire of Thinking* (New York: Basic Books, 2013).

7. Ranjay Gulati, Nitin Nohria, and Franz Wohlgezogen, "Roaring Out of Recession," *Harvard Business Review*, March 2010, https://hbr.org/2010/03/roaring-out-of-recession.

8. Daniel Kahneman, *Thinking, Fast and Slow* (New York: Farrar, Straus and Giroux, 2011), p. 119.

Chapter 12

1. Peter Krauss, *The Book of Management Wisdom* (New York: John Wiley & Sons, 2000).

2. Jim Collins, *Good to Great* (New York: HarperCollins, 2001).

3. Stanley Black & Decker, "Stanlo: Making the World, Piece by Piece," Who We Are, www.stanleyblackanddecker.com/who-we-are/our-history/responsibility/stanlo-making-world-piece-piece.

4. Paul Reilly, *The Q and A Sales Podcast*, www.theqandasalespodcast.com/.

Chapter 13

1. S. O'Farrell, J. N. Sanchirico, O. Spiegel, et al., "Disturbance Modifies Payoffs in the Explore-Exploit Trade-Off," *Nature Communications* 10:3363, 2019, https://doi.org/10.1038/s41467-019-11106-y.

2. Reilly and Reilly, *Value-Added Selling*, p. 212.

3. Reilly and Reilly, *Value-Added Selling*, p. 213.

Chapter 14

1. The Ocean Portal Team, "Gulf Oil Spill," *Smithsonian*, April 2018, https://ocean .si.edu/conservation/pollution/gulf-oil-spill.
2. CNN Wire Staff, "BP Chief to Gulf Residents: 'I'm sorry,'" CNN, May 30, 2010, www.cnn.com/2010/US/05/30/gulf.oil.spill/index.html.
3. Jon Picoult, "3 Tips for Strengthening Customer Loyalty During Difficult Times," *Forbes*, April 14, 2020, www.forbes.com/sites/jonpicoult/2020/04/14/3-tips-for -strengthening-customer-loyalty-during-difficult-times/?sh=27681fd74e1b.

Chapter 15

1. A. Bages-Amat, L. Harrison, D. Spillecke, and J. Stanley, "The Eight Charts Show How COVID-19 Has Changed B2B Sales Forever," McKinsey & Company, October 14, 2020, www.mckinsey.com/business-functions/marketing-and-sales/our -insights/these-eight-charts-show-how-covid-19-has-changed-b2b-sales-forever#.
2. *Gordon Ramsay: Uncharted*, National Geographic Channel, Studio Ramsay, 2019.
3. Dale Carnegie, *How to Win Friends and Influence People* (New York: Simon & Schuster, rev. 1981), p. 113.

Chapter 16

1. Jon Gordon, Positive U podcast, https://positiveuniversity.com/episode/coach-dabo -swinney/.
2. Ben Horowitz, *The Hard Things about Hard Things* (New York: HarperCollins, 2014).
3. Robert Rosenthal and Kermit L. Fode, "The Effect of Experimenter Bias on the Performance of the Albino Rat," Harvard University and the University of North Dakota, 1961, www.gwern.net/docs/iq/1963-rosenthal.pdf.
4. Michael Jordon, *The Last Dance*, Docuseries, ESPN Films, NBA Entertainment, episode 7, April 2020.
5. Robert Yerkes and John Dodson, "The Relation of Strength of Stimulus to Rapidity of Habit-Formation," *Journal of Comparative Neurology and Psychology* 18:459–482, 1908, via internet resource developed by Christopher Green, York University, Toronto, http://psychclassics.yorku.ca/Yerkes/Law/?null.
6. Jon Gordon, *The Energy Bus* (Hoboken, NJ: Wiley, 2007).

Chapter 17

1. *The Shawshank Redemption*, Castle Rock Entertainment, 1994.
2. Tiffany Ayuda, "How the Japanese Art of Kintsugi Can Help You Deal with Stressful Situations," *NBC News: Better by Today*, April 25, 2018, www.nbcnews.com/better/ health/how-japanese-art-technique-kintsugi-can-help-you-be-more-ncna866471.

Appendix

1. Richard Holt Hutton and Walter Bagehot, "Editor's Preface," in *Memoir of Walter Bagehot* (Hartford, CT: Travelers Insurance Company, 1891).
2. Lisa Evans, "Why Sharing Your Progress Makes You More Likely to Accomplish Your Goals," Fast Company, June 19, 2015, www.fastcompany.com/3047432/ why-sharing-your-progress-makes-you-more-likely-to-accomplish-your-goals.

Index

About the Author

PAUL REILLY is a speaker, sales trainer, and author. Reilly literally wrote the book on *Selling Through Tough Times*. Reilly also coauthored *Value-Added Selling*, fourth edition (McGraw-Hill, 2018), and hosts *The Q and A Sales Podcast*. Reilly travels the globe sharing his content-rich message of hope. In his extensive sales career, Reilly has sold through tough times and against tough competition. He is a salesperson at heart and has experienced and overcome the challenges many of you are facing.

Reilly cut his teeth in the commoditized propane industry—a notoriously price-sensitive and competitive market. Reilly competed with dozens of providers selling the same exact product. He sold tools and fasteners in the construction industry during the Great Recession. Toward the tail end of the recession, he earned Master's Club status from his employer. The Master's Club is reserved for the top ten percent of sellers company-wide. Reilly also sold medical equipment during one of the most uncertain times in the healthcare industry. In early 2010, the healthcare industry faced unprecedented change, and many ancillary providers and suppliers struggled. Amid this uncertainty, Reilly grew his distribution network and successfully relaunched their brand in a new country.

As a professional speaker and sales trainer, Reilly works with the world's best sales organizations. These organizations face constant challenges: rolling recessions, industry disruption, difficult competitors, economic downturns, and other geopolitical concerns. Reilly's mission is to help these organizations compete profitably despite their challenging environment. Reilly has the pulse of today's sales professional. On his podcast, *The Q and A Sales Podcast*, he answers the most pressing questions facing today's sales professional.

Reilly achieved his CSP (certified speaking professional) designation in 2020. Fewer than 18 percent of professional speakers have earned this designation. Reilly attended the University of Missouri, Columbia, where he earned his undergraduate degree in Business Marketing. He went on to earn his MBA from Webster University. Reilly is a frequent contributor to a variety of online and trade magazines. He is also a faculty member of the University of Innovative Distribution—UID.